I0824647

AVID

READER

PRESS

The Emerson Circle

The Concord Radicals Who Reinvented the World

Bruce Nichols

Avid Reader Press

New York Amsterdam/Antwerp London
Toronto Sydney/Melbourne New Delhi

Avid Reader Press
An Imprint of Simon & Schuster, LLC
1230 Avenue of the Americas
New York, NY 10020

First Avid Reader Press hardcover edition April 2026

Interior design by Ruth Lee-Mui

Manufactured in the United States of America

3 5 7 9 10 8 6 4 2

Library of Congress Control Number: 2025947949

ISBN 978-1-6680-9487-7
ISBN 978-1-6680-9489-1 (ebook)

To Sarah, for everything

One of the phrases . . . I think particularly descriptive of inspiration [is] "the newness." Open the uncommanded doors whence the newness comes, and I truly live.

—*The Journals of Ralph Waldo Emerson*

There were circumstances around me which made it difficult to view the world precisely as it exists . . . stranger moral shapes of men than might have been encountered elsewhere in a circuit of a thousand miles.

—Nathaniel Hawthorne, "The Old Manse"

Mediocrity is obscurity.

—Timothy Fuller, letter to his
daughter Margaret, age ten

Contents

A Note on Names

The members of the Emerson circle were fond of changing their names, which can cause confusion. For clarity and consistency, I refer to them by the names that are most famous or most preferred by themselves: Margaret Fuller (for Sarah Margaret), Henry Thoreau (for David Henry), Bronson Alcott (for Amos Bronson), and Waldo Emerson (for Ralph Waldo). Louisa May Alcott's family nickname, Louey, was used only occasionally by the immediate family, so I do not use it.

Her mother and her youngest sister were both named Abigail May Alcott, until the latter's brief marriage. Each was called Abby and sometimes Abba, until the sister reached adulthood and became known as May. Following some other biographers, I have chosen to use Abba for Mrs. Alcott throughout the text, and Abby for the daughter prior to adulthood.

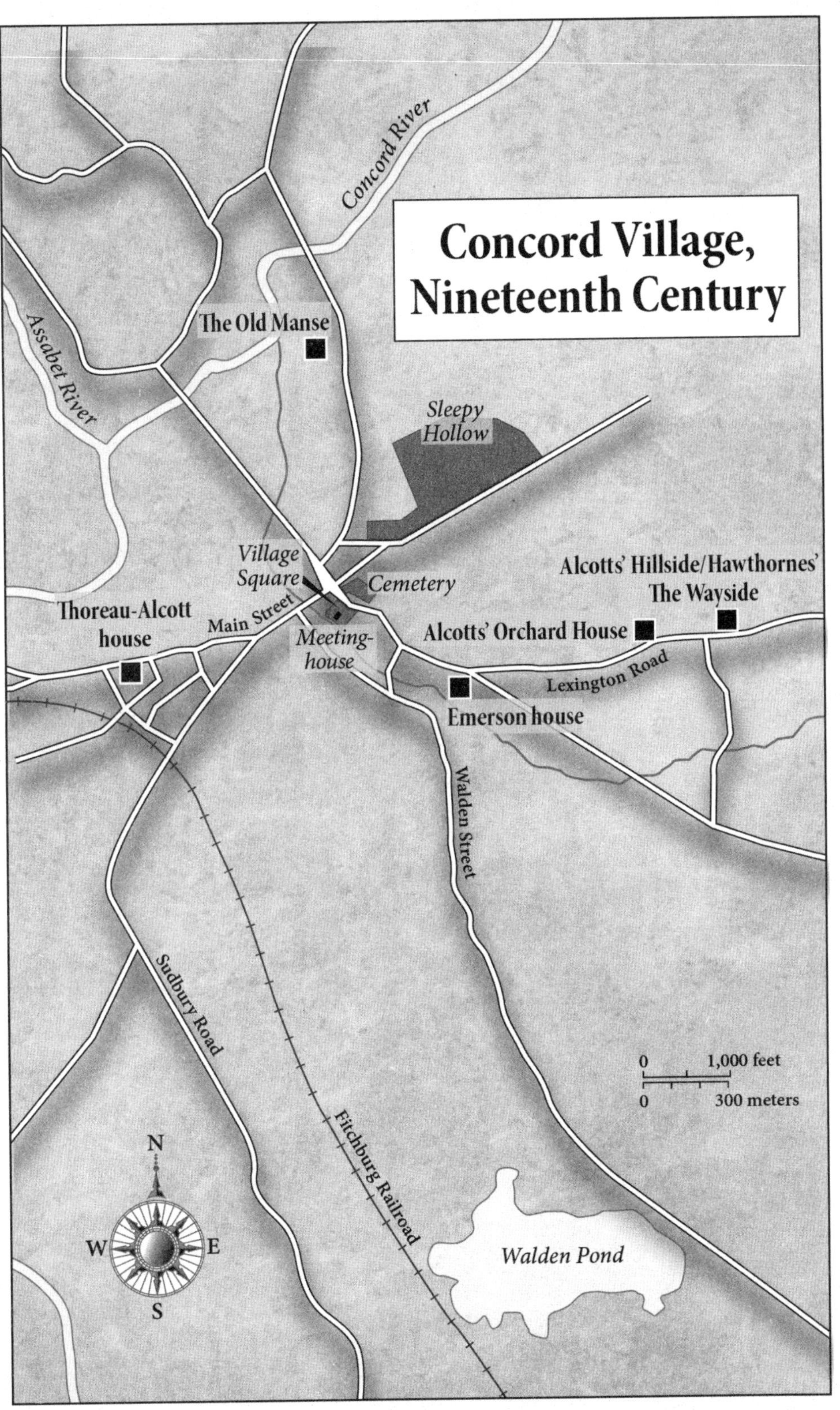
Concord Village, Nineteenth Century
Concord River
Assabet River
The Old Manse
Sleepy Hollow
Village Square
Cemetery
Thoreau-Alcott house
Main Street
Meeting-house
Alcotts' Hillside/Hawthornes' The Wayside
Alcotts' Orchard House
Lexington Road
Emerson house
Walden Street
Sudbury Road
Fitchburg Railroad
Walden Pond
0 1,000 feet
0 300 meters
N
W
E
S

Prologue

In 1830, Concord, Massachusetts, was a small town of just over two thousand people. One of them, Henry David Thoreau, was a student at Concord Academy. His father's pencil-making business provided the family's modest income. Concord had two Christian churches, and many pious believers. Henry was not allowed to play games or read books on the Sabbath.

Ten years later, Concord had become the catalyst of a radical rebirth of American culture and politics. Ralph Waldo Emerson, who moved to Concord in 1834, was locally famous and on his way to national celebrity for his lectures and essays. He had gathered a close circle of friends and allies around him, some living there, others coming to stay for weeks at a time. Emerson rejected the divinity of Christ, preferring to seek deep meaning in nature and science. He and his followers were called "Transcendentalists." His neighbor and friend Bronson Alcott, also a nonbeliever in Jesus's divinity, was a champion of school reform. Emerson's frequent guest, Margaret Fuller, argued for equal rights for women, and served as the editor of a trailblazing Transcendentalist journal. Nathaniel Hawthorne, who would live in two different Concord homes starting in 1842—one formerly occupied by Emerson, the other by Alcott—was a budding literary star. Thoreau was publishing his first poems and working on his masterful nature and travel writing. In 1840 he also taught at Concord Academy. One of his students was Bronson's daughter Anna, the older sister of Louisa May Alcott.

Historians describe antebellum America as experiencing a "market revolution," as the country expanded its manufacturing and transportation systems. That revolution—actually a long evolution, not a sudden upheaval—explains a lot, but not everything. What was truly new in the 1840s was an intellectual revolution. The many hopes and dreams of its abolitionists, freethinkers, feminists, vegetarians, animal-rights activists, teetotalers, and literary lights surround what came to be known as "the Newness." As Emerson wrote in *The Dial*, the journal he cofounded with Fuller, the reformers took aim at all aspects of society: "Christianity, the laws, commerce, schools, the farm, the laboratory; and not a kingdom, town, statute, rite, calling, man, or woman, but is threatened by the new spirit."

Transcendentalism was just one branch of the new thinking. Two generations after the Founding Fathers rejected monarchy, Americans pushed against the limits of many more institutions—the churches, government, schools, and slavery, including the Northern states' economic and legal support of it. Utopian communities sprang up throughout the states and territories. Some banned all forms of sexual contact. Some did the opposite. Some of the ideas of the reformers would become federal law—although it took a terrible war to bring about emancipation, and the better part of a century before women could vote in every election. Some of their ideas are still debated. Animal-rights activists and their vegan allies are largely unaware that their American predecessors included Bronson Alcott and Lidian Emerson, wife of Ralph Waldo. The 1840s utopian communities mostly all failed, though they inspired many subsequent attempts at collective living.

The Concord set were as radical as any group of American visionaries before or since. They were fearless. Two of them protested against the government by refusing to pay taxes. One went to jail for it. One of them attempted to storm a Boston courthouse to free a fugitive slave. And two of them worked in war hospitals close to the front lines of two different wars. Margaret Fuller, history's first female war correspondent, worked in Rome during the 1848–49 republican uprising. Louisa May Alcott witnessed pain, amputations, and death in a Georgetown hospital after the Battle of Fredericksburg.

That is not to say that Emerson and his neighbors were responsible for all the Newness, far from it. But Emerson was its fountainhead. Transcendentalism has been described as a religious movement. Yet Emerson, a trained minister who broke with his church, was interested in much more than religion, and his friends and followers pursued political, social, and economic experiments, both religious and secular. Examined in broader context, they were at the leading edge of an American impulse to reexamine and reinvent the world. As Emerson summarized their approach, "the nation existed for the individual," and "the individual is the world."

The Emerson circle also wanted to give new voices to their world. The writings of the Concord set inspired and endure as some of our greatest works of literature. These men and women thought of themselves as poets, and they all wrote poetry. But they are famous today for their prose. Emerson's *Essays*, Thoreau's *Walden*, Louisa May Alcott's *Little Women*, Hawthorne's *The Scarlet Letter*, and Fuller's *Woman in the Nineteenth Century* are just a few of their famous works. The larger literary movement that came to be known as the American Renaissance included writers connected to them: Melville, Whitman, and Poe. But it was the close interactions of the Concord set that lit the fire at the core of the Newness. Their friendships, rivalries, disagreements, and mutual support drove each of them to their highest achievements.

Their personalities ranged widely. Hawthorne was painfully shy. Fuller was overwhelmingly charismatic. Emerson was a generous catalyst who kept everyone at arm's length. His close friend, Bronson Alcott, was an enigma. He was hopeless at making his way in the world, yet he inspired deep affection among several members of the group. He was among the first of them to embrace abolitionism and a vegan diet. His controversial teaching methods have transformed into common practice today.

The youngest members, Thoreau and Louisa May Alcott, dedicated themselves to their work. Neither married. Both died young. Each wrote a masterpiece.

The Emerson Circle is the story of this small group and the movements it inspired. It is not a comprehensive group biography—there are wonderful books about each member that go into far more detail than this book can afford. Yet their collective work represents a crucial cultural moment in American history.

That moment did not last long. The looming crisis of the Civil War brought an end to the Newness. Utopian thinking, including nonviolence, largely evaporated as the conflict over slavery burst into flames. Emerson's radical idealism became more tempered as he engaged in politics, and he himself began a long mental decline. Thus, this book's story is divided into two sections: the Newness and the Crisis. Transcendentalism and most of the utopian movements failed to survive for long. Yet Emerson and his followers left a lasting mark on the world we know today.

Book I

The Newness

1

Waldo Emerson and Bronson Alcott

A great soul will be strong to live, as well as strong to think.

—Ralph Waldo Emerson

For more than four decades, they came to hear him talk. They came in towns throughout New England. They came in New York, in Philadelphia, in Cleveland, in Cincinnati. They came in Rochester, Buffalo, Syracuse, Pittsburgh; in Montreal, St. Louis, Detroit, Toledo, Dixon, Galena, Beloit, and Peoria. They came in Chicago, Jersey City, Toronto, Baltimore, Madison, Ann Arbor, Kalamazoo, Zanesville, Washington, Milwaukee, Indianapolis; in Davenport, Dubuque, Minneapolis, Cedar Falls, Des Moines, Bloomington, Kansas City, and Columbus. They came in San Francisco. They came in Richmond. Most often of all, they came in Concord, where he spoke for free.

He arranged many of these appearances himself, acting as his own producer and manager, a rarity in the crowded world of public speakers at the time. Sometimes he gave a series of lectures—twelve on the philosophy of history, ten on human life, ten on human culture. Over his life he delivered around fifteen hundred lectures in 283 towns in the United States and Canada.

His listeners, by the dozens and hundreds, saw a six-foot, slender, handsome man who stood nearly motionless at the lectern, reading from some forty pages of script in an even, measured tone. Some of those listeners may have read one of his books, or a few of his poems; but for the vast majority, to experience Ralph Waldo Emerson was to hear him in person.

There was no ad-libbing, except when he rearranged his pages and paragraphs on the spot. There was no thundering. His topics touched on almost everything: great men, natural history, Elizabethan poets, art, politics, religion, manners, ethics, prudence, heroism, the hand, the head, the heart, education, domestic life.

Emerson in his lecture stance, 1860.

Not everyone could understand him clearly. An admirer looking back from near the end of Emerson's life noted that he "always draws" a crowd, thanks to "the charm of his voice, his manner, and his matter, woven into enchanting meshes. What they do not fully understand they take on trust." Some reviewers objected to his style—one wrote that he would rather "see a perpendicular coffin behind a lecture-desk as Emerson." And some detested his philosophy. Once, after giving a talk to students at Wesleyan University, "there arose a Massachusetts minister, who stepped into the pulpit Mr. Emerson had just left, and uttered a remarkable prayer, of which this was one sentence: 'We beseech Thee, O Lord, to deliver us from ever hearing any more such transcendental nonsense as we have just listened to from this sacred desk.'"

And yet he drew crowds. He spoke to all classes and types of listeners. As one reviewer put it, "There is the saintly woman, the adored beauty, the polished gentleman, and beside them the brown-faced farmer, the rustic maiden, and the shy stripling from the Maine woods, to whom a single evening at one of these lectures is the event of the year."

Emerson was not just a towering celebrity in his own right. He was also an inspiration to a generation of radical thinkers. He urged them

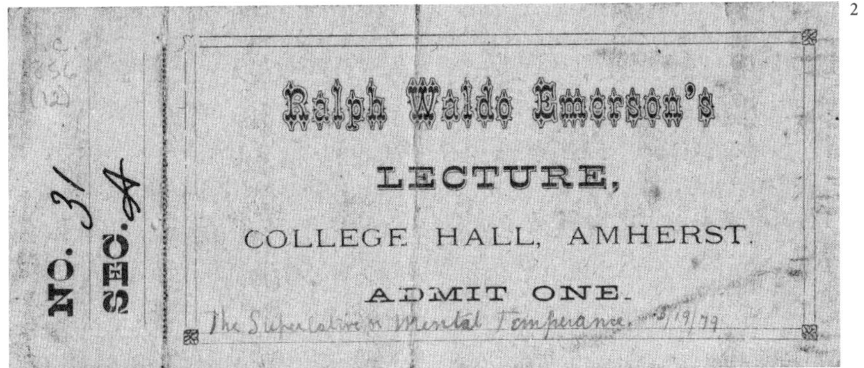

2

Henry Clay Folger's ticket to an 1879 Emerson lecture titled "The Superlative, or Mental Temperance," one of the last he gave.

to cast off the bonds of tradition and think for themselves. He believed they could be the heroes and saints of a new age. He was a relentless optimist who convinced them that their own possibilities were limitless.

Socially, he was a connector who brought them together and forged a community. He encouraged several of them to move to Concord. He cofounded a journal to publish their essays and poems. He cofounded a discussion group where they could share their ideas. To some of them, he was a source of frustration—he began as a mentor but then he drew back, keeping them at a remove. Yet he was generous to a fault, always ready to lend them money or help them find employment.

One of his closest and longest friendships was with a man who, in many ways, was his opposite. A man who failed when Emerson succeeded and eventually succeeded when Emerson failed. Each recognized the faults of the other and looked past them.

Amos Bronson Alcott, who changed his last name from Alcox and was known by his middle name, and Ralph Waldo Emerson—who was known as Waldo—became friends and allies despite differences in their backgrounds, personalities, and careers. Alcott was born and raised on a farm in rural Woolcott, Connecticut. Emerson came from Boston. Alcott received barely any education. At thirteen, his uncle tried enrolling him at Cheshire Academy, but he lasted only a month—his better-educated classmates ridiculed him. As he wrote later, "I was homesick, and soon returned to my father's, affected by the becoming [behavior] of the students." He educated himself from then on, devouring every book he could find.

Emerson, four years younger, was a graduate of Boston Latin School, Harvard College, and Harvard Divinity School. He was the son and grandson of ministers. As his aunt Mary said of Waldo and his brothers, "They were born to be educated."

Emerson and Alcott did share one childhood condition: financial struggle. Emerson's father died in 1811 just before Emerson turned eight, leaving the family in debt. Waldo was only able to attend Harvard thanks to a scholarship and a work-study position as the "President's Freshman" in his first year, running errands for President John Kirkland. Alcott's parents were, like so many rural Americans, subsistence farmers.

Alcott and Emerson also shared one career phase: They floundered before they found their callings. Emerson tried teaching and preaching. Alcott, before him, earned a teaching certificate at seventeen but couldn't find a job. He became a Yankee peddler in the South, buying and selling household goods that he carried door-to-door. He said he was learning about geography and mankind. Yet as he would prove again and again, he had no knack for business.

Eventually, Alcott returned to Connecticut and took on a series of jobs running local schools. At some point he discovered a set of six pamphlets, *Hints to Parents*, based on the theories of a Swiss education reformer named Johann Heinrich Pestalozzi. Pestalozzi believed children to be innately intelligent and moral. The parent's and educator's task was to help them uncover these natural traits, to help them flourish socially as well as intellectually.

The pamphlet series included many specific suggestions. A mother must encourage "gratitude, faith, and love" in her children, along with "unconditional, prompt, and cheerful obedience." Above all, she must bring out their intuitive moral sense and treat them as "beings holding a high rank in creation; endowed with the heavenly spark of reason."

In other words: Engage children in conversation, treat them as wise, and gently lead them to articulate what they know instinctively. Yet prompt and cheerful obedience is easier to describe than achieve. Bronson would face that problem with his second daughter, Louisa May.

Alcott's approach was a departure from the typical schooling of the day. In many schools, pupils sat silently reading at their desks until they were called to stand before the schoolmaster to recite a passage from memory. There was little conversation. Ideas went unexplored. Yet Pestalozzi's theories were gaining adherents. In 1829 in Concord, a young man named Lemuel Shattuck joined the school committee and helped reorganize the town's school along Pestalozzian lines.

3

Pencil sketch of young Bronson Alcott.

Horace Mann, the founding father of American education, described the many problems of public schooling when he became secretary of the Massachusetts Board of Education in 1837: lack of funding, lack of consistent attendance due to child labor demands, lack of standardized texts, and above all, lack of skilled teachers. As he wrote, "The business of school-keeping fell more and more into the hands of youth and inexperience." Teacher turnover was a constant problem, and many teachers struggled to maintain discipline in the classroom, using wooden rods to slap the palms of misbehaving students. Mann viewed corporal punishment as a last resort, "a relic of barbarism." Bronson joined a growing chorus arguing that it should be banned entirely.

His teaching methods were radically different from the usual. In some ways, Bronson was a pioneer of the modern technique of peer learning, by way of the Socratic method.

Perhaps because his methods were so new and strange, or perhaps because he failed to connect with his students, one after another of his postings proved a failure: four schools and five jobs in Connecticut, two schools in Boston, and two in Pennsylvania. The failures only made Bronson want to try harder. In his journal he blamed a reactionary public who considered anything new and unusual as "anarchy and confusion."

The answer to that problem? Move back to Boston and start all over again. (He would later scoff in his journal: "I have but limited faith in the moral intelligence of the Philadelphians as efficient patrons of early education.")

Fortunately, his decade of professional struggles brought great domestic happiness. In 1828, as he was preparing to launch the Salem Street Infant School in Boston, he needed an assistant. The prior year, Bronson had visited a fellow reformer named Samuel May and had been taken with his sister, Abigail, called Abba. "There was nothing of artifice, of affectation of manners; all was openness, simplicity, nature herself. There was intelligence, sympathy, piety, exemplified in the tenderness of the eye, in the beauty of moral countenance, in the joyousness of domestic performance. . . . How could we but be in love with them—with their possessor?" He was tall, with flowing hair, piercing blue eyes, and serene self-confidence. Abba, too, was smitten.

She offered to join Alcott at the new school and openly expressed her love and admiration. She had turned down a suitor approved by her parents; now she pursued a man they might not so readily accept. Yet she struggled to interpret his feelings for her. At one point, she was "convinced . . . of his indifference." He visited her. As she recorded: "I walked with him to give him an opportunity to express his opinion of my communication. His conversation was mystical. It seemed to me that the more he tried to explain the more mysterious every thing appeared to me. Did Mr. Alcott really love me?" At last, he made his feelings clear.

On May 23, 1830, they married. They would have four daughters in the following decade: Anna (1831), Louisa May (1832), Elizabeth (1835), and Abby May (1840).

Abba soon discovered that their life would not be an easy one. After losing one post in Boston in 1830 and preparing to try again in Germantown, Pennsylvania, she wrote to her brother, "My husband is the perfect personification of modesty and moderation. I am not sure that we shall not blush into obscurity and contemplate into starvation."

Two years later, when the Germantown school was failing, she wrote to her mother, "The vicissitudes of life seem to lift our principles in proportion as they disappoint our hopes and baffle our plans. . . . The harmony and symmetry of my husband's character is more and more exemplified by the pressure of adverse circumstances."

Parenthood was a chance for Bronson to test his theories. He kept journals of his daughters' progress. He hoped they would lead to a book. He drafted one manuscript based on Anna's and Louisa's first few years—"Observations on the Spiritual Nurture of My Children"—and a second after Lizzie was born: "Psyche: or the Breath of Childhood."

He would work hard on "Psyche," hoping to publish it. He called it a "prose poem . . . not a formal treatise on grave and profound topics, but a simple, unpremeditated work." It is pompous and abstract, with only occasional noteworthy anecdotes about the girls. (A taste: Spirit "fortelleth and remembereth all . . . She buildeth up around herself a lady of flesh . . . while she keepeth, as ever, the general hold on the universal." Or, just to note that it is wintertime: "Winter reigneth. External nature hath now enrobed herself in white, and sendeth man into his inner dwelling, to find the general warmth that she now refuseth him.")

Nonetheless, there are telling nuggets about his daughters in the manuscripts and in his journals. He discovered what every parent learns: Children have their own personalities. They cannot be forced into any mold. Anna was an obedient, easy child. Louisa May was not. After describing one incident when he resorted to spanking her, he noted, "Obedience has never been enforced against her determinations. . . . She resists with all her might."

• • •

Emerson, like his future friend Alcott, struggled to find his calling. Back when Alcott was traveling throughout the South, Emerson was at first a middling student at Harvard, then a teacher at the School for Young Ladies run by his brother, William, at their mother's house. They closed the school in 1824, and he entered Harvard Divinity School that fall. Nobody would have predicted that the Yankee peddler and this Harvard divinity student would cross paths, much less arrive at similar views about the world of the Spirit, the humanity of Christ, or the need to seek radical change and individual perfection.

Alcott's marriage and growing family contrast with a series of tragedies for Emerson. His father had died of stomach cancer when Waldo was young. His younger brother Edward, a standout student who went to work in Daniel Webster's law office, suffered a mental breakdown at twenty-five. He would die of tuberculosis six years later. That disease, known at the time as consumption, killed more nineteenth-century Americans than any other. Waldo and Edward's younger brother Charles would also die of it. And Waldo's first wife, Ellen Louisa Tucker, died of the disease on February 8, 1831, less than two years after their wedding.

She was already ill when they met. In late December 1828, Waldo had written, "I have now been four days engaged to Ellen Louisa Tucker. Will my Father in Heaven regard us with kindness, and . . . will he be pleased to strengthen and purify and prosper and eternize our affection!" Yet she declined steadily. Emerson's journals were mainly devoted to intellectual topics, with only occasional personal comments. On the day she died, he made one terse note: "Ellen Tucker Emerson died, 8th February, Tuesday morning, 9 o'clock."

It was a terrible blow. Later that week, he wrote of his "miserable apathy," expecting that he would only ever partially recover from it. "I shall . . . forget the graveyard. But will the dead be restored to me?"

Every day for the rest of that year and into the next while working as a pastor for Boston's Second Church, he walked to her grave in Roxbury. Once, on March 29, 1832, he opened the coffin. He wasn't ready to forget the graveyard.

Yet, as he had predicted, old duties reclaimed his energy. He continued to preach, and his thinking evolved away from church doctrine. In his journal in May, Emerson asked, "For what has imagination created to compare with the science of astronomy? . . . Who can be a Calvinist, or who an atheist? God has opened this knowledge to us to correct our theology and educate the mind." He was beginning to doubt the dogma of received religion and seek meaning directly from the natural world. And then: "The irresistible effect of Copernican Astronomy has been to make the great scheme for the Salvation of man absolutely incredible." In other words, as dorm-room discussions still question, if science has shown that we inhabit just one planet out of many others, rotating around one sun out of many others, if there is nothing in the design of the universe that suggests it was especially created for us, how can we believe that God singled us out for salvation?

At the time, the dominant religion of Boston and much of New England was Unitarianism. It was a relatively new Protestant sect: the American Unitarian Association had formed in 1825 out of a schism within the Congregational Church, one of the last "established" state churches in the country (meaning that towns were allowed to tax their residents to pay for a local Congregational church and minister). Only in 1833 would the state amend its constitution to eliminate its established church. Voters approved that amendment by a ten-to-one margin, thanks to the growing number of Unitarians, Methodists, Baptists, Quakers, and Catholics.

Unitarianism was "congregational"; each church ran its own affairs. It was also liberal, emphasizing God's benevolence and discarding the wrathful God of Puritan Calvinists. Under traditional Calvinism, God chose whom He saved and left everyone else to suffer for their sins. Under liberal Protestantism, salvation was available to anyone who embraced Jesus as their Lord. Yet the proliferating number of Protestant sects overlapped in many beliefs and practices: Most Unitarians of the 1830s still accepted the miracles of the Bible as true. Some of them questioned the divinity of Jesus, but they still believed he was God's messenger. Unitarian services typically included the reiteration of the Last Supper known as Communion. Above all, Protestants and Catholics all agreed that God sent Jesus to save mankind.

Emerson no longer accepted that orthodoxy. There were plenty of other Americans for whom religion played a minor (or no) role in their lives, but very few of them articulated an alternative path to truth and higher wisdom, as he did. He was a radical individualist who believed in spiritual truth with no need of any church or minister to help find it.

He could no longer serve the church. He created something of a crisis when he stopped offering Communion. (One parishioner said to him, "You have taken my Lord away and I know not where you have laid him.") He hailed from generations of Protestant clergy, yet he felt he had to go his own way. His aunt, Mary Moody Emerson, a major influence on him and a sharp-thinking precursor of the Transcendentalists, tried her best to argue with him, writing, "Without a personal God you are on an ocean mast unrigged for any port or object." She failed to change his mind.

Emerson's new thinking bears a relationship to Alcott's educational philosophy. Alcott believed each student had a divine spark of innate wisdom for the teacher to help develop. Emerson believed that each adult had a divine spark and could access higher truths directly. The young republic of the United States was fertile ground for these two individualists.

That summer, Emerson decided to quit. He gave a parting sermon where he tried to defend his position—the so-called Last Supper sermon—but his days of full-time ministry were over. He sold his house and furniture and in December sailed to Europe, where he spent most of 1833 traveling and meeting such writers as John Stuart Mill, William Wordsworth, Samuel Taylor Coleridge, and Thomas Carlyle. The last would become a lifelong friend.

In Paris, visiting the Jardin des Plantes and its extensive collection of plant and animal specimens, he sensed more wisdom than in any pages of scripture:

> Here we are impressed with the inexhaustible riches of nature. The Universe is a more amazing puzzle than ever, as you glance along this bewildering series of animated forms,—the hazy butterflies, the carved shells, the birds, beasts, fishes, insects, snakes, and the upheaving principle of life everywhere incipient. . . . Not a form so grotesque, so savage, nor so beautiful but is an expression of some property inherent in man the observer,—an occult relation between the very scorpions and man. I feel the centipede in me,—cayman, carp, eagle, and fox. I am moved by strange sympathies; I say continually, "I will be a naturalist."

Darwin's *On the Origin of Species* was twenty-six years in the future, yet Emerson grasped that all branches on the tree of life are connected. He wanted to pursue the spiritual truths expressed in nature rather than preach the gospel.

Upon his return to Massachusetts, a new career path opened. There were lyceums springing up in the Northeast and Midwest, organized lecture series for traveling orators. The first one, in Milbury, Massachusetts, launched in 1826. Initially, they focused on scientific and practical topics, but they quickly expanded to intellectual and ethical questions. They would soon be widespread in Massachusetts, in Boston, Cambridge, Concord, Salem, and Nantucket, and elsewhere, seventy-eight of them by 1830; and then elsewhere in the Northeast, and then beyond—some three thousand by 1845. In addition to lecturing, he could publish books and essays. He could be something new in America: a public intellectual.

2

A Temple of Learning

> [Alcott's] book is his school, in which he writes all his thoughts.
>
> —*Journals of Ralph Waldo Emerson*

Elizabeth Palmer Peabody met Emerson in 1822. She was eighteen, living in Boston and trying to launch a school for girls—one of the few employment options for women like her. She was the oldest of six children (a seventh died in infancy), and one of three Peabody sisters to become famous. The other two, Mary and Sophia, would marry prominent men—Horace Mann and Nathaniel Hawthorne. Yet Elizabeth was the most intellectually precocious of them all. At thirteen she read the New Testament thirty times in just a few months, considering different points of view on the divinity of Jesus. (One year younger than Emerson, she was far ahead of him in her theological explorations.) At seventeen, when the family moved to Lancaster, Massachusetts, she opened a school for girls and joined a series of informal gatherings of local intellectuals to discuss, among other topics, education reform. She threw herself into teaching, trying out many of the same innovations that Bronson Alcott would soon employ. She spurned one suitor—she would never marry—before moving to Boston.

She would become one of the spark plugs of the new thinking of the 1830s and '40s. She seemed to know everyone, and she helped connect and introduce them to one another, and helped them find employment when they needed it. She would stay at the Emersons' on her Concord visits, finding that Waldo "feels my infinite capacity just as I do myself." She would open a bookstore on West Street in Boston, quite possibly the first woman-founded bookstore in the country. The shop offered many American and British books alongside European texts by Goethe and others, and hosted key gatherings of what would become the Emerson circle.

She had one other suitor, this one more worthy of her: Nathaniel Hawthorne, who, in the end, chose her quieter, artistic, illness-prone sister. Elizabeth chose to live a life of the mind.

In 1822, driven to continue her self-education, she sought a tutor to help her with her Greek. Emerson, who was teaching with his brother at the time, stepped into the role. As she later wrote: "It is true that both of us were very shy (Mr. Emerson then nineteen and I eighteen years old), and we did not get into a chatting acquaintance, but sat opposite each other at the study table, not lifting our eyes from our books." When she was preparing to move to Maine to take a new teaching position and asked what she owed him, Emerson told her "he had no bill to render, for he found he could teach me nothing."

4

Elizabeth Palmer Peabody, near the end of her life.

Somewhat like Alcott, she struggled with different school posts, spending two years in Maine before moving to Brookline, Massachusetts. (Teaching was one of the only vocations available to women, yet it was not yet a highly institutionalized profession—many teachers moved frequently.) Also like him, she aroused opposition. In 1826, just as Alcott was beginning his series of teaching experiments, Peabody held a series of Saturday conversations on theology with her older students in Brookline. She was presenting Unitarian and other radical ideas. Some of the girls, and some of their parents, were outraged. She responded with the same decision Alcott would make eight years later: move to Boston and try teaching there.

She succeeded this time. She won over her occasional critics. Her school's enrollment was strong. She also flourished personally. She had already befriended William Ellery Channing, the leading Unitarian minister who preached at Boston's Federal Street Church. She began to spend time with him. He was forty-six in 1826. Since he was an older man of the cloth, she could safely spend time alone with him. She attended every sermon and then went to his house for weekly conversations. He became her intellectual mentor, introducing her to the works of Wordsworth and Coleridge. She also began writing essays. She called her new philosophy "transcendentalism," the first time anyone used the term.

She was a fountain of energy who mastered multiple languages. She proposed to Channing that they work together on publishing his sermons, with Peabody doing most of the work. She began to translate French texts, working with a printer and selling subscriptions. Yet she continued to struggle financially. She met Alcott in 1828 and wrote an admiring description of his teaching in William Russell's *American Journal of Education*. She concluded that "elementary education needs, and is receiving, great improvement in an intellectual point of view. But little, comparatively, has been done for its moral renovation. Even infant schools are too generally taught on arbitrary and mechanical methods."

Alcott shared some of his students' journals with her and she was impressed. By 1832 she was no longer teaching; she couldn't afford it. She had closed her school. She and her sister Mary were living at a boardinghouse in Boston, whose visitors included Emerson and his brother Charles. (Their aunt, Mary Moody Emerson, had urged Charles to meet Elizabeth in hopes of making a match.) Horace Mann, Mary's eventual husband, moved into the house near the end of that year.

By the spring of 1834, Elizabeth was struggling to afford her rent, so she moved to a private family home as a governess. She held semiweekly "Historical Conferences" for adult students. Yet she longed to teach children. Years later, she would found the first English-language kindergarten in America. When Alcott made plans to open yet another institution, the Temple School at the Masonic Temple on Tremont Street, she eagerly joined him to teach Latin, arithmetic, and geography. Generously, she gave him the students she had been gathering for a new school of her own.

The Temple School would prove to be the biggest success and most public failure of Alcott's teaching career. It would also prove a key turning point in the lives of several of the Concord radicals.

The school opened that fall, an early experiment in coeducation. Elizabeth described it in detail in *Record of a School: Exhibiting the General Principles of Spiritual Culture*, published in 1835. They began with thirty students, mostly young boys who were "creatures of instinct more than any thing else, with undeveloped consciences and minds . . . overflowing with animal spirits, and all but intoxicated with play."

They met in a large upstairs room at the Masonic Temple. The students sat in a semicircle facing Alcott's ten-foot custom-made desk. Behind him on top of a tall bookshelf was a large bas-relief head of Jesus. The four corners of the room featured busts of Socrates, Shakespeare, Milton, and Sir Walter Scott.

Peabody explained how Alcott achieved "cheerful obedience" among all those students, intoxicated with play. He, or the students themselves, put one student each day in charge of the children's

5

A sketch of the upstairs room of the Masonic Temple, Bronson's classroom. He sits at his desk on the right, with visitors on the couches, front right and far left center. Normally, the students' desks would face him in a semicircle, but here they have been shifted to the walls.

behavior. That student decided all punishments for misbehavior, not Alcott. As she wrote, "The worst boys, when put into that office, become scrupulously just, and get an idea of superintending themselves, which nothing else can give them."

At times, the class voted on proper punishments. Alcott even sacrificed his own body to instill guilt, insisting that a misbehaving student be forced to hurt the teacher, rather than the reverse. "They declared that they would never do it. But he soon made them understand that he was serious. . . . There was a more complete silence, and attention, and obedience, than there had ever been." A typical physical punishment of that era involved slapping a student's palm with a ferule, a twelve- or eighteen-inch wooden rod. Bronson asked the misbehaving students to slap *his* palm, instead. Decades later, a student would be ordered to slap his teacher's palm in *Little Men* by Louisa May, an act that so shamed the student that he never forgot it.

Peabody's book describes the conversations Bronson led and reproduces some of them in detail. It presents a summary journal of some five weeks of lessons, day by day, and then adds short versions of his teachings on such topics as love, faith, conscience, imagination, and the like. Throughout, the students are engaged and interested, asking good questions and wrestling with important topics.

Bronson's school gained fame. The main room featured a sofa for visitors. Emerson took the opportunity to observe Alcott and Peabody in action. In return, Alcott heard him give a lecture on Michelangelo in February 1835. As Alcott wrote in his journal, "Few men among us take nobler views of the mission, powers, and destinies of man than Mr. E. I hope the people of this city will go and learn of him the conditions of virtue and vision, by what self-denial, what exertion these are to be sought and won." They were not yet friends, but they soon would be.

The year 1835 proved pivotal for the reformers. Emerson had met Lydia Jackson in February of the previous year and had begun courting his "Lydian Queen," whom he soon renamed Lidian. In January they became engaged. In September, they married. One friend described Lidian as "almost equal to Mr. Emerson . . . Her movements are free and graceful, she is a soaring transcendentalist."

The next day, on September 15, they moved to the Concord home where they would live for the rest of their lives. As Waldo wrote to his brother William, "It is in a mean place & cannot be fine until trees & flowers give it a character of its own. But we shall crowd so many books & papers, &, if possible, wise friends, into it that it shall have as much wit as it can carry." He was prescient. The Emerson home would become a magnet for leaders and followers of the Newness.

The future author of "Self-Reliance" also now had some financial security thanks, in part, to a lawsuit against his late wife's family in a dispute over her inheritance. He prevailed and secured a meaningful sum of money.

Peabody's *Record of a School* came out in July to critical acclaim. It was the first publication that could be termed transcendentalist. Emerson recorded that he "read with great delight the *Record of a School.* It aims all the time to show the symbolical character of all things to the children, and it is alleged, and I doubt not, truly, that the children take the thought with delight." When Alcott's third daughter was born that summer, he and Abba named her Elizabeth Peabody Alcott.

Bronson had his first real conversation with Waldo in October when he visited the newlyweds and Charles Emerson in Concord. It was a three-hour ride. There was as yet no train line to Concord, so Alcott arrived on a Saturday and spent the night. They conversed all evening and much of the next day, finding a great deal of common ground. Bronson's only caveat: "Mr. E's fine literary taste is sometimes in the way of the clear and hearty acceptance of the spiritual."

Emerson found Alcott wise and "simple," completely devoted to his teaching career. "Every man, he said, is a Revelation, and ought to write his Record, but few with the pen. His book is his school, in which he writes all his thoughts." Within a year, he would describe Alcott to his brother William as a great genius. Conversely, Alcott would believe that "Emerson is destined to be the high literary name of this age."

The year 1835 also pointed toward another momentous meeting for Emerson in Concord, with a woman in Peabody's mold. Six years younger, home-schooled, and self-educated to an intense degree, she would follow Peabody's example by teaching, by holding adult-education conversations for women, and by translating key European texts both for Reverend Channing and for publication. Like Peabody, she would also connect many new thinkers to one another. She would eclipse Peabody as an author and journalist despite living less than half as long.

In the summer of 1835, she wrote to a friend that "R.W. Emerson—the reverend, and I are tottering on the verge of an acquaintance."

3

Margaret Fuller

> I now know all the people worth knowing in America, and I find no intellect comparable to my own.
>
> —*Memoirs of Margaret Fuller Ossoli*

Sarah Margaret Fuller, known by all as Margaret, lived one of the most remarkable lives of anyone in antebellum America. She was born in Cambridgeport, Massachusetts, in 1810, the oldest child of a prominent lawyer and politician who held his own views on education. When it came to the first of his seven surviving children, Timothy Fuller believed in pushing her to the limit, from an early age. She would reward his theory with prodigious learning, starting with Latin at age six. Her education in the classics and in languages would go far beyond that of most Harvard graduates. But she also suffered physically and socially.

> My father . . . instructed me himself. The effect of this was so far good that, not passing through the hands of many ignorant and weak persons as so many do at preparatory schools, I was put at once under discipline of considerable severity, and, at the same time, had a more than ordinarily high standard presented to me. . . . Frequently, I was sent to bed several hours too late, with nerves unnaturally stimulated. The consequence was a premature development of the brain,

> that made me a "youthful prodigy" by day, and by night a victim of spectral illusions, nightmare[s], and somnambulism.

She would suffer physical ailments throughout her life, and she never forgot her childhood terrors. When she was twenty-nine she wrote about them:

"For a long time I dreaded excessively going to bed for as soon as I was left alone, huge shapes . . . advanced from the corners of the room and pressed upon me, growing larger and larger till they seemed about to crush me." In one recurring nightmare she was wading in a sea of blood, grabbing at twigs and rocks to save herself, causing them to stream yet more blood upon her.

There were no pets in the house, and she had no friends her age to speak of. Her life resembled a monk's: study and more study.

Timothy Fuller's standards were uncompromising. For several years he served in Congress, away from the family for months at a time. He wrote her regularly and admonished her to study diligently and to practice her piano every day. He urged her to write him letters in Latin and French, and then he sent corrections to them.

His standards went beyond academic subjects and her piano skills. When she had to have part of a tooth removed, he wrote that he "should not be proud of you for my daughter, if you could not bear pain with courage, when it is necessary." He admonished her to keep her appearance spotless. He proscribed her reading popular fiction, urging her instead "to acquire a taste for books of *higher* order, than tales & novels. History, travels, biography, are next in rank to fiction." Better she should read *Paradise Lost*. He did not want her to read plays, especially on Sundays, but she managed to fall in love with *Romeo and Juliet* at age eight, on the Sabbath. Timothy, not pleased, ordered her to "Give me the book and go directly to bed."

He memorably summarized his views in one sentence of one letter: "To excel in all things should be your constant aim; mediocrity is obscurity." She was ten years old.

When she was fourteen, he sent her to Miss Susan Prescott's Young

Margaret Fuller, engraving by Henry Bryan Hall Jr.

6

Ladies' Seminary in Groton, a finishing school. She hated the simplistic lessons but came to like Prescott herself. She lasted one year there. It marked the end of her full-time schooling. From then on, she pursued self-education with zeal, notwithstanding her headaches. As she wrote in her journals about reading some pages by Goethe, "I read them in bed for I was very ill today—I can always understand anything better when I am ill."

In one letter to Prescott she described her daily routine: waking before five a.m. for an hour's walk, then piano practice for an hour, then breakfast at seven. Then she would read French literary history, some philosophy, and work on her Greek until noon. After more music practice and an early afternoon dinner, she would spend two hours reading Italian literature, take another walk, then do some singing or play piano to help her younger siblings settle for bed. Finally, she would retire to her room at eleven p.m. to write in her journal.

Timothy Fuller served in Congress for eight years, until shortly before Margaret turned fifteen. The family then moved to a grand house in Cambridge where they would live for eight years. Timothy required Margaret to home-school her younger siblings while she continued her own reading and language study. As she would write to one friend, "I wish to study ten-thousand, thousand things this winter—Every day I become more sensible to the defects in my education—I feel so ignorant and superficial."

The Cambridge years provided a rich social life as well as the chance to work with Channing and meet many other leading intellectuals. She was electrifying company. As one friend would later write, "She was always conspicuous by the brilliancy of her wit, which needed but little provocation to break forth in exuberant sallies, that drew around her a knot of listeners, and made her the central attraction of the hour. Rarely did she enter a company in which she was not a prominent object."

Throughout her life she would form intense attachments to both men and women, sometimes overwhelming them. When she was nineteen she became close with George Davis, a distant cousin and newly enrolled Harvard student. Of everyone in her circle of friends, he was closest to her intellectual equal. Yet he would pull away, breaking her heart. She then became close with James Freeman Clarke—a platonic, intense, lifelong relationship. She dazzled him. "With what eagerness did she seek for knowledge! What fire, what exuberance, what reach, grasp, overflow of thought, shone in her conversation!" She also fell in love with a young woman, Anna Barker, a New Yorker whom she saw only on occasion and for whom she developed powerful feelings: "We both felt such a strange mystic thrill and knew what we had never known before."

As she wrote in her journal, "It is so true that a woman may be in love with a woman, and a man with a man. . . . It is regulated by the same law as that of love between persons of different sexes; only it is purely intellectual and spiritual. . . . I loved [Barker], for a time, with as much passion as I was then strong enough to feel."

She felt that she was unattractive, and some men agreed, including Emerson. They finally met in 1836 when she came to stay with him in the summer. As he recalled:

> Her extreme plainness,—a trick of incessantly opening and shutting her eyelids,—the nasal tone of her voice,—all repelled; and I said to myself, we shall never get far. . . .[Yet] she studied my tastes, piqued and amused me, challenged frankness by frankness, and did not conceal the good opinion of me she brought with her, nor her wish to please. . . . Of course, it was impossible long to hold out against such an urgent assault.

At the time, in his journal, he called her "quite an extraordinary person for her apprehensiveness, her acquisitions & her powers of conversation. It is always a great refreshment to see a very intelligent person. It is like being set in a large place. You stretch your limbs & dilate to your utmost size."

She would come to embrace the idealism of the Transcendentalists and be welcomed into their circle. Yet she also hungered to engage with the world more directly than many of them—it would lead her out of New England, and beyond America, in her meteoric career.

Soon after Fuller visited the Emersons, Alcott and Emerson published their first books. Alcott's was a disaster. Emerson's was a significant success intellectually, if not commercially.

In the spring 1836 term of the Temple School, Alcott added a weekly session of conversations about the life of Jesus. Elizabeth Peabody transcribed them and he wished to publish the results. By now he had given her a spare bedroom in the family's apartment, since he couldn't afford to pay her for her teaching. The proximity brought tensions, as she didn't always agree with his many firm opinions.

Worse, for his book, he manipulated the students' words, rewriting her transcripts so the message was what he wanted it to be. Worse still, he identified the children by name. In June, when she took a leave to visit friends in Lowell, her sister Sophia moved in with the Alcotts to continue the project. When Elizabeth returned in July she was upset by a conversation Alcott had led on the topic of childbirth. He had asked his students, "And what did you think being born was?"

The conversation veered in a dangerous direction when one student replied, "The spirit comes from heaven, and takes up the naughtiness out of other people, which makes other people better. And these naughtinesses, put together, make a body for the child." Peabody recognized that "naughtinesses" could be interpreted as referring to sex. In the full context of the transcription, it seems clear that the student meant only that the physical world is a corruption of the spiritual—he didn't mean to say anything about sexual acts. Yet critics might seize on the quotation. She pleaded with Alcott to remove the passage. He refused, only agreeing to relegate it to a footnote.

Peabody wrote about her concerns to her sister Mary, who urged her to leave the school and the Alcotts' home. To make matters worse, Abba Alcott snooped in Elizabeth's room and found one of Mary's letters. She shared it with Bronson. They were appalled that Mary—and by implication, Elizabeth—was critical of him. Elizabeth, in turn, was appalled that Abba had invaded her privacy. Elizabeth severed relations and moved back to Salem. The Alcotts changed the middle name of their one-year-old daughter from Peabody to Sewall.

Bronson needed a new assistant. He met Fuller while she was visiting Emerson, and they spoke about it. Fuller came away confused. In late August, she wrote to him:

Dear Sir

I am not quite sure that I understood your last words at Mr. Emerson's. As I understood, you had applied to some other person to assist you in your school before you thought of me and would write to me after receiving an answer from that person. A letter since received

> *from Miss Peabody leads me to think that you may on your side be expecting to hear from me and, as I find it necessary to come to some decision about my employment for the winter, I think it best to write to you at any rate.*
>
> *Will you have the kindness to answer this letter as soon as possible informing me whether you are desirous I should take Miss Peabody's place; whether, if I do take it, you expect me to reside in your family as she did; and whether anything would be expected from me beyond the instruction in Latin or other languages which you mentioned to me. . . .*
>
> *My acquaintance with your views and character is not sufficiently thorough to give me a confidence that I could satisfy you. . . . It would be but an experiment on both sides, for, as I have never yet been subordinate to any one, I cannot tell how I should please or be pleased. But your proposal has attracted me more than any which has as yet been made to me.*

She took the job. Bronson found her to be one of the most intelligent people he had ever met. He soon came to believe that "of those who promise to add enduring glory to female literature, she seems most conspicuous among us." But their partnership at the school would last only four months. Alcott's book brought the school crashing down.

It came out in December. Reactions were scathing. Andrews Norton, a leading Unitarian clergyman, denounced it as "one third absurd, one third blasphemous, and one third obscene." The editor of the *Boston Daily Advertiser* wrote, "These conversations appear the first fruits of the new attempt to draw wisdom from babes and sucklings. It is in our opinion, a signal failure, and we cannot recommend any longer perseverance in the experiment." Alcott tried to keep his chin up, telling himself that "small men are ever in the way of great and needful changes," but the backlash was wide and deep.

Many parents withdrew their students. By the spring Alcott had to move to a cheaper apartment and auction off some of his school's prized possessions: the busts of great thinkers, furnishings, and many books. Fuller departed with no hope of ever seeing a salary. Emerson wrote to Fuller that "his book does him no justice and I do not like to see it . . . he has more of the godlike than any man I have ever seen."

While Alcott was under attack, Emerson was launching a thunderbolt in September 1836 with his first book, *Nature*. From his opening sentences Emerson called for a revolution in knowledge and spirituality.

> Our age is retrospective. It builds the sepulchres of the fathers. It writes biographies, histories, and criticism. The foregoing generations beheld God and nature face to face; we, through their eyes. Why should not we also enjoy an original relation to the universe?

In *Nature*'s mere ninety pages Emerson argues for exploring the world directly, pursuing truth through and beyond science: to perceive

7 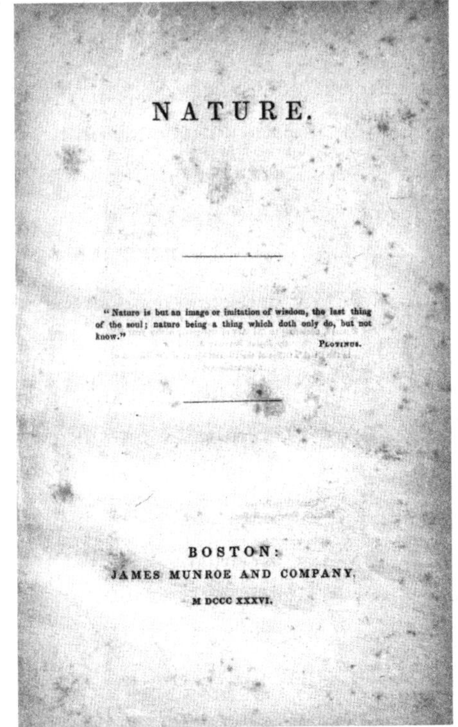

NATURE.

"Nature is but an image or imitation of wisdom, the last thing of the soul; nature being a thing which doth only do, but not know."

PLOTINUS.

BOSTON:
JAMES MUNROE AND COMPANY.
M DCCC XXXVI.

Title page of *Nature* by Ralph Waldo Emerson, 1836.

the Divine Spirit animating the world, to uncover the laws that govern us. The spiritual world expresses itself in the physical realm. Nature and the Soul are twin aspects of the universe. As he would explain in a lecture at Waterville College a few years later on "The Method of Nature": "In the divine order, intellect is primary; nature, secondary; it is the memory of the mind. That which once existed in intellect as pure law, has now taken body as Nature."

He was challenging readers to put down their books and their Bibles and seek the Divine Spirit through direct experience. But more than this, he argued that each of us contains a spark of that same spirit: "Man is conscious of a universal soul within or behind his individual life, wherein, as in a firmament, the natures of Justice, Truth, Love, Freedom, arise and shine. This universal soul he calls Reason: it is not mine or thine, or his, but we are its; we are its property and men."

One of the most quoted passages of the essay has lent itself to satire: "Standing on the bare ground,—my head bathed by the blithe air, and uplifted into infinite space,—all mean egotism vanishes. I become a transparent eyeball; I am nothing; I see all; the currents of the Universal Being circulate through me; I am part or particle of God." Emerson's friend and acolyte Christopher Pearse Cranch, a Unitarian minister, poet, and painter, caricatured Waldo in a pencil sketch as a stick figure with a giant eyeball in place of a head. It has become more famous than anything else Cranch produced.

Nature was hardly a bestseller. Emerson personally funded the anonymous publication of only five hundred copies, and it would take years for them all to be sold. Yet it had a significant impact. It became the foundational document of the Transcendentalist movement.

Alcott called it "a gem throughout." A reviewer in the *Western Messenger* hedged: "The work is a remarkable one, and it certainly will be called remarkable by those, who consider it 'mere moonshine,' as well as those, who look upon it with reverence, as the effusion of a prophet-like mind." At least one critic labeled Emerson a pantheist.

Emerson's gift for aphorism is on full display in *Nature*, as it would be in his many subsequent essays. He would become one of the most

8

Christopher Pearse Cranch's caricature of Emerson's *Nature*: "Standing on the bare ground, my head bathed by the blithe air, and uplifted into infinite space, all mean egotism vanishes. I become a transparent eyeball."

quoted writers in American history. "To go into solitude, a man needs to retire as much from his chamber as from society." "The greatest delight which the fields and woods minister, is the suggestion of an occult relation between man and the vegetable."

His aphoristic style can be a challenge. Rather than build a flowing argument, Emerson piles declaration upon declaration. As Margaret Fuller would later note in a review of his *Essays: Second Series*: "In no one essay is the main stress so obvious as to produce on the mind the harmonious effect of a noble river or a tree in full leaf. Single passages and sentences engage our attention too much in proportion. These *Essays*, it has been justly said, tire like a string of mosaics." Alcott went so far as to say (and he meant it admiringly) that "you may begin at the last paragraph and read backwards."

Nonetheless, *Nature* lit a fuse. The day before publication he met with three liberal friends, all Unitarian ministers: George Ripley, Henry Hedge, and George Putnam. They plotted a regular gathering of like-minded thinkers. On September 19, the first meeting took place at Ripley's home. The original four added one more minister, Convers Francis, and two barely educated mavericks, Orestes Brownson and Bronson Alcott. As Emerson recorded, "The conversation was earnest and hopeful. . . . The rule suggested for the club was this, that no man should be admitted whose presence excluded any one topic." The group that would come to be called the Transcendental Club was born.

In the spring of 1837, as Alcott was selling off whatever he could, the country was in the grip of a financial panic. It is commonly said that presidents cannot single-handedly cause recessions, but the Panic of 1837 nearly serves as an exception. Andrew Jackson despised national currency, and paper currency in general. He had railed against the Second Bank of the United States as an engine of elitist corruption, and he had vetoed the Senate's attempt to renew its charter in 1832. It took four years for the bank to wind down operations. In 1836, he went a step further by issuing an executive order known as the Specie Circular, requiring that public land purchases be made only in gold or silver. In his farewell address, Jackson devoted several paragraphs to the evils of paper money: "an engine to undermine your free institutions . . . those who desire to engross all power in the hands of the few and to govern by corruption or force are aware of its power and prepared to employ it." His veto, and the Specie Circular, would prove to be sour parting gifts to his vice president and successor, Martin Van Buren.

Cotton prices fell steeply in 1836, and the Bank of England began tightening credit. American banks now had to rely on their own hard currency, which ran out. The panic led to one of the longest-lasting recessions in American history. Alcott limped along with a reduced version of the school, but the end was approaching.

Fuller visited Emerson before taking a new—and this time, paying—position at the Greene Street School in Providence, Rhode Island. The school was run by Hiram Fuller (no relation) on progressive lines. As Fuller wrote to Peabody, "Mr. Fuller is as unlike as possible to Mr. Alcott. He has neither his poetic beauty nor his practical defects." Yet Margaret would last only a year and a half there. She was exhausting herself and suffering more headaches, while feeling removed from the intellectual excitement of Boston and Concord. Finally, she wrote to a friend that she wished never to teach children again—but she had "dreams and hopes as to the education of women." Like Alcott, she wanted to inspire people to seek higher truths. Unlike him, she didn't have the patience to do that with children.

At least she could visit Emerson during summer breaks, as she did in August 1837. It was good timing. On August 31, Emerson delivered an address to the annual gathering of Harvard's Phi Beta Kappa Society at Cambridge's First Parish Meeting House, just outside Harvard Yard, where Henry David Thoreau had graduated college the previous day. Fuller attended. Alcott was there. Others in the audience included Oliver Wendell Holmes, Massachusetts governor Edward Everett, and Supreme Court justice Joseph Story. If Emerson ever wanted to generate attention, this was his chance.

"The American Scholar" became a sensation—Alcott could "not forget the delight with which I heard it, nor the mixed confusion, consternation, surprise and wonder with which the audience listened to it." Orestes Brownson wrote to Emerson saying, "I do not know what the world is coming to, if such a voice as that may be heard in old Harvard. You bearded the lion in his den." Emerson published it to extend the effect. Over time it became one of his most famous works.

It was a call to arms, daring students to forsake the library and pursue original discoveries. Why read the classics when they could "read God directly"? Time is too precious to waste on Cicero, Locke, or Bacon, when they could be discovering new laws of the universe.

Students should question everything, pursuing the truth no matter where it leads. Ultimately, Emerson argued that American democracy and its spirit of inquiry would be a beacon to the world: "A nation of men will for the first time exist, because each believes himself inspired by the Divine Soul which also inspires all men."

This essay, along with "Self-Reliance," which he would publish in his first collection, in 1841, are foundational documents for the spirit of reform of the 1840s. They trumpet radical individualism, urging seekers to throw off the chains of tradition and existing institutions. They would inspire many men and women, Transcendentalist or not, to seek to change the world.

The next day, Emerson hosted a meeting of the Transcendental Club, and Fuller became one of the first three women to join its ranks. She couldn't stay long in Concord, as she was due back in Providence in just a week. But Emerson's home, and the town, were nearer to her heart than ever.

That same fall, Emerson also gained another new friend and neighbor. Henry Thoreau, with his Harvard degree, returned home and took a job as a teacher at Concord's Center Grammar School. He began just a week after Emerson's speech. He would last only ten days in the job.

4

Blasphemy

My life has been the poem I would have writ,
But I could not both live and utter it.

—Henry David Thoreau, *A Week on the Concord and Merrimack Rivers*

The call in "The American Scholar" for the fearless pursuit of truth through the direct study of nature might well have been written for one man: Henry Thoreau. The natural world inspired Emerson, but Thoreau embraced and studied it. Emerson once wrote in his journal, "If life were long enough, among my thousand and one works should be a book of nature. . . . It should contain the natural history of the woods around my shifting camp for every month in the year. It should tie their astronomy, botany, physiology, meteorology, picturesque, and poetry together. No bird, no bug, no bud, should be forgotten on his day and hour." He never wrote that book. Thoreau did.

When Emerson traveled, it was to give lectures or visit Europe's leading intellectuals. When Thoreau traveled, it was to live roughly, in the deep woods of Maine or the wilds of Cape Cod or to hike many miles to climb a mountain. He once wrote that "Emerson is too grand for me. . . . I am a commoner." Thoreau loved reading, he liked children, and he was more than capable of close friendships—but he needed the outdoors most of all. "I think that I cannot preserve my health and spirits," he wrote in "Walking," "unless I spend four hours a day at least—and it is commonly more than that—sauntering through the woods and over the hills and fields, absolutely free from all worldly engagements."

Emerson and Thoreau, mentor and mentee, close friends, fellow Transcendentalists, had different personalities. Emerson was a prudent radical who considered all sides of an issue before arriving at a conclusion. He rarely engaged in polemics. Thoreau was an outspoken radical who loved to attack manners, morals, and institutions and, often, his dinner companions. He had no use for organized religion. He once wrote, "I have much to learn of the Indian, nothing of the missionary." He had little interest in money. He was a vegetarian who disdained hunting for sport. A committed abolitionist, he did not hesitate to denounce slavery in the strongest terms. In his morality, he resembled Bronson Alcott more than Waldo Emerson.

His journals are replete with antiestablishment aphorisms:

"I hate museums. . . . They are dead nature collected by dead men."

"One man lies in his words and gets a bad reputation—
another in his manners and enjoys a good one."

"I think that the law is really a 'humbug,' and
a benefit principally to the lawyers."

"In my experience nothing is so opposed to poetry—
not crime—as business. It is a negation of life."

Such a man can be a trial to his companions. Fortunately, he had a terrific sense of humor. While Emerson could draw chuckles from his audiences, Thoreau could elicit belly laughs. He employed humor in his travel writing to great effect, and he appreciated it in others. In a review of the works of Thomas Carlyle, he wrote, "Especially the transcendental philosophy needs the leaven of humor to render it light and digestible."

Henry's brief teaching position at the grammar school ended due to one of the practices that Alcott and Peabody opposed: corporal punishment. During his second week on the job, one member of the school committee came to observe him. He did not like what he saw, telling the new teacher that he needed to enforce discipline on the unruly students. That afternoon, after the committee member had departed, Henry used a ferule on at least two of them. He hated doing it; he had hoped to avoid corporal punishment in his classroom. That evening, in an early act of civil disobedience, he resigned.

He would try teaching again, with his brother John, at a school they soon moved to the Concord Academy building—but only on his terms. The "Thoreau School" followed many of the precepts that Alcott and Peabody had championed—no corporal punishment, plentiful discussion and conversation—with an added twist: weekly field trips on Saturday afternoons. By 1840, one of their students would be Louisa May's older sister, Anna—a charity student, since Bronson and Abba could not afford the tuition.

9

Sketch of a young Henry David Thoreau by Samuel Worcester Rowse, 1854.

Exactly when Thoreau met Emerson is unclear, but by the fall of 1837 they were taking walks together. The older man encouraged the younger to start keeping a journal. On October 22, Henry began it by citing his new acquaintance: "'What are you doing now?' he asked. 'Do you keep a journal?' So I make my first entry to-day." He would enter over two million words in his journals over the next twenty-four years.

At first, Henry imitated his new friend and mentor, writing short, aphoristic entries as if he were testing ideas for possible speeches and essays. In person, he was more quick-witted. In February 1838, Emerson wrote that "Everything that boy says makes merry with society, though nothing can be graver than his meaning." Over time, Henry would do more than imitate Waldo. He would live in his house, he would join the Transcendental Club, and he would build his Walden cabin on Waldo's land.

And yet his personality was his own. His writing soon evolved

 10

Thoreau family home on Main Street.

away from Emerson's epigrammatic style, turning toward elegant essays. His natural rebelliousness fit the spirit of the age better than Emerson's prudence did. He would eventually become a political radical and devastating polemicist, though at first, in the late 1830s and '40s, he had no interest in most current affairs apart from the moral issues of Indian removal and slavery.

Emerson also dabbled in politics in the 1830s, thanks in no small part to Lidian's urging. Andrew Jackson's farewell address had boasted of America's Indian removal policy in harsh terms, stating that the states were "relieved from the evil" of the tribes. One year later, in May 1838, General Winfield Scott led the final expulsion of the last holdouts—members of the Cherokee nation in the Southeast. The operation was based on a bogus treaty, one in a long line of agreements that the US government made and broke with the once wide-ranging Southeast peoples. The evils of the Trail of Tears were by then well publicized, and Emerson had spoken against them at least once before, from the pulpit. Now, he opened a protest meeting in Concord and served as one of its speakers, then signed a petition to Congress condemning the seizure of the Cherokees' lands. When some of his neighbors asked him to go further, he wrote an open letter to the president that was published in multiple newspapers:

> Almost the entire Cherokee nation stand up and say, "This is not our act. Behold us. Here are we" . . . and the American President and the Cabinet, the Senate and the House of Representatives, neither hear these men nor see them, and are contracting to put this active nation into cars and boats, and to drag them over mountains and rivers to a wilderness at a vast distance beyond the Mississippi. . . . In the name of God, sir, we ask you if this be so. . . . Such a dereliction of all faith and virtue, such a denial of justice, and such deafness to screams for mercy were never heard of in times of peace and in the dealing of a nation with its own allies and wards, since the earth was made. . . . Will the American government steal? Will it lie? Will it kill?

He was not yet engaged in any polemics against slavery—that would come later—but the letter denouncing ethnic cleansing was a first step into a political role. The day after his Concord talk, Lidian described it to her sister, adding, "Mr. Emerson very unwillingly takes part in public movements like that of yesterday, preferring individual action."

Emerson's politics would eventually clash with his idealism and subsume it. But to some people, his theological views presented a more existential challenge. He denied the miracles of the Bible. He denied the divinity of Christ. He had been labeled a pantheist. In conservative Boston circles, these were serious charges. One criminal case in 1838 reveals some of the intense local resistance to the Newness.

Still on the books in Massachusetts was a 1782 law against blasphemy. It was clear about the red lines that could not be crossed:

> If any person shall willfully blaspheme the holy name of God, by denying, cursing, or contumeliously reproaching God, his creation, government, or final judging of the world, or by cursing or reproaching Jesus Christ or the Holy Ghost . . . every person so offending shall be punished by imprisonment not exceeding twelve months, by sitting in the pillory, by whipping, or sitting on the gallows with a rope about the necke.

The former colony of Massachusetts still carried several other outdated religious laws on its books—one 1656 act promised that any Quaker who entered the jurisdiction would be severely whipped. Most of them were ignored. But the blasphemy statute was not yet a dead letter. It came to life one last time in the summer of 1838.

Abner Kneeland was a former farmer, carpenter, legislator, and teacher who, above all, loved to preach. He began as a Baptist, then became a Congregationalist, then a Universalist, before arriving at an Emersonian pantheism. He was a provocative speaker and writer and something of a publicity hound. In 1829, he gave a series of seven lectures in New York that he later published as *A Review of the Evidences of Christianity*, beginning with a challenge to the reader:

> If thy mind is already made up, with a determination never to alter it, *right* or *wrong*, that the Bible is of divine origin, and comes to thee, claiming thy belief by divine authority, and that the christian [*sic*] doctrine is certainly true, so true, that it is *impious* to re-examine the evidences on which it is founded, then I would advise thee not to read this book.

He proceeded to argue that all early Christian apologists were "forging and lying" in their arguments; that the Bible is full of inconsistencies; that standards of evidence argue against the truth of miracles and prophecies; that the history of the Christian church is "a series of falsehoods" and "pious frauds consecrated by the highest authority; false gospels, false documents . . . false saints, false relics, false miracles"; and that religion does more harm than good.

Abner Kneeland.

Speaking of the Bible in general Kneeland asked, "Is there a book in existence that contains more filth and more falsehood?"

His rhetoric was far more extreme and obnoxious than Emerson's. His following was also much larger—in Boston in the 1830s, he preached to crowds of up to two thousand each week. Still, their ideas overlapped.

In December 1833, Kneeland wrote an article in the *Boston Investigator* that brought criminal charges. He was accused of "blasphemous libel" for four statements:

1. Universalists believe in a god which I do not; but believe that their god, with all his moral attributes (aside from nature itself) is nothing more than a mere chimera of their own imagination.
2. Universalists believe in Christ, which I do not; but believe that the whole story concerning him is as much a fable and a fiction as that of the god Prometheus, the tragedy of whose death is said to have been acted on the stage in the theatre at Athens, five hundred years before the Christian era.
3. Universalists believe in miracles, which I do not; but believe that every pretension to them can be accounted for on natural principles, or else is to be attributed to mere trick and imposture.
4. Universalists believe in the resurrection of the dead, in immortality and eternal life, which I do not; but believe that all life is mortal, that death is an eternal extinction of life to the individual who possesses it, and that no individual life is, ever was, or ever will be eternal.

In his defense, Kneeland argued that he wasn't denying the existence of God, but merely a particular conception of Him. Kneeland also argued that the blasphemy law was unconstitutional because it violated freedom of speech and the press. Today, his arguments would prevail. In the 1830s, they failed. He was convicted in January 1834. An appeal ended in a mistrial. He was tried again in November 1835 and again found guilty. His appeal to the state supreme court was heard in 1838. This time the verdict was upheld, and he was sentenced to sixty days in prison.

He made the most of the publicity. "Thus I have at length received, what I have long been expecting, A CROWN OF MARTYRDOM! and have been made a VICTIM AND SACRIFICE TO THE GOD OF SUPERSTITION, BIGOTRY AND INTOLERANCE!!"

The verdict outraged many editorialists. The Boston *Advocate* called it an "indelible page of shame on the history of Massachusetts" and compared it to the Salem witch trials.

A petition for his pardon was signed by Emerson, Alcott, and what one historian describes as "a 'Who's Who' among the reformers—dangerous radicals and eccentrics all." It did nothing. Kneeland spent the sixty days in jail.

It was the last time the blasphemy law was ever used in Massachusetts, and the last time anyone was convicted of it anywhere in the country. Kneeland faded from history after founding a utopian community in Iowa that failed soon after his death, in 1844. Yet the question remains: If Kneeland was guilty of blasphemy, why not Emerson as well? Indeed, Kneeland read one of Emerson's speeches aloud to his followers. It was a better articulation of his views than he could offer in his own words.

Kneeland's views were not transcendental—he did not believe in a Spiritual Law that exists apart from the physical world—but his arguments against Christianity resembled Emerson's. Furthermore, Kneeland's published account of his ordeal included this pithy summary, which is certainly Emersonian, as far as it goes:

> I believe in the existence of a universe of suns and planets, among which there is one sun belonging to our planetary system; and that other suns, being more remote, are called stars; but that they are indeed suns to other planetary systems. I believe that the whole

> universe is NATURE, and that the word NATURE embraces the whole universe, and that God and Nature, so far as we can attach any rational idea to either, are perfectly synonymous terms.

While Kneeland served his time in jail, Emerson presented his own public challenge to orthodoxy. It was a speech to Harvard Divinity graduates—the speech that Kneeland would read aloud. Emerson's audience consisted of just six students, plus faculty and friends such as Elizabeth Peabody and George Ripley. Emerson hoped the speech would help point Unitarian leaders toward a reformation of sorts. Instead, the faculty heard a direct challenge and an insult:

> The idioms of [Christ's] language and the figures of his rhetoric have usurped the place of his truth; and churches are not built on his principles, but on his tropes . . . the word Miracle, as pronounced by Christian churches, gives a false impression; it is Monster . . . Historical Christianity has fallen into the error that corrupts all attempts to communicate religion . . . It has dwelt, it dwells, with noxious exaggeration about the *person* of Jesus . . . The soul is not preached. The Church seems to totter to its fall, almost all life extinct . . . The stationariness of religion; the assumption that the age of inspiration is past, that the Bible is closed; the fear of degrading the character of Jesus by representing him as a man;—indicate with sufficient clearness the falsehood of our theology.

He had been invited to speak by the students. It is unknown what those six young men thought of what they heard. The faculty were outraged. Emerson would not speak there again for more than two decades.

Newspaper reviews were divided. The *Christian Register*, not surprisingly, was negative: The speech was "at war with the distinctive features of Christianity . . . tinctured with infidelity, if not with pantheism or atheism." The *Boston Investigator* responded by accusing the *Register* of "illiberality towards those who are farther advanced than themselves . . . [Emerson] is ahead of them—preaches a different and a better doctrine—and is no longer a sectarian."

Andrews Norton, a former Harvard faculty member who had become the chief Unitarian opponent of Transcendentalism, led the attack. He was known as the "Unitarian Pope" thanks to his adherence to received doctrine. He would later publish *Internal Evidences of the Genuineness of the Gospels*, arguing that the miracles in the New Testament must be true. He was firm in his convictions. Like Abner Kneeland's prosecutor, James Trecothick Austin, Norton opposed any hint of atheism as something that would undercut social order.

First, he wrote a review of Emerson's speech in the *Daily Advertiser*, accusing Emerson of rejecting "all belief in Christianity as a revelation." He amplified his arguments in an 1839 address to Divinity School alumni on "the latest forms of infidelity." He began by noting that "we meet in a revolutionary and uncertain state of religious opinion, existing throughout what is called the Christian world." He centered his argument on the miracles of Jesus—water turned into wine, illnesses cured, loaves multiplied. If you don't believe in them, you are denying the divinity and truth of Jesus.

He went on to make an argument that C. S. Lewis would repeat more than one century later: "The words of Christ . . . are accordant only with the conception of him as speaking with authority from God. They would be altogether unsuitable to a merely human teacher of religious truth. So considered, if not the language of an impostor, they become the language of the most daring and crazy fanaticism." In other words, readers of the Bible must accept Jesus as he described himself, unless they dismiss him as a lunatic. And he hardly seems insane.

Emerson did not respond publicly to Norton, and he certainly would never have employed Abner Kneeland's rhetoric. He disagreed with Kneeland's politics (Kneeland was a Jacksonian, Emerson was a Whig) and disliked his radicalism. In his private journals he dismissed "the miserable babble of Kneeland & his crew." Yet the substance of Norton's attack bothered him. In his journals, he fought back with optimism as much as radicalism:

> Divine as the life of Jesus is, what an outrage to represent it as tantamount to the universe! To seize one accidental good man that happened to exist somewhere, at some time, and say to the new-born soul, Behold thy pattern; aim no longer to possess entire nature, to fill the horizon, to fill the infinite amplitude of being with great life, to be in sympathy and relation with all creatures, to lose all privateness by sharing all natural action. . . . Renounce a life so broad and deep as a pretty dream, and go in the harness of that past individual, assume his manners, speak his speech,—this is the madness of Christendom.

This controversy, and Emerson's break with the church, explain why some scholars consider Transcendentalism to be primarily a religious movement. It offered a new path to metaphysical truth. Yet Emerson's growing fame as a radical thinker made him a magnet for many other new thinkers, Christians included. His home in Concord became a way station for them. Many apostles of the Newness wanted to change the world here on earth, never mind the hereafter.

5

Coolidge Castle

> All sorts of visitors with new ideas began to come to the house, the men who thought money was the root of all evil, the vegetarians, the sons of nature who did not believe in razors nor in tailors, the philosophers and all sorts of come-outers [people leaving their established congregations].
>
> —Ellen Tucker Emerson, *The Life of Lidian Jackson Emerson*

The Emerson home on the Cambridge Turnpike was known to the family as Coolidge Castle, or, alternatively, Bush. It became a popular destination. Elizabeth Hoar, a family friend, referred to Emerson's stream of oddball visitors as "Waldo's Menagerie." As she told Waldo's daughter, Ellen, "I looked in to the parlour one day and saw him sitting in that circle—it gave me a feeling of horror—men with long beards, men with bare feet."

Ellen recalled her mother's story of one dinner with "a whole company" of followers of Sylvester Graham, a leading vegetarian and the inventor of the graham cracker. They "bolted their potatoes and squash and beans" before "looking hungrily for the pudding, which to them was the main dinner."

Emerson's lectures in Boston—he delivered sixty-five of them in the 1830s, and others in nearby Cambridge—set minds on fire. One writer recalled that "a new course of study or a new thought was as

12

Waldo and Lidian Emerson's home, known as Coolidge Castle, or "Bush."

exciting as news of a European war could have been," and that "impressions spread rapidly; theories were infectious; phrenology, Unitarianism, vegetarianism, emancipation, Transcendentalism, worked their way from street to street like an epidemic." He added this anecdote:

> A lady remembers meeting another on Tremont Street during the full glow of the Emerson lecture epoch, and exclaiming, "Oh, there's a new idea! Have you heard it?"
>
> "Don't talk to me of ideas," retorted her friend; "I'm so full of them now that I can't make room for a single new one."

The new thinkers wanted to reform the nation. In an 1839–40 lecture series Emerson described them as "stiff, heady and rebellious . . . they hate tolls, taxes, turnpikes, banks, hierarchies, governors, yea, almost laws."

And they wanted his blessing. Emerson tolerated his visitors, rarely bothering to write about them. He felt much more strongly about his friends and disciples: Fuller, Alcott, Thoreau, and Anna Barker and

Caroline Sturgis, on both of whom he developed a crush. After meeting Barker for the first time, he wrote "I enjoyed the frank & generous confidence of a being so lovely, so fortunate, & so remote from my own experiences." His journal entries about Barker and Sturgis read much like love notes.

There were many other impressive guests at his table or in his parlor: Jones Very, a Harvard tutor who became convinced that he was the Second Coming of Christ and who spent time in an asylum; Henry James Sr.—the father of the more famous Henry and his brother, William—who complained of Emerson's "prim and bloodless friendship"; and Emerson's aunt, Sarah Alden Bradford Ripley, who was as learned and impressive as Elizabeth Peabody or Margaret Fuller. Emerson was somewhat in awe of her. "She is superior to all she knows. . . . No dust or grime could stick to the pure silver."

Ripley would move to Concord in 1845, living in the Old Manse where Emerson and Hawthorne had each resided. It had been an Emerson family home but had passed to the Ripleys after Emerson's grandmother married Ezra Ripley, Concord's longtime Unitarian minister. When she died, he bought the house and land. Sarah Ripley was an accomplished scholar of classical and modern languages who tutored young Harvard students in Greek and Latin. Like Waldo, she also read widely in modern science. One professor called her "the most learned woman I have ever known, the most diversely learned perhaps of her time, and not inferior in this respect, I venture to say, to any woman of any age."

Lidian Emerson put up with the visitors to Bush as a hostess and as someone who had her own strong views, especially on animal rights and abolitionism. She suffered periodic bouts of exhaustion and illness, which her daughter Ellen blamed on an old episode with scarlet fever. It must also have been a trial for her to witness Waldo's infatuations. As Emerson wrote in his journal: "How joyfully would I form permanent relations with the three or four wise & beautiful whom I hold so dear, and dwell under the same roof or in a strict neighborhood."

The Emerson marriage had been strained by the arrival of their first child, Waldo, born in the fall of 1836. In that era, when a mother was breastfeeding, the parents refrained from sexual intercourse on the theory that it harmed the quality of her milk. Of course, the arrival of an infant can upend any household in any era. In his poem "Holidays," Emerson wrote:

Year by year the rose-lipped maiden,
Playfellow of young and old,
Was frolic sunshine, dear to all men,
More dear to one than mines of gold.

Whither went the lovely hoyden?
Disappeared in blessed wife;
Servant to a wooden cradle,
Living in a baby's life.

One biographer, speaking of Emerson's feelings for Fuller, Barker, Sturgis, and Sam Ward, the young man who soon married Barker, goes so far as to suggest that "in the early 1840s Emerson was living emotionally, though not physically, in what would now be called an open marriage."

Yet Lidian was able to poke fun at the Newness. To Waldo's delight, she wrote a satire she called the "Transcendental Bible":

> Never hint at a Providence, Particular or Universal. It is narrow to believe that the Universal Being concerns itself with particular affairs, egotistical to think it regards your own. Never speak of sin. It is of no consequence to "the Being" whether *you* are good or bad. It is egotistical to consider it yourself; who are you?
>
> Never confess a fault. You should not have committed it and who cares whether you are sorry? . . .
>
> Loathe and shun the sick. They are in bad taste, and may untune us for writing the poem floating through our mind. . . .

Lidian Jackson Emerson.

13

> If you have refused all sympathy to the sorrowful, all pity and aid to the sick, all toleration to the infirm of character, if you have condemned the unintellectual and loathed such sinners as have discovered want of intellect by their sin, then are you a perfect specimen of Humanity.

Emerson pulled it out for repeated readings.

Alcott came to Bush often. At one point he sensed a touch of insincerity in his new friend. "He seems not to be fully in earnest. He writes and speaks for effect. Fame stands before him as a dazzling award, and he holds himself somewhat too proudly, nor seeks the humble and sincere regard of his race." Many others, including Fuller and Thoreau, would express similar frustrations with Emerson.

Conversely, Emerson never wavered in his support for Alcott, who greatly needed it. The attacks on his book, and the death spiral of his school, caused what one scholar calls "a serious physical and emotional collapse" in the summer of 1837. The serene philosopher suffered from serious depression.

By the fall he was recovering. He worked on his lengthy manuscript *Psyche* every day, and enjoyed visits to Concord. His confidence returned. As he insisted in his journal, "I shall not always be dependent, and helpless. My influence shall spread."

He wrote this even as the Temple School continued to decline. In June 1838 he had to give it up. He tried one last attempt as a teacher at the family's home on Beach Street, which attracted twenty students in early 1839, but when he accepted a Black girl named Susan Robinson, the other families objected. Coeducation, they liked; integration, they refused. As he tersely recorded, "My Patrons . . . urge the dismissal of Robinson's child (coloured) from the School. Decline dismissing the child, and, June 22nd, have five children remaining as pupils." Three of them were his own daughters.

By June 1839, Bronson's teaching career was finished for the foreseeable future. It would be years before he had a steady income again. Still, he believed in himself. In his journal that summer, he wrote that "God shall provide a way in his own due time."

How else could he earn a living? If not conversations with children, perhaps conversations with adults. He would lead many of them over the rest of his life. Some received press attention, but only a few were transcribed in detail. At one point he thought he might publish some of them as a book, and Ednah Dow Cheney agreed to transcribe a conversation on "Self-Knowledge." It makes for humorous reading. At one point a member "in the frankest manner" stated that "he should not have understood him, but for knowing his theory." Another "seemed to think that we were wasting time for want of a more outward method." Alcott responded that the point was not to reach a conclusion; the point was to go on a journey.

Alcott's conversations were often one-way affairs in which he talked and talked, while his audience only spoke occasionally. They covered many topics but always circled around his version of idealism. He liked especially to dwell on Plato, history's most famous idealist.

As with Emerson's lectures, there were some Alcott listeners who were baffled.

The years 1839 and 1840 brought the Transcendentalist movement to new prominence. For some time, Emerson, Alcott, Fuller, and George Ripley had considered launching a journal. In late 1839 they decided it should be a quarterly. Alcott came up with a name: *The Dial.* Fuller agreed to serve as editor, with Emerson and Ripley assisting. The first issue appeared in July 1840.

Fuller was living in Boston by now, having left her final teaching post. She led successful conversations for women along the model set by Elizabeth Peabody and Bronson Alcott—attendees paid for a thirteen-week series. Her first attempt attracted twenty-five women, including many friends and former students of Peabody. The conversation focused on Greek mythology, by which she hoped to address the "great questions" for women: "What were we born to do? How shall we do it?"

As one attendee—probably Elizabeth Palmer Peabody—recorded, "Miss Fuller's most important thoughts . . . were expressed with much illustration—& many more ideas were mingled with them—& all was expressed with the most captivating address & grace—& the most beautiful modesty."

She would continue them over the next two years. Her audiences may have included Elizabeth Cady Stanton, future organizer of the 1848 Seneca Falls Convention calling for women's rights, and definitely did include Julia Ward, better known today as Julia Ward Howe, author of the "Battle Hymn of the Republic." Yet when Fuller opened them up to men in early 1841, it did not go well. The men, including Emerson and Alcott, talked too much. Emerson later admitted, "Margaret spoke well,—she could not otherwise,—but I remember that she seemed encumbered, or interrupted, by the headiness or incapacity of the men . . . who fancied, no doubt, that, on such a question, they, too, must assert and dogmatize."

The Dial would take up much of her remaining time. It would never make much money.

The first issue filled 136 pages with poems, essays, reviews of music and literature, and one unfortunate set of epigrams by Bronson Alcott. He called them "Orphic Sayings." The first of the fifty gives a flavor:

> *Thou art, my heart, a soul-flower, facing ever and following the motions of thy sun, opening thyself to her vivifying ray, and pleading thy affinity with the celestial orbs. Thou dost:*
> *The livelong day*
> *Dial on time thine own eternity.*

The New York *Knickerbocker* spoofed them with "Gastric Sayings": "The poles of potatoes are integrated; eggs globed and orbed. . . . As the magnet the steel, so the palate abstracts matter, which trembles to traverse the mouths of diversity, and rest in the bowels of unity."

Emerson did not like them, but he hadn't wanted to reject them. He had written to Fuller that "you will not like Alcott's papers . . . & yet I think, on the whole, they ought to be printed pretty much as they stand, with his name in full." Every other contribution was either unsigned or signed only with an initial. Emerson thought readers should know that the "Orphic Sayings" were Alcott's.

Fuller contributed an essay on criticism—a critic "should not be merely a poet, not merely a philosopher, not merely an observer, but tempered of all three"—and a review of a major exhibition of the famous painter Washington Allston. Theodore Parker contributed the text of an old sermon, "The Divine Presence in Nature and in the Soul." Henry Thoreau contributed two poems.

The critical reaction was mainly negative. Alcott's sayings received the worst of it.

A review in the *Boston Times* was particularly harsh:

> One of the most . . . ridiculous productions of the age. . . . The mixture is as unintelligible as the confusion of tongues at Babel. . . . Duck tracks in the mud convey a more intelligible meaning.

The Dial would last for just four years and sixteen issues. The first eight were edited by Fuller, the latter eight by Emerson, with Thoreau's help.

Years later Emerson would diagnose the journal's problem: there were too few contributors, no money to pay any of them for their work, and not enough clarity of focus. Thus "the journal did not get [anyone's] best work, but his second best . . . the magazine was so eclectic and miscellaneous, that each of its readers and writers valued only a small portion of it." Fuller's editions had covered literary and cultural topics. Emerson had wanted to focus on politics and philosophy.

Some of Fuller's greatest essays appeared in *The Dial*, including "The Great Lawsuit: Man versus Men. Woman versus Women," her first call for equal rights for women. In the journal's third issue, two years earlier, she also published a pioneering feminist essay by Sophia Ripley, George's wife, originally written for Fuller's conversation class. Ripley complained about women's lack of property rights ("woman possesses not; she is under possession") and their second-class status ("she is only half a being, and an appendage"). She did not explicitly call for equal rights, but she made a strong case for women to think for themselves, and for men and other women to pay heed.

During its first year, in addition to his poems, Thoreau submitted an essay titled "The Service." Fuller sat on it for a time and then rejected it: "The essay is rich in thoughts, and I should be *pained* not to meet it again. But then the thoughts seem to me so out of their natural order, that I cannot read it through without *pain*."

Thoreau set it aside. Reading it alongside the essays that Emerson was then preparing for his first collection, it almost appears as if the younger writer was satirizing the elder. He was certainly trying to imitate him:

> Most things are strong in one direction; a straw longitudinally; a board in the direction of its edge; a knee transversely to its grain; but the brave man is a perfect sphere, which cannot fall on its flat

> side, and is equally strong in every way. . . . Mankind, like the earth, revolve mainly from west to east, and so are flattened at the poles.

It is possible to read the essay without pain, but not without confusion.

Fortunately for the sake of American literature, in the summer of 1839 Thoreau embarked on a different venture. He and his brother John had built a wooden boat they named the *Musketaquid*, the Algonquin for the Concord River (meaning "grassy plain"). No photos of it exist, but replicas have been attempted based on his description. It was a two-man, four-oared, two-masted boat. The main sail doubled as a tent for overnight camping.

In late August and early September, they took the boat out on the Concord and Merrimack Rivers, followed by a ten-mile hike to Concord, New Hampshire, a forty-mile stagecoach ride to Plymouth, and more hiking to reach the base of Mount Washington, which they scaled, before riding, rowing, and sailing back home. Emerson marveled in his journal: "Now here are my wise young neighbors who, instead of getting, like the woodmen, into a railroad-car, where they have not even the activity of holding the reins, have got into a boat which they have built with their own hands, with sails which they have contrived to serve as a tent by night, and gone up the Merrimack to live by their wits on the fish of the stream and the berries of the wood."

It would take several years, including the famous stay at Walden Pond, for Thoreau to turn this trip into his first book, *A Week on the Concord and Merrimack Rivers.*

The brothers were close, notwithstanding a rivalry over a love interest. Ellen Devereux Sewall was seventeen in 1839, and a frequent visitor to Concord with her family. Henry and John had met her when she was a child, but by now she was a beautiful young woman. Henry spent lots of time with her, always with a chaperone, in his boat on the river, on walks, and berry-picking. But John also saw much of her, and he was the older, more gregarious of the brothers. In late September, John visited her at her home in Scituate. He did so again at Thanksgiving, and at Christmas with Henry. Both men were in love.

In the summer of 1840, the competition came to a head. Ellen visited Concord in June, and Henry took her out on the water. In July, John went to Scituate and proposed. She accepted, but her mother insisted she break it off. Ellen's father was a strict Unitarian, and it was out of the question that his daughter marry a Transcendentalist, especially one who wasn't wealthy. Henry tried his own proposal by mail, but the objections remained.

Henry would never again propose to anyone. He would even refuse a bold proposal made to him. He maintained male friendships, but also wrote that it is better to see friends only infrequently. From now on, he would live for his walks, his travels, and his writing and speaking. Like Emerson, Alcott, and Fuller, he would remain an idealist, but his inclinations and habits increasingly shaped him as a naturalist, interested in the lives of plants and animals above all.

In April 1840, Concord gained a new resident family, the Alcotts. Emerson's close friend was now within walking distance of Coolidge Castle. A few months earlier, Emerson had fretted that "Alcott seems to need a pure success. If the men and women whose opinion is fame could see him as he is and could express heartily . . . their joy in his genius, I think his genius would be exalted and relieved of some spots, with which a sense of injustice and loneliness has shaded it."

Bronson and Abba moved to Hosmer Cottage (the model for Dovecote, Meg and John's house in *Little Women*). Their fourth daughter, Abigail (Abby) May, was born in July. The family would spend three years in that house, after Abba vetoed an invitation from Emerson that they move into Coolidge Castle. (As she explained to her brother, "I cannot gee and haw in another person's yoke.") Louisa would spend mornings at the Emersons', where, initially, a tutor taught her and her younger sister Lizzie lessons. She would also spend some afternoons with her older sister Anna, joining Henry Thoreau's class field trips.

 14

The Alcotts' first Concord home.

A popular, perhaps apocryphal, story has emerged from those years in which Henry Thoreau took young Louisa for walks. Spotting a cobweb, he asked her if she knew what it was. When she named it correctly, he said no, it was a handkerchief dropped by a fairy. (He did enjoy metaphors of the sort; in the spring of 1854, in his journal, he described cobwebs as "little dewy nets of gauze—a faery's washing.") Over the years, apocryphal quotes attributed to Thoreau and Emerson would grow like mushrooms.

In the latter months of 1840, as Emerson was polishing essays on love and friendship, he and Fuller struggled to define their own relationship. They had each had strong feelings for Anna Barker, and each felt attracted to Sam Ward. The news that Ward and Barker were engaged and would marry in October was a blow to both. Emerson wrote to Caroline Sturgis that the news "affected me at first with a certain terror.

I thought that the whole spirit of our intercourse at Concord implied another resolution." He had thought that Barker wanted to establish "ideal relations" with him, not someone else. He and Fuller proceeded to exchange a series of letters of which, sadly, only his have survived. All but one of hers have not. Nonetheless they trace an emotional arc.

September 13: "I will study to deserve my friends—I abandon myself to what is best in you all. I have a great deal to say on this head but will not trust myself with it now."

September 25: "Absent from you I am very likely to deny you, and say that you lack this & that. . . . [Please] do say, for I am willing & resolute for the sake of an instance to fix one quarrel on you, that I am yours & yours shall be."

Margaret's reply: "How often have I left you despairing & forlorn. How often have I said, This light will never understand my fire. . . . This simple force will never interpret my need of manifold being."

Waldo to her, on October 1: "Today I think I shall not reply to your seven chords of melody which came to me last night. I do not know how I have ever deserved any friends."

After several more letters he ended the discussion on October 24: "I ought never to have suffered you to lead me into any conversation or writing on our relation. . . . I see very dimly in writing on this topic. It will not prosper with me. Perhaps all my words are wrong. Do not expect it of me again for a very long time."

As she would later say, Emerson's God was Truth; hers, Love. The twain did not always meet.

In his essay on the topic Emerson wrote that "friendship, like the immortality of the soul, is too good to be believed. The lover, beholding his maiden, half knows that she is not verily that which he worships; and in the golden hour of friendship we are surprised with shades of suspicion and unbelief." And: "We are armed all over with subtle antagonisms, which, as soon as we meet, begin to play, and translate all poetry into stale prose."

His social inclinations lay somewhere between those of Thoreau and Fuller. He valued his solitude as much as his friendships. He could not give Fuller the emotional connection she desired. Of all the Concord set, it was Alcott whose friendship with Emerson proved the strongest, with the fewest problems. They were opposites who appreciated each other deeply.

In the midst of Emerson and Fuller's exchange, on October 18, Waldo hosted a meeting of Fuller, Alcott, and George and Sophia Ripley, at the Ripleys' request. George was in the process of resigning from his Boston Unitarian church after fourteen years in the pulpit. He explained to his parishioners that he would now focus on "social reform and the advancements of the age . . . which are met by some with frowns, and by others with ridicule."

The Ripleys intended to launch a new project: a utopian community on the outskirts of the city, one that treated everyone equally and elevated them all. Along with Alcott, in August, he had hiked sixty miles to attend the "Groton Convention"—a gathering of many different types of utopianists who were comparing notes on their various experiments.

Now, in Concord, Ripley made his pitch. He would purchase five hundred acres. He needed to raise $50,000. The community would be a joint-stock company, with members purchasing shares at a guaranteed rate of interest to protect their investment.

Emerson mostly listened. Fuller was unimpressed, writing to a friend that the "talk was useless."

Three weeks later, Ripley wrote with a revised plan and asked if Emerson would invest:

> *My Dear Sir,—Our conversation in Concord was of such a general nature, that I do not feel as if you were in complete possession of the idea of the Association which I wish to see established. . . . I wish to submit the plan more distinctly to your judgment, that you may decide whether it is one that can have the benefit of your aid and cooperation.*
>
> *Our objects, as you know, are to insure a more natural union*

> *between intellectual and manual labor than now exists; to combine the thinker and the worker, as far as possible, in the same individual; to guarantee the highest mental freedom, by providing all with labor, adapted to their tastes and talents, and securing to them the fruits of their industry; to do away the necessity of menial services, by opening the benefits of education and the profits of labor to all; and thus to prepare a society of liberal, intelligent, and cultivated persons, whose relations with each other would permit a more simple and wholesome life, than can be led amidst the pressure of our competitive institutions.*

He scaled down the size and the cost, to $30,000—still a substantial sum, roughly a million in today's dollars—and proposed that the land be used both for farming and a school, with free tuition for investors and paid tuition for outsiders. He wanted "three or four families" to take possession in April. He already had some interest, adding up to perhaps $10,000. Bringing Emerson on board would make a difference. "Your decision will do much towards settling the question with me, whether the time has come for the fulfillment of a high hope, or whether the work belongs to a future generation." What would Waldo do?

6

The Satirist in Paradise

> The better life! Possibly, it would hardly look so now; it is enough if it looked so then.
>
> —Nathaniel Hawthorne, *The Blithedale Romance*

After agonizing, Waldo turned Ripley down. "The ground of my decision is almost purely personal to myself. . . . That which determines me is the conviction that the Community is not good for me." He needed independence. He enjoyed his neighbors and friends, but ultimately, he wished to seek universal truths on his own.

He had been lecturing and would publish essays on great men of history—his *Representative Men*—including Plato, Swedenborg, Montaigne, Shakespeare, Napoleon, and Goethe. He aspired to join their ranks. "Nature seems to exist for the excellent. The world is upheld by the veracity of good men: they make the earth wholesome."

Besides, thanks to so many visitors to his Concord home, he already had a version of group living.

Ripley should not have been surprised. Bronson Alcott was also uninterested in Brook Farm, but for different reasons: It wasn't radical enough, or, as he put it, "not pitched sufficiently above the current economics of our social system."

What *is* surprising is that the Ripleys' original ten subscribers to Brook Farm, which would become the most prominent utopian community in Massachusetts, included a struggling yet decidedly non-utopian writer: Nathaniel Hawthorne.

Hawthorne was thirty-six, the same age as his fellow Salem neighbor friend, Elizabeth Palmer Peabody. His family had roots in Salem that were deep and haunting. His great-great-grandfather, John Hathorne (Nathaniel added the *w*, possibly to distance himself from his ancestors), had been a prominent judge during the witch trials. John assumed that the girls and women he interrogated were guilty, and he never apologized for that terrible episode. By contrast, Abba Alcott's great-great-grandfather, Samuel Sewall, was a witch-trial judge who did apologize and repent.

Nathaniel's immediate family was impoverished despite the prominence of several of his forebears. His father died when Nathaniel was four years old. His mother moved Nathaniel and his two sisters back and forth to Maine, twice, to live with or near their uncle Richard while still sending Nathaniel to school in Salem. When it was time for Nathaniel to attend college he went to Bowdoin, where his classmates included Henry Wadsworth Longfellow and Franklin Pierce.

He was determined to be a writer. At seventeen he had written to his mother: "I have not yet concluded what profession I shall have." He ruled out politics—"of course out of the Question"—and the law, as there were too many lawyers already. Then he asked, "What do you think of my becoming an Author, and relying for support upon my pen[?] . . . But authors are always poor Devils, and therefore Satan may take them."

After college he tried but failed to interest publishers in a collection of stories. He apparently burned the manuscript in frustration. In 1828, age twenty-four, he used a small inheritance to publish his first novel, *Fanshawe: A Tale*, anonymously, to meager sales. He later tried to suppress it. For a man without much money, he had chosen a challenging career path.

Living in the family home in Salem, he started publishing stories anonymously in an annual anthology called *The Token*—ten stories in three years (1831–33). As he entered his thirties, he published more stories where he could, but never for much reward. He moved to Boston to take a job editing a monthly magazine, but his modest salary went unpaid and the company soon went bankrupt.

Back in Salem, in 1837, he at last managed to publish a story collection under his own name. *Twice-Told Tales* initially included nineteen stories, later expanded to thirty-nine for a second edition in 1842. Some are gothic, some historical, some gently humorous, with flashes of caustic satire ("she was that wisest but unloveliest variety of woman, a philosopher"). Among its stories are several seeds of *The House of Seven Gables* and some interesting experiments in viewpoints; one story is narrated by a village water pump.

Though sales of both editions were modest—and his first publisher went out of business during the Panic of 1837—the book proved to be a turning point. Reviews were strong. One by Longfellow appeared in the *North American Review*. One by Margaret Fuller appeared in *The Dial*: "It is not merely the soft grace, the playfulness, and genial human sense for the traits of individual character, that have pleased, but the perception of what is rarest in this superficial, bustling community, a great reserve of thought and strength never yet at all brought forward. . . . We wait new missives from the same hand." She recognized his genius and his potential, even as she criticized his "frigidity and thinness of design" which "usually bespeaks a want of . . . deeper experiences."

Twice-Told Tales includes a story set within a Shaker community, featuring a pair of lovers who join it for purely financial reasons. Was it inspired by Hawthorne's own decision to join Brook Farm?

By 1840 he had a secret fiancée, and he needed a potential home for them. Some believed him to be engaged to Elizabeth Peabody, but they had the wrong sister. Hawthorne had met his fellow Salem residents, the Peabody sisters, a few years earlier. He had given Elizabeth a copy of his book. She admired it greatly and became a lifelong supporter of his work. She also seems to have fallen in love with the shy, handsome writer. When they first met at her Salem home, she ran upstairs to her sister: "Oh Sophia, Mr. Hawthorne and his sisters have come, and you never saw anything so splendid—he is handsomer than Lord Byron!

15

Nathaniel Hawthorne, portrait by Charles Osgood, 1840.

You must get up and dress and come down." Sophia demurred. Elizabeth was struck by Hawthorne's shyness, but "as soon as he forgot himself in conversation, all this passed away, and the beauty of the outline of his features, the pure complexion, the wonderful eyes, like mountain lakes seeming to reflect the heavens, made a wonderful impression."

For a time in 1838, Elizabeth had believed she was the one who would marry him. But when Hawthorne met Sophia, who had been bedridden with recurring headaches and sickness, he was taken with her. In the spring of 1838, he wrote to a friend, "I have heard recently the interesting intelligence that I am engaged to two ladies in this city. It was my first knowledge of the fact. I do trust that I shall not get married without my own privity and consent." By the beginning of the following year, he and Sophia were secretly engaged. He showered love letters on "my dove."

Anyone who thinks of Hawthorne as a gloomy author (anyone who has read only *The Scarlet Letter*) will change that opinion by spending a few minutes with his many passionate love letters. "Often, while holding you in my arms, I have silently given myself to you, and received you for my portion of human love and happiness, and have prayed Him to consecrate and bless the union."

Her letters to him do not survive. He burned them, exclaiming to a friend that "now they are all ashes. What a trustful guardian of secret matters fire is! What should we do without Fire and Death?"

Despite any wounded feelings, Elizabeth did what she could for him. She sent copies of his book to several potential supporters, including Wordsworth. She pestered friends until she managed to get Hawthorne appointed as a customs inspector for the Port of Boston. Hawthorne, in turn, urged John L. O'Sullivan, editor of the *Democratic Review*, to publish articles that Elizabeth wrote.

Hawthorne was happy to correspond with various friends, but he shunned public gatherings. He wrote to Sophia in late 1839 that "I was invited to dine at Mr. Bancroft's yesterday, with Miss Margaret Fuller; but Providence had given me some business to do; for which I was very thankful." At one point Sophia invited him to attend one of Emerson's lectures; he declined.

In 1840 at her West Street store, Elizabeth began publishing books. Included among them was Hawthorne's historical stories for children, *Grandfather's Chair*. Meanwhile, in June, Nathaniel and Sophia debated where they might live after they married. He could not yet afford a house. Worse, in November, after William Henry Harrison defeated Martin Van Buren in the presidential election, Hawthorne had to resign from the Customs House. His finances were as shaky as ever.

Money, not idealism, explains why he and Sophia decided to move to Brook Farm when the community began operations in the spring.

• • •

A few months later the couple decided that only Hawthorne should make the move at first. He purchased two shares of stock (one for each of them) for a total of $1,000 and took a room in the farm's main building.

Brook Farm covered a beautiful 170 acres in rural West Roxbury along the Charles River, just eight miles from Boston. When Ripley purchased it, it had only a few buildings, including a good-sized farmhouse with open spaces and a sizable kitchen on the first floor, and some smaller rooms on the second. Brook Farmers dubbed it the Hive. It became the center of their indoor activities and meals.

Brook Farm stood out from America's growing number of utopian communities in several ways. It was close to Boston, whereas most of the new experiments were outside New England. It was secular, unlike those of the long-established Shakers. It was not socialist; investors held stock that they could, in theory, sell—but it was democratic

 16

Brook Farm, painting by Josiah Wolcott, 1844.

and regulated. All labor was valued at the same rate. Total daily work hours were limited to ten from May to October, eight from November to April.

The members ate plain food together in the dining room, with one table reserved for vegetarians. Everyone sat on pine benches. After breakfast, they went to work, initially as farmers, but eventually also as manufacturers of useful items, such as shoes. In the afternoon, the workers changed clothes and became teachers. The Brook Farm school was its biggest attraction, bringing in tuition-paying students, including one of Margaret Fuller's brothers.

The Brook Farmers also had some fun. An "Amusement Group" planned "charades, tableaux, dances, picnics, theatricals, readings, games, [and] diversions in the woods or in the house." Hawthorne, in his notebooks, describes one "picnic party" at the farm:

> I strolled, after dinner, with Mr. [George] Bradford; and in a lonesome glade, we met the apparition of an Indian chief, dressed in appropriate costume of blanket, feathers, and paint, and armed with a musket. Almost at the same time a young gipsey [*sic*] fortune teller came from among the trees, and proposed to tell my fortune; which while she was doing this, the goddess Diana (known on earth as Miss Ellen Slade) let fly an arrow and hit me smartly in the hand. . . . Accompanied by these denizens of the wild wood, we went onward, and came to a company of fantastic figures, arranged in a ring for a dance or game. There was a Swiss girl, an Indian squaw, a negro of the Jim Crow order, one or two foresters; and several people in Christian attire; besides children of all ages. Then followed childish games, in which grown people took part with mirth enough—while I, whose nature it is to be a mere spectator both of sport and serious business, lay under the trees and looked on. Meanwhile, Mr. Emerson and Miss Fuller, who had arrived an hour or two before, came forth into the little glade where we were assembled. Here followed much talk.

Brook Farm's school became the main source of income for the group. Its faculty included some of the best-educated men and women in America: George and Sophia Ripley, several other Harvard graduates, and several intellectual women. The students, apart from Margaret Fuller's brother Lloyd, included relatives of such Newness leaders as Emerson (his nephew), Orestes Brownson (his son), Theodore Parker (his ward), and George Bancroft (two sons). Yet those boarders were not investors, and even as their numbers swelled, the farm struggled.

From the beginning, due to its location, Brook Farm was a magnet for visitors. Alcott was one of the first to seek it out, in April. Fuller spent a few days there in early May. Soon, Emerson, the Alcott family, Thoreau, and Elizabeth Peabody each came, and Fuller visited so often that a room in the Hive was reserved for her. Peabody would give her thoughts on the farm's first year in *The Dial*. After admiring its principles, she cautioned, "The very liberality, and truth to nature of the plan, is a legitimate reason for fearing it will not succeed as a special community in any given time." Like Fuller, she was not convinced that communities could depend so heavily on goodwill. As Fuller wrote to a friend, "Utopia it is impossible to build up."

Brook Farm failed to make money in each year of its brief existence. Emerson did not regret his rejection of Ripley's offer. As he wrote in his journal, "'And fools rush in where angels fear to tread.' So say I of Brook Farm."

Hawthorne arrived during a snowstorm on April 12, 1841. He was among the first to move in. He wrote his first letter to Sophia on the thirteenth. "Here is thy poor husband in a polar Paradise!" He was in good cheer, writing with optimistic humor about the farm's cows. "We have eight of our own, and the number is now increased by a transcendental heifer, belonging to Miss Margaret Fuller. She is very fractious, I believe, and apt to kick over the milk pail." He took up a pitchfork and set to work spreading manure.

By July he was having second thoughts. He had to do so much manual work that he had no time to write fiction. He complained about Ripley to a friend, and expressed concern that the enterprise might fail. In late August, he wrote to Sophia, "Thou and I must form other plans for ourselves; for I can see few or no signs that Providence purposes to give us a home here." By the end of September, he told Ripley he would not spend the winter there. By November he was gone for good.

Years later he would use Brook Farm as the inspiration for *The Blithedale Romance*, the third of his 1850s novels after *The Scarlet Letter* and *The House of the Seven Gables*. Blithedale is the name of a Brook Farm–like colony. Hawthorne began the book with a preface datelined "CONCORD (Mass.), May, 1852," noting that although he wrote it with Brook Farm "in his mind," the story is "an available foothold between fiction and reality." He added that the characters are "entirely fictitious" and that it would be "a most grievous wrong" to suppose otherwise. It would prove a vain hope.

The book's strong female protagonist, assumed by many readers to be based on Fuller, is Zenobia ("not her real name . . . [but] her magazine signature"). Unlike Fuller at Brook Farm, Zenobia is a resident of Blithedale, and the most compelling character there. She is a woman of "noble courage" and magnetic charisma. "One felt an influence breathing out of her, such as we might suppose to come from Eve, when she was just made, and her Creator brought her to Adam, saying, 'Behold! here is a woman!'"

What unfolds is a drama concerning a zealous Blithedale member, Zenobia's secret past, a mysterious half sister, and a climactic suicide. It is a human drama more than a satire, yet many readers could not separate the novel from its inspirations. Speaking of Zenobia, Emerson huffed that "no friend who knew Margaret Fuller could recognize her rich and brilliant genius under the dismal mask which the public fancied was meant for her in that disagreeable story."

Hawthorne loved to satirize the Newness. In his *American Notebooks* he had tossed out one idea for a short story: "A sketch to be given of a modern reformer,—a type of the extreme doctrines on the subject of slaves, cold water, and other such topics. He goes about the streets haranguing most eloquently, and is on the point of making many converts, when his labors are suddenly interrupted by the appearance of the keeper of a mad-house, whence he has escaped. Much may be made of this idea."

When Alexis de Tocqueville wrote his famous *Democracy in America* based on his travels to the country in 1831 and early 1832, he commented on Americans' love of associations, large and small: "As soon as several of the inhabitants of the United States have conceived a sentiment or an idea that they want to produce in the world, they seek each other out; and when they have found each other, they unite."

Brook Farm was a medium-sized example, but smaller versions could take place within a single home. While Hawthorne was moving to Brook Farm, Emerson was looking to change his domestic arrangements. He had suggested that the Alcotts move in. Now he invited Thoreau to "live with me & work with me in the garden & teach me to graft apples." Henry accepted. Fuller was glad of both decisions, writing to Emerson, "I am glad Henry T is coming to you; *that* seems feasible." Henry would prove to be a useful handyman, a boon companion to the children, and—during Emerson's lecture-tour absences—good company for Lidian. Yet his fractiousness simmered beneath the surface. In his first journal entry from his new home, Thoreau wrote that "the civilized man has the habits of the house. His house is a prison, in which he finds himself oppressed and confined, not sheltered and protected." Not exactly an omen of domestic bliss.

Fuller wrote to her brother about Emerson's new houseguest, "an earnest thinker [who] intends being a farmer." He had taken her out on a boat ride.

Thoreau enjoyed paddling on the river at nighttime. He would take his flute and improvise "a tinkling stream [of music] which meandered with the river, and fell from note to note as a brook from rock to rock."

17

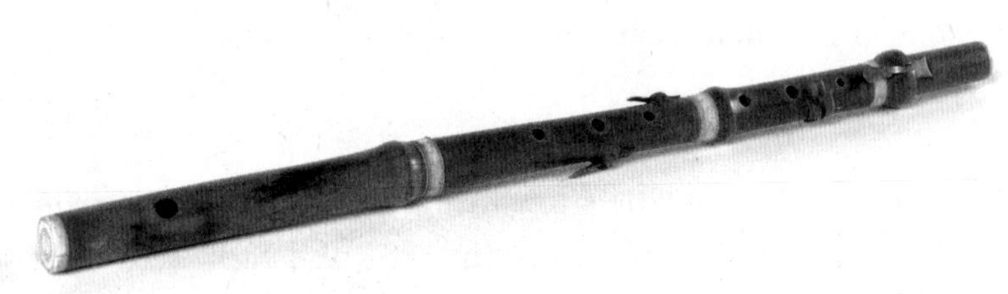

Thoreau's wood flute, on which he etched his name below those of his father and brother.

That spring, Emerson published "Man the Reformer" in *The Dial*, the essay that argued that every statute, institution, and vocation was "threatened" by the new spirit. He excoriated America's reliance on the products of enslaved labor and even condemned "the whole institution of property." His article appeared two years ahead of a famous letter in which Karl Marx called for "a ruthless criticism of everything existing," which makes many of the same points.

Yet Emerson still believed that moral revolutions were individual affairs, each man and woman reaching for their own perfection. He was not yet engaged deeply in politics.

At heart, Emerson was a thinker more than an activist. He was slower to embrace abolitionism than Lidian or Bronson Alcott. Brook Farm was not the only utopian experiment he would shun—after meeting two leaders of another utopian movement he wrote to Lidian that he "cannot content them. They are bent on popular actions. I am, in all my theory, ethics, and politics, a poet." He wanted to sit in his study or walk in the woods, to contemplate universal truths. Put another way, as he said in one early lecture, "Progress is not for society. Progress belongs to the individual."

His first volume of essays came out in March 1841. Among its twelve pieces are three of his most famous: "Self-Reliance," "The Over-Soul," and "Circles." One biographer hails "Self-Reliance" as "perhaps the most brilliant display of Emerson's literary strategy in all his essays." It is certainly the most quoted of anything Emerson wrote:

"Society everywhere is in conspiracy against the
manhood of every one of its members."

"Whoso would be a man, must be a nonconformist."

"What I must do is all that concerns me, not what the people think."

"A foolish consistency is the hobgoblin of little minds,
adored by little statesmen and philosophers and divines."

"If we live truly, we shall see truly."

"Insist on yourself; never imitate."

"Trust thyself: every heart vibrates to that iron string."

"Self-Reliance" may well be the most influential essay by any American writer in the nineteenth century. Yet its popular aphorisms give a distorted picture of its meaning. "Self-Reliance" is not merely an exhortation to trust yourself and bravely set your own course. It is also profoundly transcendental—celebrating the "ever-blessed ONE . . . the Supreme Cause" that animates nature and life. We should reject old thinking if it impedes us from pursuing the truth of that Supreme Cause. Be brave, but only in the service of the moral law, common to all.

Near the end, Emerson takes a swipe at politics and reform movements:

"The political parties meet in numerous conventions; the greater the concourse, and with each new uproar of announcement, The delegation from Essex! The Democrats from New Hampshire! The Whigs of Maine! . . . In like manner the reformers summon conventions and vote and resolve in multitude. Not so, O friends! will the God deign to enter and inhabit you, but by a method precisely the reverse." You cannot find the truth in social movements. You will only find it in yourself.

It is no wonder he stayed home in Concord rather than move to

Brook Farm, and no wonder that he was slow to embrace abolitionism.

"The Over-Soul" is his most mystical essay, the only one of the twelve that he had not tested out on the lecture circuit. "We live in succession, in division, in parts, in particles. Meantime within man is the soul of the whole; the wise silence; the universal beauty, to which every part and particle is equally related; the eternal ONE." We not only all have access to moral law, we carry it within ourselves.

One other essay from the collection reveals his ambitions: "Compensation." Emerson had long wished to unlock the laws of nature and culture as Newton had unlocked the laws of motion. "Compensation" was an attempt at it. The title refers to the idea that for every action and every part of nature, and human nature, there is a reaction. "Polarity, or action and reaction, we meet in every part of nature; in darkness and light; in heat and cold; in the ebb and flow of waters; in male and female; . . . in the systole and diastole of the heart."

He had no inkling of entropy, a concept first proposed only later in the nineteenth century, and it is easy to turn his compensation principle into a mystical jumble. But it is characteristic of his thought that he would consider the opposite of every phenomenon, and the problem of having too much of any good thing.

Boston newspapers had already poked fun at Emerson's lectures. Now, in late 1841, the *Boston Courier* joked: "Mr. Emerson will give a lecture upon the Times, entitled, 'the perfunctory cognoscence of ephemeral ineffabilities,' and another upon the Notion, entitled, 'the hebdomadal indagation of subsultory periodicities.' The style is to mount up with its subject, to the highest empyrean of starry transcendentalism."

At least seven American journals reviewed the essays. Most of them praised his style but condemned the obscurity of his meaning and/or the egotism of his philosophy. Nonetheless, the *Essays* attracted new followers for Emerson. In the UK, Thomas Carlyle was so enthusiastic that he wrote a preface for a British edition, which sold widely.

At Coolidge Castle, Emerson was delighted with his new housemate. In June he wrote that "the good river-god has taken the form of my valiant Henry Thoreau here and introduced me to the riches of his shadowy, starlit, moonlit stream, a lovely new world."

Emerson was less of a fan when it came to Thoreau's thinking. In September, he wrote in his journal, "I am very familiar with all his thoughts,—they are my own quite originally drest [dressed]. But if the question be, what new ideas has he thrown into circulation, he has not yet told what that is which he was created to say." He was correct in one sense: Thoreau was not interested in the vague philosophizing of such essays as "Compensation." He was much more interested in observing nature to unlock its secrets.

That fall, Fuller came for another visit. She was exhausted by her unpaid efforts for *The Dial* and concerned by the news that her younger sister Ellen was engaged to William Ellery Channing, a nephew and namesake of the Unitarian minister. This Ellery was a poet who had dropped out of college and abandoned a brief effort to study law. Channing was erratic. She feared, correctly, that he was a bad match for Ellen. (The marriage was an unhappy one, and the couple eventually separated.)

Channing would become an important Concord addition, a hiking companion for Thoreau and Hawthorne. Some of his poems would be featured at major local events. Yet his poems are uneven and hardly remembered today. Emerson wrote in his journal that "Ellery . . . is a very imperfect artist [who] does not even like to distinguish between what is good and what is not, in his verses, would fain have it all pass for good,—for the best,—and claim inspiration for the worst lines."

Nonetheless Waldo encouraged Ellery and Ellen to move to Concord. For Margaret, though he could not prevent her sister's marriage, he at least could relieve her of editing *The Dial*, a duty he would assume the following March despite misgivings: "I wish it to live but do not wish to be its life." It seems that their conversations in Concord were not unlike their letters and talks of the previous fall. Emerson wrote of his "strange, cold-warm, attractive-repelling conversations with Margaret, whom I always admire, most revere when I nearest see, and sometimes love,—yet whom I freeze, and who freezes me to silence, when we seem to promise to come nearest."

Emerson succeeded in gathering some of his friends to his town, and some to his house. What he could not do was guarantee happy results.

7

Compensations

The South-wind brings
Life, sunshine and desire,
And on every mount and meadow
Breathes aromatic fire;
But over the dead he has no power,
The lost, the lost, he cannot restore;
And, looking over the hills, I mourn
The darling who shall not return.

—Ralph Waldo Emerson, from "Threnody"

The year 1842 began with tragedy. On New Year's Day John Thoreau was stropping a razor when he nicked a finger. He didn't think much of it; he bandaged it up and kept working. Yet that nick introduced an invisible bacteria into his bloodstream. Emerson, in *Nature*, had marveled at the profound connections between all living beings. He had no knowledge of the relations between visible beings and invisible microorganisms. One week after that shaving accident, John was ill with tetanus. Henry rushed home from the Emersons'. John died in Henry's arms on January 11.

Soon afterward, Henry also came down with symptoms of the disease. Emerson returned to Concord from a Boston lecture to the frightening news. He wrote to his brother, "My pleasure at getting home on Saturday night at the end of my task was somewhat checked by finding that Henry Thoreau, who has been at his father's since the death of his brother, was ill & threatened with *lockjaw*! His brother's disease. It is strange—unaccountable—yet the symptoms seemed precise & on the increase."

Henry managed to recover, and his suffering may have been sympathetic or psychosomatic rather than an actual case of tetanus. But he emerged to terrible news: young Waldo Emerson, five years old, had contracted scarlet fever. The disease could be deadly, especially for young children.

Louisa May recalled her first memory of the Emerson home from those terrible days. "I was sent to inquire for little Waldo, then lying very ill. His father came to me, so worn with watching and changed by sorrow, that I was startled, and could only stammer out my message. 'Child, he is dead!' was his answer. Then the door closed, and I ran home to tell the sad tidings. I was only eight years old, and that was my first glimpse of a great grief, but I never have forgotten the anguish that made a familiar face so tragical, and gave those few words more pathos than the sweet lamentation of the 'Threnody.'" Emerson's poem about young Waldo is a heartbreaking lament.

Henry tried to assuage Waldo's grief in a letter in March. "Death is beautiful when seen to be a law, and not an accident—It is as common as life. . . . When we look over the fields we are not saddened because these particular flowers or grasses will wither. . . . The herbage cheerfully consents to bloom, and wither, and give place to a new." It is hard to imagine Emerson finding comfort in such a thought. Instead, in "Threnody," he expressed only pain and frustration:

Nature who lost, cannot remake him;
Fate let him fall, Fate can't retake him;
Nature, Fate, men, him seek in vain.

The rest of 1842 brought happier rites of passage. Hawthorne and Sophia Peabody made their engagement public. In early May they went house-hunting in Concord. It was Sophia's idea to move there, to the first of two Concord homes for the couple. Nathaniel was drawn to the Emerson circle even as he kept them, and their ideas, at a critical distance. Emerson's step-grandfather, Ezra Ripley, had passed away; the Old Manse was available for rent. Emerson met them there and struck a deal, then asked Thoreau to plant a garden for the soon-to-be newlyweds.

Emerson was delighted by his new neighbors and wanted more like them. As he mused, "Here is a proposition for the formation of a good neighborhood: [Henry] Hedge shall live at Concord, and Mr. Hawthorne; George Bradford shall come then; and Mrs. [Sarah] Ripley afterward. Who knows but Margaret Fuller and Charles Newcomb would presently be added." (Hedge, Bradford, and Newcomb were all apostles of the Newness.) He never managed to bring the entire Transcendental Club to the town, but he succeeded with Mrs. Ripley; Elizabeth Hoar (former fiancée of his late brother Charles); Ellery Channing and Ellen Fuller; and the Alcotts.

In July, after getting married in Elizabeth Peabody's West Street parlor, the Hawthornes moved in. Nathaniel was as happy as a newlywed can be. "Happiness has no succession of events; because it is a part of eternity; and we have been living in eternity, ever since we came to this old Manse."

Despite his intense shyness, Hawthorne received visitors, including Emerson, Channing, and Thoreau. He found Thoreau to be "a singular character—a young man with much of wild original nature still remaining in him; and so far as he is sophisticated, it is in a way and method of his own. He is as ugly as sin, long-nosed, queer-mouthed, and with uncouth and somewhat rustic, although courteous manners, corresponding very well with such an exterior. But his ugliness is of an honest and agreeable fashion, and becomes him much better than beauty."

After one dinner Thoreau took Hawthorne out on his boat and offered to sell it to his new neighbor for seven dollars (Thoreau needed cash). Hawthorne agreed. Yet he did not have Thoreau's experience on the water, wishing he could acquire Thoreau's skills at "as reasonable a rate." Hawthorne would befriend Thoreau and spend time with Emerson, Alcott, and Fuller, yet in his writings he would consistently grapple with their ideals.

Hawthorne complained that the house had no running water—"Only imagine Adam trudging out of Paradise with a bucket in each hand, to get water to drink, or for Eve to bathe in! Intolerable!" Outside the Manse he swam in the river at least once a day. Inside, he enjoyed imagining Emerson's grandfather William watching the Battle of Lexington and Concord from an upstairs window, and his step-grandfather writing his sermons at an upstairs desk. Just outside the door, he enjoyed working in the vegetable garden and the orchard and picking flowers for Sophia.

He took walks with Emerson. On one, they met Edmund Hosmer. Hawthorne couldn't help contrasting the Sage with this local farmer: "The mystic, stretching his hand out of cloud-land, in [a] vain search for something real; and the man of sturdy sense, all whose ideas seem to be dug out of his mind, hard and substantial, as he digs potatoes, beets, carrots, and turnips, out of the earth."

Fuller came to stay with Emerson for a month before moving to Cambridge, where she would begin writing "The Great Lawsuit: Man versus Men. Woman versus Women." It would grow to be one of the longest essays ever published in *The Dial*. She also visited Hawthorne.

After a visit in which she left a book behind, Hawthorne walked to Emerson's house to return it, and then returned home through the Sleepy Hollow garden area, the future site of a town cemetery. There was "Margaret herself. She had been there the whole afternoon, meditating or reading." He stopped and chatted about all sorts of topics: autumn, the "pleasures of getting lost in the woods," crows, childhood influences, beautiful views, and "other matters of high and low philosophy." Eventually, Emerson came along and joined the chatter.

Hawthorne's feelings about Fuller would sour, but there was no sign of tension on that summer day.

Hawthorne's walks with Emerson included one two-day hike to

the town of Harvard, a trip of some fifteen miles in each direction. They wanted to visit the local Shaker community—for Emerson, the farm was an interesting social experiment; for Hawthorne, it was a literary inspiration. At home in Concord, however, Hawthorne wasn't getting a lot of writing done. He hoped for another political appointment "which would do away the necessity of writing for bread." In his three years renting the Old Manse, even at a very favorable rate of $100 per year, he fell into arrears.

Fuller also faced some tensions at Coolidge Castle. Her relations with Waldo had settled into a form of détente after the drama of 1840. "My expectations are moderate now: it is his beautiful presence that I prize, far more than our intercourse." Yet there was trouble between Margaret and Lidian, who was feeling ill and spent much of her time in her room. One day she asked Fuller to take a walk with her, and when Fuller replied that she had promised to walk with Waldo, Lidian burst into tears. "The family were all present, they looked at their plates. Waldo looked on the ground, but soft & serene as ever." When Fuller hurried to say that she would certainly accompany Lidian, the response was icy: "I do not want you to make any sacrifice. . . . With you, I should have courage, but go with Mr E. I will not." Throughout this exchange, Waldo said nothing.

In 1842 Bronson Alcott was still in need of the "pure success" that Emerson had wished for him. Now Emerson came to his financial rescue. Thanks to Elizabeth Peabody's book, Alcott's educational methods had inspired reformers in London. Three of them had launched Alcott House and corresponded with Bronson. Unlike the Temple School, theirs was a success. He wished to visit but could not afford the trip. Emerson paid his way.

As Bronson prepared to depart, Abba wrestled with her feelings. In February, three months before he left, she wrote, "I dread and yet desire this separation." Yet when he finally departed in early May, she was devastated. "Rose early, feeling sick and sad . . . no appetite . . .

weeping most hysterically." She concluded that women were destined for hardships. "Some flowers give out little or no odor until crushed."

Emerson wanted his friend to meet with Thomas Carlyle, but he struggled to write a letter of introduction. He tested out several paragraphs in his journal, comparing Alcott's pluses ("a man of ideas, a man of faith") with his minuses: "it is speculation which he loves, and not action. Therefore he dissatisfies everybody and disgusts many."

He was not wrong to worry about Alcott's impression on the dour, fiery Scotsman. The two did not make a good match. After their first two meetings, Carlyle described Alcott as a "genial, innocent, simple-hearted man, of much natural intelligence and goodness, with an air of rusticity, veracity, and dignity withal, which in many ways appeals to one . . . a venerable Don Quixote, whom nobody can even laugh at without loving!" Yet after a third encounter, he wrote to Emerson that "the good Alcott and I have prospered, I am afraid, almost as ill as it was possible for two honest men kindly affected towards one another to do." Bronson, for his part, dismissed Carlyle as "all sounding brass, the tinkling cymbal's empty note."

Alcott found London to be "costly, elegant, magnificent . . . But all is for the body; all seems body." It wasn't *spiritual.* But when Charles Lane, one of the Alcott House leaders, brought Bronson there, the school enchanted him. He described Lane to Abba as "the deepest, sharpest intellect" he had ever met.

Lane was an uncompromising reformer. Like the Shakers, he was militantly celibate; like Bronson, he abhorred the use of animals for food, clothing, or farm work. He would come to irritate Thoreau, Abba, and Louisa May Alcott, but he enthralled Bronson.

Alcott found Lane's partner Henry Gardiner Wright to be "the first man and only man whom I have found to see and know me even as I am seen and known by myself." He compared the school favorably to his former Temple School and was certain "that we might become cooperators in the work of carrying the same to its ultimate issues, whether here or in America."

Alcott House combined a cooperative community with a

progressive school. Members rose early; ate mostly raw, mostly cold, and entirely vegetarian meals; drank no stimulants; and maintained strict celibacy. The school, inspired by Bronson, utilized his teaching methods, with students from within the community and beyond. Naturally, Bronson loved it, calling Alcott House an "abode of divine purposes and loveliest charities."

Apart from Lane and Wright, no other Englishmen seemed to impress him. Nor was England the right place for a new project with his two new friends. "Britain, with all her resource and talent, is not the scene for the education of humanity: her spirit is hostile to human welfare, and her institutions averse to the largest liberty of the soul."

In August he was ready to return. He wrote to Abba that Wright, his wife and child, and Lane would come with him or follow soon after. He blithely let her know that his colleagues might interfere with her parenting, since Wright "will begin his labours on our own Children, who serve as the nucleus of the new institution." Once again, parenthood afforded him opportunities to test his theories. And this time, his theories aimed high: not just for a school but a way of life.

18

Charles Lane, with a cane and top hat.

In the end, Wright would come alone—his wife did not want to subject their newborn to an ocean crossing—but the divorced Lane would come with his son. Together with Alcott, they boarded a ship in September. They would become houseguests for Bronson, Abba, and the girls.

Thoreau, like Alcott, needed financial help. He served as surrogate father to Emerson's children while Emerson was traveling in 1843, and he guest-edited an issue of *The Dial*, but none of these activities paid anything. He wrote to Emerson, who was visiting his brother William on Staten Island, that he needed to find a source of income beyond lectures and writing. He wondered if Waldo had any ideas. Waldo and William came up with an offer: move to William's home and tutor his seven-year-old son, Willie, in exchange for room, board, and a salary of $100.

In early May Thoreau traveled by boat, arriving at the Battery in lower Manhattan for his first, and, as it turned out, only attempt at living away from Concord. He fended off cabdrivers and was dismayed by the crowd: "a confused jumble of heads, and soiled coats dangling from flesh-colored faces, all swaying to and fro, as by a sort of undertow. . . . A sad sight."

He complained about city living. He needed "a whole continent to breathe in," and he disliked the noises and crowds. He found the city "a thousand times meaner" than he had imagined.

Emerson, who had given lectures in New York since 1840, was not a fan of the city either. A few years later, hosting a visit by a noted reformer and women's rights advocate named Elizabeth Oakes Smith, the two discussed the merits of New York versus Boston. He asked her how she thought Boston compared to New York society. She defended her home city:

"I must say I think New York far superior to Boston. If society represent humanitarian and progressive ideas, they are about equal; but it seems to me that society for genial, social purposes is almost lacking in Boston." Waldo responded that "society in New York is more shallow and the knowledge more superficial."

Thoreau sent his most intriguing letters from Staten Island to Lidian. During his first residence at the Emersons' he had developed feelings for her, and biographers have long wondered how to categorize them. In May 1843 he wrote to her as "My Dear Friend": "I shall not hesitate to know you. I think of you as some elder sister of mine, whom I could not have avoided—a sort of lunar influence—only of such age as the moon, whose time is measured by her light. You must know that you represent to me woman."

A month later Lidian was "My very dear Friend," and she was more than an elder sister. She seemed "to speak out of a very clear and high heaven . . . Your voice seems not a voice, but comes as much from the blue heavens, as from the paper." Henry worshiped Lidian as Waldo never did.

Thoreau traveled to Manhattan from Staten Island on occasion, where he had brief encounters with Henry James Sr., the utopianist Albert Brisbane (who "did not impress me favorably. He looks like a man who has lived in a cellar, far gone in consumption"), and a "refreshing" Horace Greeley. Yet his career prospects languished. By September he complained to Emerson that "literature comes to a poor market here." To his mother, after listing some of the human tides in Manhattan, including "Whole families of immigrants cooking their dinner upon the pavements," he recoiled, finding them "of less firm fibre" than the people he knew. He was home by December, still uncertain how to make a living but now very certain that city life was not for him.

He had already spent some time improving his father's pencil business in the late 1830s, when he used Harvard's library to study how German pencil-makers mixed graphite with Bavarian clay. He managed to purchase some clay from the New England Glass Company, and he and his father developed a machine to grind graphite into fine particles, creating a pencil that wrote smoothly. In 1843 he returned to the family business, inventing a saw to slice lengths of baked lead to fit into grooved pencil halves before they were glued together. Then he found a way to bake the graphite mixture into cylinders, and invented a machine that drilled a hole in the wood to slip them in. Thoreau pencils became some of the best on the market. But he had no interest in making a career as a manufacturer. Among other things, the industry relied on wood from Florida red cedar trees harvested by slaves—which must have bothered Henry's mother, who refused to allow sugar in their home for similar reasons.

A few years later, when asked what profession or trade he practiced, he wrote, "I will give you some of the monster's heads. I am a Schoolmaster—a Private Tutor, a Surveyor—a Gardener, a Farmer—a Painter, I mean a House Painter, a Carpenter, a Mason, a Day-Laborer, a Pencil-Maker, a Glass-paper Maker, a Writer, and sometimes a Poetaster."

Thoreau's meeting with Horace Greeley would prove to be his most useful accomplishment in New York. From humble origins, Greeley had become a powerful newspaper magnate. Greeley grew up on a farm in Vermont and spent an apprenticeship at a local newspaper. The paper failed when he was nineteen years old. He arrived in New York in 1831 "with all his clothes in a bundle carried over his back with a stick, and with but ten dollars in his pocket." He worked as a printer and launched an inexpensive paper, unsuccessfully. He then founded *The New-Yorker*, a weekly, which achieved some renown before it failed after seven years. (It bears no relationship to its modern namesake). He befriended Whig leaders who hired him to run *The Jeffersonian*, a partisan paper, as were so many in that era.

The election of 1840 brought him more fame, as his weekly campaign paper *The Log Cabin* achieved high circulation. In 1841, he borrowed funds to found the *New-York Tribune*, a daily and soon also a weekly. It would become the country's largest weekly, and a profit-maker and kingmaker. He faced competition. In its first few days, the owner of New York's leading penny-press paper, *The Sun*, "entered into a conspiracy with their own newsboys, first to bribe, and then to flog, any urchin found selling *The Tribune* in the streets." He used "strapping young men" to put an end to that campaign.

Whitelaw Reid, his assistant and the eventual next owner of the *Tribune*, cited financial figures that should have made Greeley wealthy.

19

Horace Greeley, daguerreotype by Matthew Brady, c. 1851.

Yet "he lacked business thrift, inherited a disposition to indorse for his friends, and was often unable to distinguish between deserving applicants for aid and adventurers."

Greeley's influence would become vast, as his paper grew to the highest circulation in the country. His passions drove much of its content, and he loved reform. Experiments in socialism intrigued him. He opposed slavery and the Mexican War. He embraced women's rights. He was a strict vegetarian who refused to wear leather. He would become one of the founders of the Republican Party, and eventually, a Democratic and Liberal Republican candidate for the presidency against Ulysses Grant in 1872. In 1842 he was also determined to help launch America's most popular utopian movement—so long as he could profit from it.

8

Utopia

> We are all a little wild here with numberless projects of social reform. Not a reading man but has a draft of a new Community in his waistcoat pocket. . . . One man renounces the use of animal food; and another of coin; and another of domestic hired service; and another of [the] State; and on the whole we have a commendable share of reason and hope.
>
> —Emerson to Thomas Carlyle, October 30, 1840

In Nathaniel Hawthorne's short story "The Hall of Fantasy," the narrator describes a grand building, paved with white marble, with a spacious hall topped by a dome. Marble statues of Homer, Aesop, and Dante sit alongside "more ephemeral" idols made of wood: contemporary thinkers and visionaries. Visitors cluster around their favorites: believers in El Dorado, would-be inventors of impossible machines, and "most of the noted reformers of the day . . . the representatives of an unquiet period, when mankind is seeking to cast off the whole tissue of ancient custom like a tattered garment."

Ultimately, the narrator faces "one theory that swallows up and annihilates all others" when he is brought to meet William Miller, the rural New York preacher.

• • •

Utopian thinking—a tradition as old as the republic, and still with us today—surged in the 1840s. One scholar counted 119 communal societies founded in the first six decades of the century. Half of them, fifty-nine, fell in that single ten-year span. They came in many flavors, religious and secular, capitalist and socialist. Utopian communities were founded by "free lovers, nonlovers, vegetarians, communists, abolitionists, anarchists, Swedenborgians, atheists, spiritualists, Adventists, and teetotalers." A few managed to last for decades, including the Oneida Community, founded in 1848 in upstate New York by religious perfectionist and free-love advocate John Humphrey Noyes. Most burst into life and almost immediately collapsed—including those inspired by Miller. The average life-span of the fifty-nine communities of the "Mad Forties" was just two years.

William Miller was an upstate New York farmer with little formal education but an intense love of books—especially the Bible. He studied it, making complex calculations based on various passages to conclude that the Second Coming of Christ would happen during a one-year window beginning in March 1843. He gave dozens of lectures throughout New England, New York, and the South, warning of the coming end times to growing crowds. He inspired other so-called Second Adventist preachers to do the same.

The movement grew throughout the target year. One preacher, John Starkweather, generated especially feverish reactions. On September 13 at a Starkweather revival in Windsor, Connecticut, one woman became convinced that she could walk on water. She had to be prevented from striding into the Connecticut River.

In late 1843 and early 1844 Miller gave eighty-five lectures in eight weeks throughout New York state, followed by more in Boston and New York City. At one appearance there appeared to be at least five thousand people in attendance. The final date within Miller's predicted window, March 21, 1844, loomed.

When that day passed uneventfully, and un-Adventfully, Miller wrote an open letter to his followers: "I *confess my error*, and *acknowledge my disappointment*; yet I still believe that the day of the Lord is

20

William Miller, 1851 lithograph with the caption, "I remain as ever looking for the Lord Jesus Christ unto eternal life."

near, even at the door; and I exhort you, my brethren, to be watchful, and not let that day come upon you unawares." He thought he must have made a math mistake. Some Second Adventists had made their own calculations about Christ's return, and he came to agree with them. The new date was specific and soon: October 22, 1844.

As that day neared, people set up camps, dressed themselves in white "Ascension Robes," and closed their businesses. One Philadelphia tailor put a sign in his window: "This Shop is closed in honor of the King of Kings, who will appear about the 23rd of October. Get ready, friends, to crown him Lord of all."

The new deadline came and went, with no miracles but plenty of drama. One man attached turkey wings to his back, climbed into a tall tree, and leaped out, expecting to fly to heaven. He broke his arm. This non-advent of Judgment Day became known among Miller's followers as the Great Disappointment.

Some continued to argue for Jesus's imminent return. Eventually, one Millerite strand created the Seventh-Day Adventist Church. As "Adventist" suggests, the church teaches that Christ's return is imminent, if not precisely predictable. "Seventh-Day" refers to the church's recognition of Saturday as the Sabbath, after the biblical commandment to work the first six days of the week before resting on the seventh.

It might seem paradoxical to link Adventism with the burgeoning communities seeking utopia on earth. Many of Miller's followers were farmers and shopkeepers who had little in common with the Newness disciples of Brook Farm. Yet in practice, the many experiments of the 1840s attracted a fluid population of seekers, many of whom would sample one version after another. It is telling that a Unitarian minister, avid abolitionist, and reformer named Joshua Himes, of Boston's Chardon Street Chapel, coordinated Miller's movement. When Himes saw the power of Miller's message, he "became the manager and publicity agent of the enterprise, founding journals, arranging camp meetings, and devising the extensive tours of a group of evangelists, with the biggest tent the country had ever seen."

New religious and utopian movements attracted people for many different reasons during this age of spiritual upheaval. Joseph Smith, who grew up amid the Second Great Awakening in Vermont and western New York, published the Book of Mormon in 1830. By the time of his death in 1844, he had tens of thousands of followers who believed he would lead them to the millennial kingdom.

One of the oldest utopian movements in America, the Shakers, combined religious zeal with practical rules for living. The founder, Ann Lee, was born in 1736 in Manchester, England. By twenty-three she had become a follower of local Quakers, believers in Jesus's imminent return. Members of the group were jailed on multiple occasions for disturbing the Sabbath. During one prison stay, Lee experienced a vision of Christ and the Fall of Man that convinced her that sexual relations were the original sin of mankind, a sin that must be eradicated to achieve salvation. She emerged as Mother Ann Lee, the charismatic head of a new movement.

She called it the United Society of Believers in Christ's Second Appearing. Unofficially, her followers were called Shakers, because their ecstatic worship services included dancing and speaking in tongues.

The Church of England opposed them. Guided by another vision, she and her small group set sail for America in 1774. In the New World they established a small number of Shaker communities thanks to ceaseless travel and proselytizing by Ann and others. As a female preacher, she was an object of fascination. They built their first community in upstate New York. A second community developed in Harvard, Massachusetts.

Their rules were strict: Joiners had to renounce marriages and families. Converts had to sell their land and donate their money and possessions to the collective. By 1783, just before Mother Ann died, they had attracted at least a thousand converts. By 1796, under Joseph Meacham, they grew to eleven settlements. By 1831, after two more changes in leadership, their members numbered four thousand. Their villages had large-scale kitchens, bakeries, barns, and workshops, carefully arranged and kept spotless. Indoors, they worshiped with standardized hymns and dances, men on one side of the room, women on the other. They produced and sold seeds, brooms, and medicines, and later, their famous furniture, sturdily made items based on plain, ornament-free designs.

They continued to recruit and grow, issuing a list of 125 rules (the "Millennial Laws") to govern every aspect of life. For example:

> When two Shakers walk together . . . they must walk in step. When walking indoors, they should be as quiet as possible . . . there should not be any rugs at all; devils hide in rugs. Shakers should not play with cats. . . . When praying, a Shaker should fold the right thumb over the left, never the left over the right.

As they grew—they would peak in the late 1850s at around six thousand members—they added more rules. Men and women could not pass each other on staircases. Men's clothing could not hang to dry beside women's clothes. It was forbidden to watch animals having sex.

As a group that could not produce biological children, they needed to recruit new members or adopt children from outside the community. Despite that challenge, they achieved remarkable longevity. Today, one active community survives at Sabbathday Lake Shaker Village, in Maine. It has two members.

Communal living had advantages in America's preindustrial farm economy. By dividing all labor among dozens or even hundreds of people, the groups could magnify the talents of their members, including their tinkerers. As one historian notes, these communities produced a host of useful inventions: "the flat broom, the lazy Susan, the clothespin, a new mop ringer, a hernia truss, motorized washing machines, a new mousetrap, vacuum-sealed cans, the circular saw, cut nails, a superior animal trap, a cheese press, a corn cutter, a pea sheller, an elastic women's sneaker, and new types of barns and houses."

Yet most of the communities set up in the 1840s failed to attract a critical mass of members. In some cases, the members who did join were not practical or skilled. Brook Farm faced both problems—through its first two years, Ripley had to take on three mortgages to cover the farm's costs. Brook Farm had twenty residents at the end of its first year, and sixty by the following summer, but they were far more talented as teachers than farmers. Ripley needed to bring in tradesmen who could help manufacture goods to sell, and he needed to expand the population.

In late 1843, he decided to change the farm's constitution and join it to the most rapidly expanding utopian movement of all. Brook Farm would become a "phalanx," a community based on the theories of Charles Fourier.

• • •

21

Charles Fourier, portrait by Jean Gigoux, 1836.

Fourier had died in 1837, leaving only a handful of followers. One of them, an energetic New Yorker named Albert Brisbane, almost single-handedly made "Fourierism" a success in America. Brisbane is to Fourier what Joshua Himes was to William Miller, or Joseph Meacham was to Mother Ann—or Paul to Jesus, or Brigham Young to Joseph Smith—the practical follower who turned an original inspiration into a movement.

Brisbane was a wealthy man thanks to his father's real estate investments. The family lived in Batavia, but his father wanted him to have a better education than that town offered, so he sent Albert to a boarding school on Long Island and then supported his move to New York to study with tutors. At age eighteen, he departed on a six-year trip to Europe that included studies in Paris and Berlin. In 1832, Brisbane

22

Albert Brisbane self-portrait, age eighteen.

encountered one of Fourier's books in which the Frenchman explained how to reorganize society and reinvent economic relations.

The book left Brisbane thunderstruck. "I had studied, as well as I could at my age, all the philosophies of the world; and in this vast speculative realm of the human mind I had not found one new idea, one single truly original conception. . . . Now, for the first time, I had come across an idea which I had never met before—the idea of *dignifying* and *rendering attractive* the manual labors of mankind."

Somehow, this young man of leisure was certain that the world of wage work needed an overhaul. In Berlin at the time, he set out for Paris to meet the aging philosopher. He convinced Fourier to tutor him and then returned to New York in 1834 to proselytize for his new cause. Walt Whitman, encountering him in the city, described him as "a tall, slender man, round-shouldered, chin stuck out, deep-set eyes, sack-coat. His step is quick, and his arms swing awkwardly, as if he were trying to knock his elbows together behind him. . . . Somehow or other he always looks as if he were attempting to think out some problem a little too hard for him."

Fourier was the son of a successful merchant who hated the world of business. He was seventeen when the French Revolution toppled the monarchy, and the ensuing violence of the Terror—especially in Lyon, where he was living—horrified him. He decided that human society needed to be reorganized, and that laws of social science could make it harmonious. He was, in most ways, the opposite of William Miller: he sought utopia in this world, not the next; he believed in science, not the Bible. Yet the two men shared one tool in their search for truth: mathematics.

Fourier argued that there are twelve basic human passions: five based on the senses, four based on social passions (familism [i.e., parenthood], love, ambition, friendship), plus three different self-governing "passions": the cabalist, the butterfly, and the composite (don't ask).

Furthermore, any individual can exhibit these twelve passions to different degrees and in different combinations. The math gets fuzzy, but Fourier's equations produced 810 distinct personality types, distributed randomly throughout any given population. Much like William Miller's biblical math, it may have made sense only to its author.

Fourier loved to categorize things and make lists: twelve types of unproductive workers, sixteen causes of despair among working people, sixteen misfortunes in married life, and forty-nine types of cuckold, including "the presumptive cuckold," "the imaginary cuckold," and "the health-conscious cuckold," who cannot have sex due to medical reasons. "His wife has no choice but to appeal to substitutes, and her spouse is not entitled to take offense."

Fourier believed that God would not have created these passions and types if He didn't want them expressed and encouraged. All our impulses are natural; it's only our arbitrary moral customs that force us to suppress them. He dismissed members of society as "civilizees." He sought to liberate them from their hangups.

He envisioned settlements that would have two of each personality type, that is, 1,620 people. Of these, 830 should be male, 790 female. (Again, don't ask.)

It is hard to read Fourier's writings without dismissing him as a lunatic. He believed that no previous book about human civilization had any value, so it was up to him to reinvent the world and build a new system of knowledge from scratch, no matter how bizarre that system might become. One scholar summarizes his view of cosmology, for example, as "a vast field of copulation with planets engaging in sexual relations which affected the tone and degree of the passions throughout the universe."

Fourier predicted massive population increases thanks to his settlements, which he called phalanxes, expecting them to number in the millions. In order for Earth to accommodate them all, someone would have to reorient the North Pole to warm up the Arctic and open it up to agriculture. He was certain it could be done, but he wouldn't say how. "I am waiting to make these means known when the time is right."

He also believed the future would bring thirty-five thousand years of expanding passions, affecting the Earth in other dramatic ways: the oceans would transform from saltwater into lemonade, the air would become a perfumed mist, and fleas, rats, crocodiles, and lions would transform into friendly creatures. Human life-span would stretch to 144 years. After sixteen generations, people would develop tails of "immense" length, terminating with a small hand, "as strong as the claws of an eagle or a crab."

His vision for the phalanxes was detailed. On an average summer day, members would sleep from 10:30 p.m. to 3:30 a.m., take in the news of the day at 4:00, eat breakfast at 4:30, and then engage in a series of tasks and meals (five meals in total), no task lasting more than an hour and a half: hunting, fishing, planting seeds, attending Mass, working with fish tanks and sheep, then shopping, and so on. There would be no marriage, only a series of liaisons depending upon everyone's passions, up to and including orgies.

He wrote often about orgies and polygamy. He attacked the hypocrisy of monogamy, asserting that "nine-tenths of all civilizees are bigamists or polygamists." He described how, in a phalanx, one male and one female leader would act as minister and pontiff to help organize orgies. Nobody would be left out; everyone would play a role that suited their character. "Civilizees may think that the [phalanx] orgy is an assembly of pure sensuality, as is the foul civilizee orgy; but the two have nothing in common . . . orgies are prepared by the minister and the female pontiff who arrange delightful reunions and cumulative sympathies that heighten one another." Emerson described it as "a calculation how to secure the greatest amount of kissing that the infirmity of human constitution admitted."

Fourier struggled to make a living. He attracted only a few

23

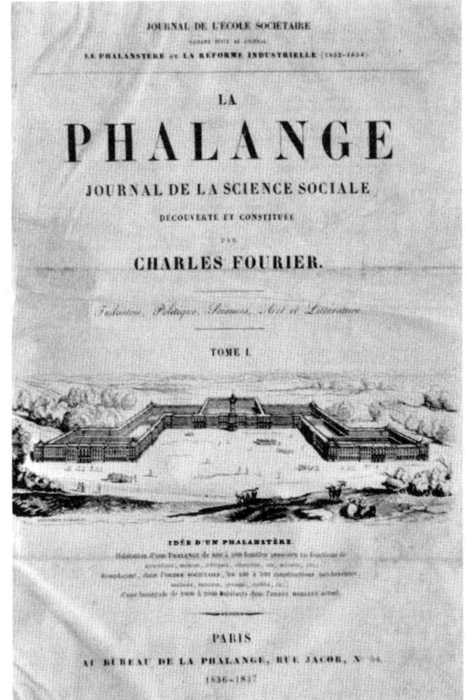

JOURNAL DE L'ÉCOLE SOCIÉTAIRE

LE PHALANSTÈRE OU LA RÉFORME INDUSTRIELLE (1832-1834)

LA

PHALANGE

JOURNAL DE LA SCIENCE SOCIALE

DÉCOUVERTE ET CONSTITUÉE

PAR

CHARLES FOURIER.

Industrie, Politique, Sciences, Art et Littérature

TOME I.

IDÉE D'UN PHALANSTÈRE.

PARIS

AU BUREAU DE LA PHALANGE, RUE JACOB, N° 54.

1836-1837

Design for a phalanstery, from the title page of Fourier's journal, *La Phalange*.

followers; he had difficulty getting his books published, and sales were poor; his articles were routinely rejected by journals and newspapers. His disciples begged him to explain key parts of his theories, yet he refused to do so—he claimed that plagiarists would steal them. He acted strangely. According to one disciple, "When walking in the streets, [he] habitually talked to himself almost aloud; which caused him to be noticed and to be considered by the unreflecting crowd as an individual of extreme eccentricity and almost as a crazy man." He spent most of his time writing in two-hour blocks, interrupted by those eccentric walks.

As to his personal life, even his disciples had no clue. All that could be said on the subject was that Fourier was gallant, and that he argued for women's equality throughout his writings.

Fourier had analyzed his own passions and decided that he was one of the 26,400 living humans who had a mania for "Sapphianism," meaning "the love of lesbians and the eagerness to aid them in every way possible." Since he estimated that the entire planet contained only twenty-six thousand lesbians, and that not even one percent of them were behaving according to their natures, he faced long odds of sexual fulfillment.

Fourier's disciple Brisbane, in the words of his third wife—one of two at the time; he was a bigamist—shared one personality trait with Bronson Alcott: "His very mental constitution rendered it impossible for him ever to attain to a commonplace, common-sense appreciation of the matter-of-fact world; and he never dealt successfully with either men or matter. This was . . . why his imagination projected an ideal transcending all possible practical realization." Yet he returned to the United States with a cause, and the funds to pursue it. He and his brother would eventually inherit almost half a million dollars.

First, he decided that he could ignore some of Fourier's theories, since "Fourier's fertile mind was full of the strangest fancies, the most far-fetched conceptions on every conceivable subject in the universe." He translated passages from Fourier's writings with no mention of orgies, no lemonade oceans, no copulating planets. He also changed Fourier's requirements for a community, reducing the minimum number of members to four hundred.

By 1839 he had enlisted several earnest adherents and needed a publisher for his translations. He funded much of the work but needed a distributor. A colleague exclaimed: "There is Horace Greeley, just damned fool enough to believe such nonsense."

His memory was a little off, as he didn't meet Greeley until 1840. Yet Greeley did become an enthusiastic supporter—for a price. He was planning to launch the *New-York Tribune*, and in March 1842, he let Brisbane have a prominent, front-page column there, but he charged him for it. Just how much the wealthy Brisbane paid for this real estate is unclear—one source names a price as high as $150 per week, nearly $4,000 in today's dollars.

Brisbane used the column to announce a "North American Phalanx." Forty other papers either carried or discussed his column. Fourierist clubs began to mushroom and make their own plans for phalanxes, and Brisbane organized regional conferences to bring them together and attract new support in Boston, New York, and the West.

Brisbane's argument rested on making work attractive to everyone. He was certain that most workers were miserable. In the phalanxes, labor, just like sex, would become "attractive" rather than "repugnant." If a sufficient variety of individual characters joined the community, each person could do the work most appealing to him or her. Nobody would be forced to work at the same task for hours on end. Somehow members would enjoy doing everything that needed to be done.

The details become both specific and murky. There would be "Groups" with twelve or sixteen people divided into three "wings"; the Groups would combine into much larger "Series." And yet "the members of an Association will choose freely the Groups which they wish to join; they will consult their own tastes, and no dictation or control will be exercised by the Association." He was proposing an army with companies, platoons, and battalions, but no officers.

Greeley wasn't the only editor who gave Brisbane a place to publish his writing. When Emerson took over editorial duties for *The Dial*, he agreed to print Brisbane's "Means of Effecting a Final Reconciliation Between Religion and Science." Yet he wrote an introduction of more than four pages on "Fourierism and the Socialists," undermining his guest author:

> Mr. Brisbane pushes his doctrine with all the force of memory, talent, honest faith, and importunacy. As we listened to his exposition, it appeared . . . the system was the perfection of arrangement and contrivance. . . . Our feeling was, that Fourier had skipped no fact but one, namely, Life. He treats man as a plastic thing, something that may be put up or down, ripened or retarded, moulded, polished, made into solid, or fluid, or gas, at the will of the leader.

Between 1842 and 1846 there were twenty-four attempts to build Fourierist communities in America. A few more were founded in the 1850s. They sprang up everywhere from Hopedale, Massachusetts, to Indiana, Ohio, Pennsylvania, and Wisconsin. Most had fewer than one hundred members, some as few as thirteen or twenty. The largest, in Dallas in the mid-to-late 1850s, had 350. The membership in most of them turned over regularly, even during their brief life-spans. Yet there were many more followers of Fourierism than these numbers suggest—one historian estimates that the movement attracted a hundred thousand followers by the end of 1843.

It is a measure of the upheavals of the times that Brook Farm became one of the most famous Fourierist experiments. Ripley needed a new strategy for his farm, and he hoped that reorganizing into a phalanx would bring financial support from Greeley and Brisbane, as well as an influx of new members. It did swell the population with new tradesmen. In the six months after the reorganization, eighty-seven applicants were admitted, including shoemakers, carpenters, printers, and a cabinetmaker. Thanks to the newcomers, the farm began generating pewterware, shoes, and sashes and blinds. Yet Brook Farm's finances worsened. The residents needed a new building (the "Phalanstery") to house the newcomers, and supplies were expensive.

They reduced their budget for food and drink. They sold off some of their animals. Hawthorne filed a lawsuit to recover $524.05 still owed on his original investment. In December 1845, Brisbane delivered the bad news that Brook Farm would not receive any outside financial aid, as he had decided to focus his attention on a new community in Red Bank, New Jersey, where sixty people had declared themselves the North American Phalanx and started a farm in 1843.

The end began in March 1846. The carpenters working on the new Phalanstery lit a woodstove in the basement of the building to keep themselves warm during the day. In the evening, sparks flew. The nearly finished, massive structure was destroyed. Members soon began to leave the farm. It dissolved in October 1847.

Historians tend to describe utopian communities as either "social" or "moral" in approach. For the former, the problem to be fixed is structural—perhaps it is capitalism, perhaps the nuclear family. If you replace the rules of society with a new set of rules, you can achieve heaven on earth. For the latter, the problem is personal—you need to bring together a group of purified seekers, people with pure motives, to solve the greater problems of civilization. You might still need new rules, but first, you have to be certain of including only ideal individuals. Many of the 1840s communities were both—rejecting "the common view that economic behavior could be treated separately from moral concerns." This helps explain the fluid membership between the various experiments. Many Americans believed society needed reinvention, and they were willing to try different solutions based on different theories.

Bronson Alcott's new friend Charles Lane was a full-bore moralist. So was Alcott. They mostly agreed on what was "spiritual" and what wasn't. A spiritual diet was not just vegan, it also excluded vegetables that grew downward into the soil (e.g., potatoes or carrots) versus those that grew upward, toward heaven. All stimulants were proscribed—no coffee, no tea, no alcohol. Wearing leather was forbidden, and animals were not to be exploited, not even by using their manure for fertilizer. Wearing cotton was banned, since it was produced by slaves.

Cold baths were spiritual, hot baths were not. As for sex, the divorced Lane opposed it. The married Alcott was ambivalent. Mrs. Alcott disagreed with Lane. When the men had first arrived in Concord in October 1842, Abba had been overjoyed. "Happy days these!!! Husband returns accompanied by the dear English-men; the good and true—Welcome to these shores, this house—to my bosom!" One month later, Lane's rigid rules were irritating her as she decried "this invasion of my rights as a woman and a mother."

The two men visited the Shaker community in Harvard, and Lane wrote about it in *The Dial*. He was impressed by the seriousness of their sexual abstinence, but the Shakers weren't as purely spiritual as he wished. They kept animals in a barn, which he compared to a prison. They were bringing in revenue by selling seeds—including to Alcott and Lane—which, to the latter, "is far too great an involvement in money affairs." They ate meat and drank milk, tea, and coffee. Still, their simplicity impressed him, as did their withdrawal from the trappings of civilization.

The trip was a short hike for the two men, as they were coming from their own Harvard utopian experiment. Though Henry Wright had declined to join it, the six Alcotts, two Lanes, and a few others had launched a grand experiment on ninety acres purchased by Lane. They called it Fruitlands. It had no orchards.

In his essay "Prudence," Emerson had written, "A gay and pleasant sound is the whetting of the scythe in the mornings of June, yet what is more lonesome and sad than the sound of a whetstone or mower's rifle when it is too late in the season to make hay?" He had been lecturing on the topic since 1837. Sadly, Bronson Alcott did not take his words to heart.

From the start, Fruitlands was a folly. The initial inhabitants were too few and too late in the planting season to launch successful crops,

24

The farmhouse at Fruitlands.

arriving only on June 1. And they were eccentric: apart from the founders' families there were just two men. One believed swearing was purifying ("Good morning, damn you!"). The other was a former asylum inmate who had changed his name repeatedly. Soon, they would be joined by one ascetic, one hermit, and a nudist. None of these people would last long. Alcott and Lane frequently departed on trips to try to recruit new members or give lectures, forcing Abba and the five children to do much of the work.

In June, Lane wrote to Thoreau in a vain attempt to convince him to join. No luck.

Lane and Alcott did manage to spread the word about Fruitlands. One intriguing footnote to their experiment is that Sojourner Truth, the spellbinding Black preacher, abolitionist, and women's rights advocate, considered joining. The former slave was a mystic who sampled and considered a range of religious and communal groups before she became nationally famous. In New York City in the 1830s, still using her given name of Isabella, she joined the household of the millennialist fanatic Prophet Matthias, whose cult was "infamous for free love and murder." The cult broke up in 1835 after Matthias was imprisoned for assaulting his daughter (though he was acquitted of a separate murder charge).

Isabella remained in the city until the day of Pentecost, June 1, 1843, when she changed her name and departed that "second Sodom" to preach the gospel. She began in Brooklyn, appearing at Millerite revivals. When she witnessed the extreme fanaticism—speaking in tongues, for example—at one of John Starkweather's meetings in Connecticut, she broke with the Adventists. By the late fall, when she needed to settle somewhere for the coming winter, she considered three possibilities: a Millerite home in Springfield, Massachusetts, a Shaker community in Enfield, Connecticut, and Fruitlands. Her Millerite friends recommended yet a fourth option: the Northampton Association for Education and Industry. It wasn't millennial; it was focused on perfecting life on earth. It would last just four and a half years in total, but its members espoused racial equality and it attracted more Black members than most such experiments. She went there, staying until the association dissolved. Frederick Douglass had visited and commented that "the air was full of isms—Grahamism, mesmerism, Fourierism, transcendentalism, communism, and abolitionism," while that community, by contrast, was "an assertion of the paramount importance of human brotherhood."

When Alcott had described his plans to Emerson in late 1842 Waldo had reacted pessimistically in his journal. "Their whole doctrine is spiritual, but they always end with saying, Give us much land and money." When he visited Fruitlands in July 1843, he wrote, "I will not prejudge them successful. They look well in July. We will see them in December." He was prescient; Fruitlands barely made it to the end of the year.

Louisa May began writing her first journal there, at age ten. For the most part, its few entries are sparse lists of the work, lessons, and play of each day. On September 1, she began, "I rose at five and had my bath. I love cold water!" Years later, when she reread her youthful journals, she added parenthetical commentary. An entry from November 2, when the small population had dwindled and the children had no time for play, described her spiritual lessons at the end of a long day of work: "In the evening Mr. Lane asked us, 'What is man?' These were our answers. A human being, an animal with a mind, a creature, a body, a soul and a mind. After a long talk we went to bed very tired. [No wonder, after doing the work and worrying their little wits with such lessons.—L.M.A.]"

By late July Alcott was fearful that the project would fail. Ellery Channing visited and reported to Emerson that Alcott was terribly sick and depressed. Late in the summer, just as it was time to harvest its barley, Alcott and Lane departed for New York to try to recruit new members and raise money. They would be gone for two weeks, during which Abba and the children raced to save the cut barley from a rainstorm. Returning in mid-September with no recruits, Lane left

25

Bronson Alcott in middle age.

again to visit Emerson in Concord. By late October, all of the nonfamily members had departed.

Conditions were dire. Notwithstanding the rule against using animals, they had relied heavily on a local farmer with one ox and one cow. It wasn't enough to produce a meaningful harvest. Lane annoyed Abba Alcott, for good reason. He did little manual work while she and her daughters exhausted themselves, and he blamed the farm's lack of members on her affection for her husband and family, which went against his principles. She wrote desperate letters to her brother, seeking an escape valve. She managed to send Anna to Boston to visit with a cousin. By late November, the Alcotts and Lane were openly discussing "separating" from the community. Louisa wrote, "Father and Mr. L. had a talk, and father asked us if *we* saw any reason for us to separate. Mother wanted to, she is so tired. I like it, but not the school part or Mr. L."

On New Year's Day, the Alcotts decided to take up an offer from local friends to rent three rooms until spring, while Lane chose to join the Shakers. As Louisa recalled in a fictionalized account, her father "lay down upon his bed, turned his face to the wall, and waited with pathetic patience for death." She may have been conflating this period with the prior August, when Channing found him so depressed, but the failure of his utopia was certainly a bitter pill.

Louisa recorded that memory in "Transcendental Wild Oats," a short story written in 1873 that mixes fact, fiction, and satire, not always easily distinguished. She described the early arrival of two members: "One a dark, melancholy man, clad in homespun, whose peculiar mission was to turn his name hind part before and use as few words as possible. The other was a bland, bearded Englishman, who expected to be saved by eating uncooked food and going without clothes." The character standing in for her father is "Brother Lamb," with a "face shining with the light and joy of the splendid dreams and high ideals hovering before him"; the Lane character is "Brother Lion," a stern taskmaster who refuses to roll up his sleeves and get to work.

After the collapse of the experiment, Brother Lamb manages to recover from depression because of his love for and attachment to his family. "In the early dawn, when [his] sad wife crept fearfully to see what change had come to the patient face on the pillow, she found it smiling at her, saw a wasted hand outstretched to her, and heard a feeble voice cry bravely, 'Hope!'"

The utopian failures demonstrated that reform and reinvention had their limits. Still, they did not quench the optimistic spirit of the age so much as underscore it.

9

Transcendence Abroad

> I have met with but one or two persons in the course of my life who understood the art of Walking.
>
> —Henry David Thoreau, "Walking"

Members of the Emerson circle who chose not to pursue utopia could take another path to deep truths: travel.

The nineteenth century was a golden age of travel writing. George Palmer Putnam, a publisher, reportedly told one of his authors that "travels sell about the best of anything we get hold of. They don't always go out with a rush, like a novel by a celebrated author, but they sell longer and in the end, pay better." Seemingly anyone who went anywhere tried to write about it. Some books were adventure memoirs, like Richard Henry Dana Jr.'s *Two Years Before the Mast* (1840). Others, like Emerson's *English Traits* (1856) or Hawthorne's *Our Old Home: A Series of English Sketches* (1863), were mixtures of observation and analysis for serious or humorous ends.

Margaret Fuller and Henry Thoreau each launched their authorial careers with a book of travel writing, and they each stretched the boundaries of the genre almost beyond recognition.

Fuller's first book was *Summer on the Lakes, in 1843*. She had traveled to the Great Lakes and visited Niagara Falls, Buffalo, Chicago, and Milwaukee, meeting some members of the Ottawa and

Chippewa tribes along the way. She traveled with Cary Sturgis as far as the falls, and then, after traversing Lakes Erie, Huron, and Michigan by boat, she took covered wagons led by William Clarke, brother of her close friend James, and their sister Sarah and mother Rebecca, from Chicago to the Mississippi River and back, before reversing her steps.

She mixed social observations with travelogue, some stories told by others, a fictionalized tale of part of her childhood, poems, and discussions of books and even of one painting. The result is difficult to classify, with flashes of poetic description, musings on the hard lives of settler wives, "the aversion that the white man soon learns to feel for the Indian on whom he encroaches," and the "disgust" and "loathing" that white women feel toward the indigenous peoples. It veers from topic to topic, author to author, yet it contains many profound thoughts. At one point, after a long digression using several lengthy passages from a German book about a clairvoyant, she echoes Bronson Alcott's transcendentalism:

> The fashioning spirit, working upwards from the clod to man, proffers as its last, highest essay, the brain of man. In the lowest zoophyte it aimed at this; some faint rudiments may there be discerned; but only in man has it perfected that immense galvanic battery that can be loaded from above, below, and around . . . whose right hand is memory, whose life is idea, the crown of nature, the platform from which spirit takes wing.

As part of her research, she managed to convince Harvard authorities to grant her access to the university library—the first woman ever to enjoy that privilege.

To Emerson, she pretended not to care for the book, writing, "Don't expect any thing from the book about the West. I can't bear to be thus disappointing you all the time." Yet when it came out in the summer of 1844 she followed the reviews closely, writing to a friend that "it is much read already, and esteemed 'very entertaining'!" Emerson had helped her secure a publishing arrangement with Little and Brown in Boston, together with Charles S. Francis in New York.

For Thoreau, travel writing would be a lifelong pursuit, engaging with the people he met but even more with the natural world. Back in February 1843, before the move to Fruitlands, Lidian Emerson had hosted Alcott and Lane for a conversation on nature and prophecy. Thoreau attended, along with a handful of others. Waldo was away on a lecture tour. As Lidian reported to her husband, "Mr. Lane decided, as for all time and the race, that this . . . love of nature—of which Henry was the champion . . . was the most subtle and dangerous of sins; a refined idolatry, much more to be dreaded than gross wickednesses." Thoreau snapped back that Lane and Alcott did not know what they were talking about. Alcott condescended to reply that "it was because they went beyond the mere material objects, and were filled with spiritual love and perception (as Mr. T. was not), that they seemed to Mr. Thoreau not to appreciate outward nature."

She found the whole discussion "ineffably comic." Yet it pointed to a profound difference between Thoreau and the other Transcendentalists. Henry respected and revered nature, but above all, he sought to understand it. For Alcott, and even for Emerson, nature was a gateway to the Over-Soul, with its moral laws and spiritual truths. Emerson loved to take long walks, but he loved human company even more, if the company were stimulating. Thoreau, conversely, often avoided or challenged his dinner companions.

For Emerson, travel meant visiting cities for lectures or going to Europe to meet great thinkers. For Thoreau, travel meant diving into the deep woods of Maine, or climbing the mountains of New England, or walking up and down the arm of Cape Cod. He had no interest in utopian communities—his version of living "deliberately" would be his solo stay at Walden Pond. Yet his travels provided the material for some of his greatest writing, and for a form of idealist thinking.

His first book, *A Week on the Concord and Merrimack Rivers*, took years to write after his boating and hiking trip with his brother. As with Fuller's, it was far more than a simple travelogue.

The trip had lasted two weeks, but Thoreau created a seven-day structure, omitting Mount Washington and adding digressions on all sorts of topics—Homer, reformers, politics, ancient Greek and Roman writers, Hindu scripture, the New Testament, history, Goethe, and one of his hiking trips, as well as many poems by himself and others. As with Fuller's book, he sprinkles profound thoughts among this jagged structure: "Men do not fail commonly for want of knowledge, but for want of prudence to give wisdom the preference." His view of reform is that it must be personal, not communal: "The reform which you talk about can be undertaken any morning before unbarring our doors."

After a long, tortured path, *A Week* would finally be published in 1849. Initially, Thoreau could not secure a contract for it. Emerson encouraged his friend, editor and publisher Evert Augustus Duyckinck, to include it in a series of new American authors with Wiley & Putnam, noting that Thoreau "has done nothing half so good as his new book." Yet Duyckinck lost his position at the house and the manuscript was rejected. The publishers offered only to print and distribute it if Thoreau would pay for everything.

Thoreau wrote to Emerson in November 1847 that four different publishing firms had declined to take it on at their own risk, but any of them would do it if he paid for it. He was inclined to "let it lie" as he did not yet "like the book well enough." Emerson argued with him—he thought the book should be published as soon as possible, and that Thoreau would face little or no danger in taking on the financial risk. It was bad advice.

Thoreau finally published *A Week* with James Munroe and Company, agreeing to reimburse the firm if the thousand-copy printing failed to sell. It was a costly mistake: Sales were miserable despite reviews that mixed criticism with praise. *The Athenaeum* was almost completely dismissive of the book's grab-bag of prose essays and poems:

> The Concord and Merrimak [*sic*] are not rivers which would be likely to yield much matter of interest to the traveller—even if he sought for it,—which Mr. Thoreau does not. . . . The book would therefore be better described as a series of essays on love, poetry, religion—and so on. The matter is for the most part poor enough; but there are a few things in the volume, scattered here and there, which suggest that the writer is a man with a habit of original thinking, which with more careful culture may produce a richer harvest in some future season. The manner is that of the worst offshoots of Carlyle and Emerson: all Mr. Thoreau's best things are spoilt in the utterance.

Of the thousand copies printed, the company sold only about two hundred over four years. Thoreau had to pay Munroe $290 (nearly $9,000 in today's dollars) to take back the unsold copies. It took him several years to wipe out the debt. He joked wanly, "I have now a library of nearly nine hundred volumes, over seven hundred of which I wrote myself."

He was especially upset by Emerson's reaction, or lack thereof. Emerson had declined the chance to review the book for the *Massachusetts Quarterly Review*, explaining that it would be inappropriate for him to critique someone of his own "clan & parish." The *Quarterly Review* turned to James Russell Lowell, just one year after Lowell's popular satiric poem, *A Fable for Critics*, had attacked Thoreau as a mere mimic or even a plagiarist of Emerson: "to see him's rare sport / Tread in Emerson's tracks with legs painfully short . . . He follows as close as a stick to a rocket, / His fingers exploring the prophet's each pocket."

Lowell's eleven-page review was not entirely damning, but Lowell complained of the many digressions that "thrust themselves obtrusively out of the narrative." And he objected that "Mr. Thoreau, like most solitary men, exaggerates the importance of his own thoughts."

Thoreau despaired about Emerson in his journal in September:

> I had a friend, I wrote a book, I asked my friend's criticism, I never got but praise for what was good in it—my friend became estranged

> from me and then I got blame for all that was bad,—& so I got at last the criticism which I wanted.
>
> While my friend was my friend he flattered me, and I never heard the truth from him, but when he became my enemy he shot it to me on a poisoned arrow.

The relationship between the two men had frayed before this episode, when Emerson grew cool to Thoreau's obstreperousness. He wrote in his journal that Thoreau was always on the attack, without the cheerfulness that makes a friend valuable.

For the next decade, Thoreau would wrestle with his feelings about his neighbor. At one point he would go so far as to write, "And now another friendship is ended. I do not know what has made my friend doubt me, but I know that in love there is no mistake, and that every estrangement is well founded. . . . With one with whom we have walked on high ground we cannot deal on any lower ground ever after. We have tried for so many years to put each other to this immortal use, and have failed."

Yet just a few weeks later he reversed course, noting that just as he was trying to sever relations, he found them nearer and dearer to each other. The friendship made him a "helpless prisoner." He concluded on a philosophical note: "Those whom we can love, we can hate; to others we are indifferent."

His struggles with *A Week* hardly dissuaded him from traveling and writing about it. In essays, eventually collected in two other books, Thoreau's travel writing spanned his entire career. In 1843, he and William Fuller (Margaret's brother) hiked thirty miles to climb Mount Wachusett, which became his first essay for a large audience, "A Walk to Wachusett," published in *The Boston Miscellany*. In 1844, he agreed to meet Ellery Channing in Pittsfield at the western edge of Massachusetts. He chose a two-week-long route to get there: He began with a train to Mount Monadnock in southern New Hampshire. He climbed it, and then hiked to Mount Greylock, eighty miles west, followed by yet more hiking to reach Channing. He carried no water.

He would travel to Maine three times and Cape Cod four, writing essays about the trips which he tried to sell to magazines. He proved to be a difficult author. When *The Atlantic Monthly* published the first of three installments about one Maine excursion, "Chesuncook," he was outraged when a single sentence was omitted without his approval. The sentence paid homage to a pine tree: "It is as immortal as I am, and perchance will go to as high a heaven, there to tower above me still." Thoreau's letter to editor James Russell Lowell was blistering:

> I do not ask anybody to adopt my opinions, but I do expect that when they ask for them to print, they will print them, or obtain my consent to their alteration or omission. . . . I am not willing to be associated in any way, unnecessarily, with parties who will confess themselves so bigoted and timid as this implies. I could excuse a man who was afraid of an uplifted fist, but if one habitually manifests fear at the utterance of a sincere thought, I must think that his life is a kind of nightmare continued in broad daylight. It is hard to conceive of one so completely derivative. Is this the avowed character of the Atlantic Monthly?

Perhaps it is no wonder that he published so little in his lifetime. He did manage to publish an account of his first Maine trip, to Mount Katahdin, in five installments in 1848, thanks to Horace Greeley's connections with the *Union Magazine of Literature and Art*. Greeley paid him $25 up front and then more when he sold the essay.

Thoreau's travel writing yields many riches—some of his best humor, some of his most profound observations, and much of his philosophy. He disdains the trappings of civilization. He writes of the limits of friendship, noting that too much time spent with a friend can do more harm than good, and he "must withdraw religiously into solitude and silence, the better to prepare ourselves for a loftier intimacy."

Conversely, when he meets up with woodsmen, he has only good things to say. They are the pioneers who have experienced the world and gained "information more general and far reaching than the villager's."

On one of his Maine trips, with a handful of companions determined to shoot a moose, the group hired a Penobscot Indian guide named Joe Polis. Thoreau had no interest in the hunt and was repulsed when the group finally slaughtered a moose. It was Polis who interested him. Thoreau was fascinated to learn everything he could from his guide.

Henry and Joe traded information on the local fauna. Polis taught Thoreau how to distinguish between varieties of spruce trees, and Thoreau learned as much Penobscot vocabulary as he could. "I told him that in this voyage I would tell him all I knew, and he should tell me all he knew, to which he readily agreed."

He admired the woodcraft of the Indians he met, yet, like Margaret Fuller, he could not escape condescension toward them, and like Emerson, he believed that the so-called red man, as a race, was inherently inferior to the white man, and destined to wither away. Both Fuller and Thoreau accused white settlers and the US government of terrible abuses toward the native population, but it was only Emerson who would write a polemic on the subject. Thoreau, who became a fierce polemicist against slavery, said almost nothing about Indian removal—a paradox that scholars continue to ponder.

Thoreau's nature writing often combines observation with poetic contemplation:

> I sit now on a stump whose rings number centuries of growth. If I look around I see that the soil is composed of the remains of just such stumps, ancestors to this. The earth is covered with mould. I thrust this stick many aeons deep into its surface, and with my heel make a deeper furrow than the elements have ploughed here for a thousand years. If I listen, I hear the peep of frogs which is older than the slime of Egypt.

He could be correspondingly brutal about the timber industry as it "ransacked" virgin forests. "The Anglo-American can indeed cut down, and grub up all this waving forest, and make a stump speech, and vote for Buchanan on its ruins, but he cannot converse with the spirit of the tree he fells, he cannot read the poetry and mythology which retire as he advances." Taken together, his views on nature, and man's place in it, can be summed up in one famous line from his essay "Walking": "In Wildness is the preservation of the World."

To experience and record everything possible about the Wildness of New England, he withstood hardships that no other Emerson acolyte would dare to face.

He bushwhacked up mountains. When he and his companions hiked to Mount Katahdin, there were no trails to guide them. He set his compass and tried to proceed on a straight line, occasionally stopping to climb to the top of a tall tree to get a view and reorient himself. When the group became tired and ready to bed down on the side of the mountain, he plunged ahead, scrambling up steep, boulder-strewn slopes until he reached the clouds and had to turn back. The next day he tried again with the others, but again he had to give up. "Nature was here something savage and awful, though beautiful."

When he hiked to Mount Greylock, the highest peak in Massachusetts, as part of his long walk across the state, he picked raspberries for food and occasionally bought a loaf of bread at a farmhouse. He carried a knapsack with one change of clothing, a hatchet, and a dipper for drinking and cooking. He plotted his own course. When he reached the highest house on the slope, he left the trail—which veered sideways for a more gradual ascent—to bushwhack upward for two miles. The farmer at the house had warned him against it, but "I knew that I was more used to woods and mountains than he, and went along through his cow-yard, while he, looking at the sun, shouted after me that I should not get to the top that night."

He did make it to the top, where the ruins of an old observatory stood. He became thirsty, so when he found some horseshoe tracks that had small puddles of standing water, he lay down flat and drank each one. Then he returned to a damp spot he had passed and used sharp stones to dig a two-foot well, which provided water. "I filled my dipper, and, making my way back to the observatory, collected some dry sticks, and made a fire . . . [and] cooked my supper of rice, having already whittled a wooden spoon to eat it with."

He slept on the summit, as he had done on Mount Monadnock at the start of that trip. He grew cold, so he collected wooden boards near the old observation tower and lay down with his head near the fire, encased in wood. He even managed "to put a board on top of me, with a large stone on it, to keep it down, and so slept comfortably."

He was deeply respectful of nature but not in the least respectful of other people. In 1844, he and Concord neighbor Edward Hoar were preparing to cook some fish near Fair Haven Pond on a dry, windy day. They lost control of their fire. It spread quickly and burned over three hundred acres. When he wrote about it in his journal, he was more haughty than regretful:

> I once set fire to the woods. . . . Presently I heard the sound of the distant bell giving the alarm & I knew that the town was on its way to the scene—Hitherto I had felt like a guilty person—nothing but shame & regret—But now I settled the matter with myself shortly—& said to myself—who are these men who are said to be the owners of these woods & how am I related to them? I have set fire to the forest—but I have done no wrong therein. . . . It was a glorious spectacle & I was the only one there to enjoy it.

Some of his neighbors never let him forget it, calling him the "woods burner" whenever they saw him.

His trips to Cape Cod brought out his sense of humor. He liked puns. "As for Sandwich [Massachusetts], I cannot speak particularly. Ours was but half a Sandwich." He could also poke fun at the Cape's hardscrabble residents:

> A strict regard for truth obliges us to say that the few women whom we saw that day looked exceedingly pinched up. They had prominent chins and noses, having lost all their teeth, and a sharp W would represent their profile. They were not so well preserved as their husbands; or perchance they were well preserved as dried specimens. (Their husbands, however, were pickled.)
>
> But we respect them not the less for all that; our own dental system is far from perfect.

Perhaps his most famous humorous passage is "The Wellfleet Oysterman," from his first trip to the Cape, in 1849. He was traveling with Ellery Channing. The trip began with a disturbing scene of bodies and wreckage from a lost ship washing ashore in Cohasset. They took a train to the base of the Cape and then a stagecoach to Orleans before beginning their hike to and from Provincetown. In Wellfleet, near the top of the peninsula, they knocked on the door of one of the few houses they saw. They were greeted by a "suspicious" man who appeared to be sixty or seventy.

John Newcomb turned out to be eighty-eight. He was old enough to remember hearing the guns of the Battle of Bunker Hill when he was a boy, echoing over the water. "'I was fourteen year old at the time of Concord Fight,—and where were you then?'

"We were obliged to confess that we were not in the fight."

After deciding that the two travelers were acceptable, he said, "Well, walk in, we'll leave it to the women." They spent the evening in conversation, while Newcomb's wife and daughter served them dinner and Newcomb's son, "a fool," sat muttering about all the "Damn book-pedlers,—all the time talking about books. Better do something. Damn 'em. I'll shoot 'em."

As for Newcomb himself, Thoreau writes, "They said that he was old and foolish, but he was evidently too knowing for them." His portrait is amusing and respectful. He gleaned as much as he could from Newcomb about the oystering business, the Cape's kettle ponds, and the shifting sands around Wellfleet.

Thoreau never failed to observe people, their settlements, and their environments. As he would do in his journals, especially in his later years, he loved to combine precise descriptions with soaring metaphors, finding universal truths in a single tree, plant, or animal. The sentence that was cut from *The Atlantic Monthly* was part of the conclusion of a passage about human exploitation of the woods, and what it might mean:

> I have been into the lumber-yard, and the carpenter's shop, and the tannery, and the lampblack factory, and the turpentine clearing; but when at length I saw the tops of the pines waving and reflecting the light at a distance high over all the rest of the forest, I realized that the former were not the highest use of the pine. It is not their bones or hide or tallow that I love most. It is the living spirit of the tree, not its spirit of turpentine, with which I sympathize, and which heals my cuts. It is as immortal as I am, and perchance will go to as high a heaven, there to tower above me still.

Bronson Alcott believed that Thoreau's journals were his greatest achievement. At first, Thoreau struggled to find his voice. But over time his journals evolved into a naturalist's notebook based on each day's excursions, usually one at dawn, another in the afternoon. As he put it, "A journal is a record of experiences and growth, not a preserve of things well done or said. . . . The charm of the journal must consist in a certain greenness, though freshness, and not in maturity." He would interrupt his observations with philosophical and political comments. Many of his most famous quotes come from these pages. But the journals reveal a naturalist and a poet at work, trying to understand and appreciate the flora and fauna around him.

He was scientific—measuring and cataloguing animal and human tracks, nests, eggs, birds, rocks, plant life, and more—yet he disdained science unless it was tethered to something higher. "To the indifferent and casual observer the laws of nature are science—To the enlightened and spiritual they are morality—or modes of divine life." When the Association for the Advancement of Science sent him a questionnaire, asking which branch of science was his greatest interest, he mused, "The fact is I am a mystic—a transcendentalist—& a natural philosopher to boot. Now I think of it[,] I should have told them at once that I was a transcendentalist—that would have been the shortest way of telling them that they would not understand my explanations."

Yet fellow naturalists, then and now, would have no trouble understanding his interests and obsessions: his long walks, his minutely detailed observations, his experiments. He loved to capture animals and bring them home for a night—a flying squirrel, a snapping turtle, even a screech owl. His attic was stuffed with plants, pressed flowers, seeds, nests, feathers, rocks, skulls, insects, and shells. He enjoyed wordplay and paradox, as he did in social situations. Edward Waldo Emerson, Waldo and Lidian's surviving son, recalled that "when Thoreau came, rather unwillingly, by invitation to dine with company, it often happened that he was in a captious mood, amusing himself by throwing paradoxes in the way of the smooth current of the conversation." The paradoxes in his journals have the same effect. When Thoreau writes, " 'Tis healthy to be sick sometimes," it brings the reader up short. Upon inspection, the profundity dissolves. Given that his loved ones died of tuberculosis and tetanus, it might have been healthier to have had vaccines.

Like Emerson, Thoreau knew how to craft an epigram, and he is one of America's most frequently quoted authors. But he also wrote entire paragraphs that are poetic. Consider this excerpt from a January journal passage on the miracle of snowflakes: "Wheels of the storm-chariots . . . What a world we live in! Where myriads of these little disks, so beautiful to the most prying eye, are whirled down on every traveler's coat, the observant and the unobservant, and on the restless squirrel's fur, and on the far-stretching fields and forests, the wooded dells, and the mountain-tops. . . . There they lie, like the wreck of chariot-wheels after a battle in the skies."

He often paused to express admiration and delight. "Why was there never a Poem on the cricket?" "How well-behaved are cows!"

He not only strove to live deliberately but also to write deliberately. His journals pause to comment on the importance of writing, reflecting, and finding poetry in the world.

Ultimately, Thoreau transcended Transcendentalism. The meaning he found in nature was not an invented abstraction, it was a sincere exploration of how the world worked. In his lecture "The Transcendentalist" Emerson had tried to distinguish between materialists and idealists, the former proceeding only from the "data of the senses," the latter perceiving that the senses only give us "representations of things, but what are the things themselves, they cannot tell." In other words, the physical world is an imperfect manifestation of an ideal world, and the job of the transcendentalist is to uncover that hidden essence.

The arguments of Lane and Alcott on that February 1843 night in Concord were extreme forms of idealism. They denied that the physical world carried its own meaning. It reflected spiritual truth but, if anything, nature was a corruption of the spiritual.

Thoreau, by contrast, was a keen observer and a practical man. He made money as an occasional surveyor and handyman. He spent days surveying Walden Pond when it was frozen over, using an ax to cut over one hundred holes and placing over twenty sighting posts to measure its length and breadth, and using a plumb line to measure its surprising depth (102 feet at the deepest point). He corresponded with Louis Agassiz, the great biologist, geologist, and Harvard professor, sending him new species for his natural history work. In 1853, the Association for the Advancement of Science named him a member. He loved to express poetic thoughts, but they were always in the service of understanding the world as it is.

When Darwin's *On the Origin of Species* was published in the United States in January 1860, Thoreau was an early, enthusiastic, and close reader of it. In February he copied extracts into six pages of his notebooks. He shared Darwin's talent for close observation and ingenious experimentation. He acknowledged the truth of interspecies competition and adaptation, which he had witnessed countless times. He believed in inductive reasoning—first, observe the world closely, and only then derive principles to explain that data.

He was a born scientist even more than a born poet. Alcott, and to an extent Emerson, were the opposite. Ultimately, Emerson came to recognize that his former protégé had exceeded the accomplishments of his mentor. Many years after his death, Emerson spent time reading Henry's voluminous journals and pondering his legacy:

> In reading Henry Thoreau's journal, I am very sensible of the vigour of his constitution. That oaken strength which I noted whenever he walked, or worked, or surveyed wood-lots, the same unhesitating hand with which a field-labourer accosts a piece of work, which I should shun as a waste of strength, Henry shows in his literary task. . . . In reading him, I find the same thought, the same spirit that is in me, but he takes a step beyond, and illustrates by excellent images that which I should have conveyed in a sleepy generality.

Thoreau's utopia was the natural world, and it contained more than enough to occupy his mind and body.

10

How to Live at Home

Where do we find ourselves?

—Ralph Waldo Emerson, "Experience"

By the mid-1840s Waldo Emerson was an established celebrity, settled permanently at Coolidge Castle with his lecture career at its height. Yet the other members of his circle were all still seeking their place in the world. Travel was one thing, but where, and how, should they live? They would answer those questions very differently from one another, revealing quite a lot about their inclinations and needs, and the trajectory of the Newness.

Emerson's own thinking had evolved from his brash optimism toward a more nuanced, pragmatic idealism, as witnessed by some of the essays in his second collection, published in 1844. For many modern readers, "Experience" is his greatest of all because it faces the gap between ideal and real: "Illusion, Temperament, Succession, Surface, Surprise, Reality, Subjectiveness,—these are . . . the lords of life." We cannot avoid subjectivity, because "we do not see directly, but mediately, and . . . we have no means of correcting these colored and distorting lenses." Yet we must find ways to act in the world as it exists. The final sentence of "Experience" points toward a new engagement with the messy world: "The true romance, which the world exists to realize, will be the transformation of genius into practical power." But does politics ever allow for idealism?

The other members of his circle were struggling with even more basic questions: Where to live? How to live? Hawthorne still needed money. In Concord, he fell behind even his low rent due to the Manse's owner, Samuel Ripley, so he and Sophia returned to his family home in Salem in the fall of 1845. His second story collection for adults, *Mosses from an Old Manse*, failed to sell when it was released in June 1846. Finally, he managed to find a new post at the Salem Custom House thanks to the intercession of John L. O'Sullivan, who published several of his stories in his *Democratic Review*, and who had connections within the Democratic Party. Readers of the preface to *The Scarlet Letter* can see Hawthorne's satirical portrait of his new office—he did not love the work, and he did not admire his colleagues. But it was a financial lifeline.

Mosses received mixed reviews. Margaret Fuller wrote a front-page notice for the *New-York Tribune*, confessing her disappointment that Hawthorne's writing had not evolved beyond that of his previous collection. She complained that "Hawthorne intimates and suggests, but he does not lay bare the mysteries of our being."

Mosses from an Old Manse includes twenty-three stories and sketches, mostly but not entirely fictional. As he would do with *The Scarlet Letter*, Hawthorne appended a preface, "The Old Manse." It describes his house and its history, noting "the most delightful little nook of a study" where Emerson wrote *Nature*, and where Emerson's grandfather, William Emerson, may have looked out his window at the Battle of Concord. The North Bridge adjoined the Manse's backyard.

Hawthorne noted the upstairs library, packed with volumes from the many generations of clergymen in Emerson's ancestry, including the most recent inhabitant, Ezra Ripley. He described an outing on the water with Ellery Channing. And he noted the many strange "moral shapes of men," "hobgoblins of flesh and blood" who were attracted there by Emerson, whose "mind acted upon other minds of a certain constitution with wonderful magnetism."

The stories include fables and allegories, with notable satires of

Transcendentalism ("The Celestial Rail-road") and utopians ("The Hall of Fantasy"). Hawthorne repeatedly displays a cranky aversion to progress. He even rails against woodstoves ("the cheerless and ungenial stove"), which were replacing the fireplaces he loved. He echoes Thoreau when he adds that "the inventions of mankind are fast blotting the picturesque, the poetic, and the beautiful out of human life."

Hawthorne's allegories attack contemporary reformist fads. In "Earth's Holocaust" he imagines a massive bonfire of the vanities, including all jewelry, all bottles of liquor, all weapons, all books, and all cash. He adds a couple of jokes, including when "an American author, whose works were neglected by the public, threw his pen and paper into the bonfire and betook himself to some less discouraging occupation." Standing to the side and observing throughout is the devil in disguise, untroubled by the zealous reformers. He knows that he "shall see good days yet. There is one thing that these wiseacres have forgotten to throw into the fire, and without which all the rest of the conflagration is just nothing at all." That thing is "the human heart itself."

Hawthorne never forgot that people are sinful and never pretended to seek Emersonian perfection.

Edgar Allan Poe, who had previously praised the stories in *Twice-Told Tales*—"they belong to the highest region of Art—an Art subservient to genius of a very lofty order"—panned the new collection. He found it "monotonous" and complained that "the strain of allegory . . . completely overwhelms the greater number" of the stories. He blamed the Newness:

> Indeed, *his* spirit of "metaphor run-mad" is clearly imbibed from the phalanx and phalanstery atmosphere in which he has been so long struggling for breath. . . . He has the purest style, the finest taste, the most available scholarship, the most delicate humor, the most touching pathos, the most radiant imagination, the most consummate ingenuity; and with these varied good qualities he has done well as a mystic. . . . Let him . . . come out from the Old Manse, cut Mr. Alcott, [and] hang (if possible) the editor of "The Dial."

Poe believed the Newness was strangling Hawthorne's imagination. In this view, optimistic politics is worse than naive; it makes art impossible.

The Alcotts, after leaving Fruitlands in early 1844, were similarly in dire straits. At first, they found accommodations with a family in nearby Still River. That summer they met young Frederick Willis, a rare male playmate for the girls. Like Laurie in *Little Women*, he joined Anna and Louisa in playacting. As he later recalled, they would hike to a pond, carrying lunch and some books in a wheeled cart, and create impromptu dramas: "We christened a favorite nook, a beautiful rocky glen carpeted with moss and adorned with ferns opening upon the water's edge, 'Spiderland.' I was the King of the realm, Anna was the Queen, and Louisa, the Princess Royal."

He remembered Louisa as "full of spirit and life; impulsive and moody, and at times irritable and nervous. She could run like a gazelle. She was the most beautiful girl runner I ever saw. She could leap a fence or climb a tree as well as any boy and dearly loved a good romp."

Bronson considered moving in with the Shakers, as Charles Lane had done, or the Northampton Association, where Sojourner Truth lived. Yet he decided against joining either. Once again, he found utopian experiments to fall short of his grand hopes. As he wrote to his brother, "I am unwilling to join any of the Communities in Mass—they aim at little, and are but new phases of the Spirit of Old Society." He wanted something of "vastly nobler aim."

By the fall the Alcotts were back in Concord, staying with a neighbor of Emerson's and hunting for a house to purchase, thanks to money inherited by Abba. Yet Bronson still desired some form of community. "I cannot consent to live solely for one family: I would stand in neighborly relations to several." Finally they purchased the house they called Hillside, with Abba's money supplemented by a $500 gift from Emerson. They moved in in April 1845.

It was the start of a pivotal period for Louisa. Over the next several years she became a frequent visitor to the Emerson household. Waldo

26

The Wayside, with Nathaniel and Sophia Hawthorne, formerly the Alcotts' Hillside.

let her borrow books from his library, which she devoured. She was twelve when she first arrived in the town, and she developed a preteen crush on Emerson. "I wrote letters to him, but was wise enough never to send them, [and] left wild flowers on the doorsteps of my 'Master.'"

She and her sisters were taught lessons at home, mostly by Bronson and Abba. She continued to enjoy vigorous exercise. She and Abba could each challenge Bronson. At one point in his diary he wrote, "Two devils, as yet, I am not quite divine enough to vanquish—the mother fiend and her daughter."

The Alcotts would not live at Hillside for many years, but it proved a congenial home after a long series of short-term arrangements. Bronson spent much of his time making improvements to the interior and the surrounding landscape, and educating his daughters. He had a talent for all three tasks. None of them produced any income.

The more famous new homestead in the town was its smallest. In late March 1845, Henry Thoreau borrowed Alcott's ax, walked to the shore of Walden Pond, chopped down a few trees, and started building a cabin. The land was Emerson's. Thoreau designed and built the cabin—he called it a house—using boards from a nearby shanty that he purchased from an Irish railroad worker for $4.50. By early May, he was ready to raise the frame with the help of Emerson, Alcott, Channing, and other neighbors. Henry built a trapdoor in the floor to reach a modest cellar hole where he could store potatoes. He laid a chimney foundation with cobblestones from the pond. The cabin measured ten by fifteen feet. He moved in on the Fourth of July. He would add plaster to the walls and finish the chimney in time for the colder weather in the fall.

Just as the frame-raising required neighborly help, so did the farming. In the spring he hired a team of oxen and a driver to plow two and a half acres where he planted beans, potatoes, peas, turnips, and sweet and yellow corn. He intended to sell the beans.

For the next two years Thoreau mostly lived there, alone. He was well known in town. He had served as secretary of the Concord Lyceum and given talks there; he and his brother had run the Concord Academy; he had set fire to the woods; and he had lived in Emerson's famous house. Yet he was now creating a persona both strange and very public. It turned him from a curious neighbor into a famous eccentric.

He walked into town on many days, shopping and chatting with people. He walked home every Sunday to drop off his laundry and have dinner with the family. He hosted a steady stream of visitors, prompting his famous line: "I had three chairs in my house; one for solitude, two for friendship, three for society."

He was deeply embedded in Concord life. He memorialized one visit by Bronson Alcott in *Walden*: "I think he must be the man of the most faith of any alive. His words and attitude always suppose a better state of things than other men are acquainted with, and he will be the last man to be disappointed as the ages revolve."

His family visited him frequently. He dined at the Emersons' and the Alcotts'. He continued to take handyman jobs. He was no hermit; he even threw annual melon parties in town. Yet he immersed himself in his life in the woods. Frederick Willis recalled a visit by himself and the Alcotts, and Thoreau's unusual greeting:

"'Keep very still and I will show you my family.' Stepping quickly outside the cabin door, he gave a low and curious whistle; immediately a woodchuck came running towards him from a nearby burrow. With varying note, yet still low and strange, a pair of gray squirrels were summoned and approached him fearlessly. With still another note several birds, including two crows, flew towards him, one of the crows nestling upon his shoulder. . . . He fed them all from his hand, taking food from his pocket, and petted them gently before our delighted gaze." Afterward, Thoreau took all five children out on the water in his boat and played the flute for them.

His purpose wasn't just to "live deliberately," as he put it at the start of *Walden*. He also meant to turn his notes and drafts of *A Week on the Concord and Merrimack Rivers* into a book. He believed he had finished it by the spring of 1847. When Lidian Emerson invited him to move back into her house in September, to keep the family company while Waldo went to Europe for a year-long trip, he closed the cabin

27

Interior replica of Thoreau's Walden Pond cabin.

and sold it to Emerson. The hermit of legend returned to a bustling household.

It would take him two more years to publish *A Week*, and five beyond that to finish *Walden*. His masterpiece would draw from his journals over several years, not just his time in the cabin.

Thoreau never lived alone again, yet he remained solitary in one important way. In November, he declined a marriage proposal from Sophia Foord. She was forty-five, fifteen years older than he. She had come to Concord from the Northampton Association in 1845 to live initially with the Alcotts, then the Emersons, to tutor their children. As Henry described it to Waldo, "She really did wish to—I hesitate to write—marry me—that is the way they spell it. . . . I sent back as distinct a *No*, as I have learned to pronounce after considerable practice, and trust that this No has succeeded. . . . I really had anticipated no such foe as this in my career." She remained in love with Thoreau until her death, writing letters to Louisa about him for decades.

If any other eligible woman had any interest in him, no record of it survives. Once, when he was thirty-four, he reluctantly attended a party and spoke with two younger women. He dismissed them harshly: "The society of young women is the most unprofitable I have ever tried. They are so light & flighty that you can never be sure whether they are there or not there." Scholars have pored over his writings about women and men—the former, rarely admiring except for mother or sister figures; the latter, often admiring of their appearance and character—and speculated about his sexuality, while agreeing that the record has no sign of actual sexual relations with anyone. Thoreau rarely addressed the topic directly, saying simply that "there is a . . . crust over my heart."

Emerson sold Thoreau's cabin to his gardener, who, in turn, sold it to two farmers, who moved it across town. By 1868, it was dismantled. Yet Waldo had liked the idea of a small writer's retreat of his own, so he hired Alcott to build one for him, with Thoreau's help. Alcott invented a structure based on his own spiritual ideas—there were nine joists, one for each of the Muses; he omitted standard framing and simply wove and lashed branches together for the walls. At one point,

28

May Alcott's sketch of Tumbledown Hall.

Thoreau asked Alcott, "Did you ever study geometry?" Emerson joked to his wife that he would name it "Tumbledown Hall." It was open to rain and mosquitoes, and hardly used by Emerson, but it stood for several years. Emerson, a generous friend, continued to pay Alcott to repair it.

Margaret Fuller made the boldest move of the Emerson circle. In the fall of 1844, she temporarily moved to Fishkill Landing on the Hudson River to complete *Woman in the Nineteenth Century*, the expansion of her essay for *The Dial* that Horace Greeley had promised to publish. As part of her research and at the invitation of a friend from Brook Farm who was now working at Sing Sing prison, she visited the women incarcerated there. Most of them were imprisoned for prostitution.

She had written in the essay that "if there is a misfortune in woman's lot, it is in obstacles being interposed by men." In the book she would go further: when "husbands tell their wives that it is folly to expect chastity from men, it is inevitable that there should be many monsters of vice." Meeting these inmates lit a fuse for social reform in Fuller. She had lived a life of reading, writing, and conversation. It was now time to engage more directly with the world.

New York City, and employment at Greeley's *New-York Tribune*, beckoned. Greeley recognized that she was "the best instructed woman in America." His offer of employment made her the first woman to serve on the editorial staff of a major newspaper. Both projects—the book and her journalism—would help her reach a much larger audience than that of any of the other transcendentalists to date. Her journalism would also help her engage with New York from its elite to its most impoverished members. Unlike Emerson and Thoreau, she was hungry to take it all in.

Woman in the Nineteenth Century was one of the first books published in America to call for equal rights for women, following Sarah Grimké's *Letters on the Equality of the Sexes.* (Sarah and her sister Angelina, born into a slaveholding family in Charleston, South Carolina, had renounced slavery and become pioneering speakers and writers on behalf of abolition and women's rights.)

Fuller's arguments went beyond Grimké's. They were all present in her 1843 *Dial* essay, but she expanded them greatly, discussing reform issues and sharpening her rhetoric for the book. Unlike *Summer on the Lakes, Woman in the Nineteenth Century* intently focuses on its great topic.

By the standards of modern feminism, Fuller's book can feel both prescient and outdated. She argues that there are fundamental and distinct characteristics of the male versus the female, and that "woman is the weaker party." She, like Emerson, makes the Transcendentalist case that the ideal masculine and ideal feminine form a spiritual dichotomy that could be manifested in any individual—that was the point of her original title's "Man *versus* Men. Woman *versus* Women": the ideals of the two sexes were juxtaposed against living people. Yet in one famous passage, she anticipates modern concepts of gender fluidity: "Male and female represent the two sides of the great radical dualism. But, in fact, they are perpetually passing into one another. . . . There is no wholly masculine man, no purely feminine woman."

The book is less philosophical than polemical and practical. She was engaging with the world more directly and urgently than Emerson. Fuller demolished popular arguments in favor of limiting women's sphere. To start, women are not too weak to enter public life. "Those who think the physical circumstances of woman would make a part in the affairs of national government unsuitable, are by no means those who think it impossible for the negresses to endure field work, even during pregnancy, or the sempstresses to go through their killing labors." She also argued that the fact that women have been held back in so many arenas is not just bad for them, it is bad for men.

She decried the hypocrisy of laws that limit women's property rights; she tied the emancipation of women to the abolition of slavery and called for radical liberation. She was silent on the topic of voting rights, though she had privately supported the idea in her journal. Her most famous line: "But if you ask me what offices they [women] may fill, I reply—any. I do not care what case you put; let them be sea-captains, if you will."

She finished the book in a rush in November, writing to a friend that she "felt a delightful glow as if I had put a good deal of my true life in it, as if, suppose I went away now, the measure of my foot-print would be left on the earth." When Greeley published it in March the first printing sold out in a week. He paid her $85. It made her newly famous.

She moved to New York, taking a room in the Greeleys' home in rural Turtle Bay, and began a meteoric journalistic career. She would write three or four articles a week for Greeley's *Tribune* while she lived there, a total of 250 over eighteen months. It was a prodigious output by normal standards—but never enough for Greeley, who could write even faster and always wanted more from her.

She wrote on a wide range of topics: social reforms of prisons, asylums, and poor houses ("Never was punishment treated more simply as a social convenience, without regard to pure right, or a hope of reformation"); social prejudices about the Irish (combating the popular view of "their incorrigible habits of falsehood and evasion"); on the rich and the poor; on her hopes for women; and more.

She wrote many literary and music reviews, including of the *Essays: Second Series* by Emerson, and the *Narrative of the Life of Frederick Douglass* ("It is an excellent piece of writing, and on that score to be prized as a specimen of the powers of the Black Race, which Prejudice persists in disputing").

In what may be her most cutting review of a book, she criticized Longfellow's poems: "We must confess to a coolness toward Mr. Longfellow, in consequence of the exaggerated praises that have been bestowed upon him. When we see a person of moderate powers receive honors which should be reserved for the highest, we feel somewhat like assailing him and taking from him the crown which should be reserved for grander brows." The scathing review caused a storm. Poe and Duyckinck both admired it, but Emerson, a few years later, urged Greeley not to include it in her collected works.

She wrote cultural commentary, including "The Rich Man—An Ideal Sketch," in which she decried economic inequality: "radical reform is needed." On the Fourth of July 1845, she went further, arguing that the entire country was in need of rebirth, that it had become polluted by the lust for power and money.

She still suffered headaches, and pain caused by curvature of the spine. She began each day with treatments from a mesmerist. She would sit on a stool with the back of her dress unbuttoned while the doctor "held his right hand horizontally, close against the vertebral column, the fingers pointing towards but never touching it. Slowly he moved his hand from the very end of the spine to the base of the brain, charging it with his vigorous magnetism." She believed it helped.

She admired and liked Greeley, finding him "a man of genuine excellence, honorable, benevolent, of an uncorrupted disposition, and, in his way, of even great abilities. In modes of life and manners he is the man of the people."

She also fell in love. She met James Nathan, a German-Jewish banker, at a New Year's Eve party not long after she arrived in the city. By February they were attending exhibitions, concerts, and lectures together. She began writing a flurry of letters to him. By March, she told him that "my mind has been enfolded in your thought, as a branch with a flame" despite frustration that he was not writing her as frequently as she hoped. And then: "I hear you with awe assert power over me and feel it to be true. . . . Are you my guardian to domesticate me in the body, and attach it more firmly to the earth?"

Again, she was unlucky in love. Nathan had a secret mistress at his downtown apartment. In late March she learned the truth—the mistress was an English woman whom he had seduced and abandoned when he departed Europe for America fifteen years earlier. The woman had followed him and had been living with him for years.

The news devastated Fuller. Nathan attempted to explain and defend himself, claiming that the mistress was merely an "injured woman" whom he had taken in and was hoping to reform. Fuller replied, admitting that "yesterday was, perhaps, a sadder day than I had in all my life. . . . Since then, I have your note. . . . Yet forgive [me], if I say one part of your note and some particulars of your past conduct seem not severely true."

Yet she chose to accept his excuses and continued to see him. She had understood that the prostitutes in Sing Sing were victimized by men. Now, she seemed unable to avoid her own victimization.

Nathan toyed with her. He told her he planned to travel to Europe in June without her, and he apparently told her he did not love her. She wrote to him in anguish: "You have touched my heart and it thrilled at the centre. . . . But your heart, your precious heart (I am determined to be absolutely frank), that I did long for . . . you have cruelly hung it up quite out of my reach, and declare: I never shall have it."

At one point, alone together, something happened that deeply troubled her. It has troubled her biographers ever since. Afterward, she compared the ruins of her feelings for him to the violence of the French Revolution: "the sweet little garden, with which my mind had surrounded your image, lies all desecrated and trampled by the hoofs of the demon . . . You know how we did meet. You seemed dissatisfied." As one biographer wonders, "Was it an assault?"

We will never know. Yet it didn't destroy her feelings. When Nathan left for Europe, Fuller continued to write to him.

In August 1846, she had the chance to take a trip of her own, when a friend invited her to accompany them to Europe. It was the grand tour she had long desired. She convinced Greeley to pay her an advance against some travel dispatches, "Things and Thoughts in Europe." It was also a chance to meet up with Nathan.

11

War, Part I

> [When] a whole country is unjustly overrun and conquered by a foreign army, and subjected to military law, I think that it is not too soon for honest men to rebel and revolutionize. What makes this duty the more urgent is that fact that the country so overrun is not our own, but ours is the invading army.
>
> —Henry David Thoreau, "On the Duty of Civil Disobedience"

Fuller was now directly engaged in the world, which would change some of her thinking. As for the others in Emerson's circle, two issues would have that same effect: war and slavery. Their public activism would eventually spell the end of the Newness. Philosophical contemplation and idealistic thinking would inevitably give way to the urgency of politics and violence.

The presidential election of 1844 was fought largely over land annexations. Two former Speakers of the House, James K. Polk and Henry Clay, faced each other, and differed only marginally from each other. They were both Southerners—Polk lived in Tennessee; Clay lived in Kentucky—and they both owned slaves. They both supported states' rights to maintain slavery or not, as each state might choose.

Clay was much more famous, yet Polk advocated for American expansion more aggressively. His campaign slogan, "Fifty-four Forty or Fight," referred to the latitude line at the top of the so-called Oregon Country, bordering Alaska, much of which was in dispute between the United States and Great Britain. But the fate of Texas, far to the south, proved to be the most contentious issue between the candidates. It had been in dispute ever since that territory rebelled from Mexico, in 1836, and became the Republic of Texas. For eight years the United States had hesitated to bring Texas into the Union out of fear of war with Mexico. Abolitionists opposed adding Texas to the Union for a different reason: it would add another slave state.

The increasing number of Anglo-American settlers in Texas forced a decision. During the campaign Polk promised to expand the Union wherever possible—not just in the Oregon Country, but also by annexing Texas and acquiring California from Mexico. Clay equivocated. Initially he opposed Texas annexation. When he saw how strongly the public disagreed with him, he switched positions, but it was too late. On Election Day the lesser-known but more bullish Polk edged out the famous "Great Compromiser"; it was Clay's third defeat in a presidential election. American voters believed in their so-called manifest destiny. Texas joined the Union one year later.

Polk now faced a likely war with Mexico, whose government had obstinately refused to recognize the Republic of Texas. He made an offer to purchase California and New Mexico from Mexico for $30 million—but only if the two countries could agree on the Rio Grande as the new border. He also sent an army under General Zachary Taylor to the Rio Grande in March 1846. Mexico spurned the offer and demanded Taylor's army retreat to the Nueces River, 150 miles to the north of the Rio Grande. War was on.

Over the course of 1846 and 1847, regular and irregular American forces seized Santa Fe and the settlement at Los Angeles before landing at Veracruz and marching to Mexico City. When the capital fell to the invaders in September 1847, the war was over. In February the two countries signed a treaty that gave the United States virtually all of today's states of California, Nevada, Utah, and New Mexico, along with most of Arizona and Colorado and parts of Oklahoma, Kansas, and Wyoming for only $15 million. Whether or not it was destiny, the western and southwestern borders of the continental United States were now manifest (with one small addition, the Gadsden Purchase, south of the Gila River, to come in 1853).

The United States had been the aggressor. Horace Greeley wrote column after column denouncing the Polk administration in the strongest possible language: "People of the United States! Your Rulers are precipitating you into a fathomless abyss of crime and calamity!" When war supporters claimed that Mexico was to blame, Margaret Fuller called them out. The Mexicans "were fighting in defense of their rights, and we for liberty to do our pleasure."

Henry Thoreau and Bronson Alcott were seasoned tax resisters. They had each refused to pay an annual poll tax of $1.50, for different reasons. Alcott had done it in 1842 and 1843 to protest the very existence of government. His Fruitlands partner Charles Lane had explained, in a *Dial* essay, that they denied the validity of all "governments, creeds, and institutions," declaring their allegiance only to "Universal Love." Or, as Alcott put it, "Why should I need a State to maintain me and protect my rights? The Man is all. Let him husband himself. . . . That is a great age when the State is nothing and Men are all."

In 1843 a constable had come to arrest him, but when the two men reached the jailhouse, the jailer wasn't there. Alcott waited for two hours. By the time the jailer returned, Judge Samuel Hoar had paid his tax for him. He was released.

Thoreau's tax resistance began even earlier. Initially, in 1840, he agreed to be taxed in support of the First Parish Church. One year later, he reversed himself, writing to the town clerk, "I do not wish to be considered a member." From then on, he avoided paying the poll tax and suffered no consequences. His famous arrest and one-night imprisonment in 1846 was likely due to the simple fact that the tax collector and constable, Sam Staples, was in his final year of office and needed to come up with overdue taxes or he would be required to pay them himself. As Staples later recalled, "Henry knew that I had a warrant for him, but I didn't go to hunt for him, 'cause I knew I could git him when I wanted to." In late July, he did just that. By now, Thoreau was protesting both slavery and the war with Mexico, not just the First Parish Church budget.

By his standards, one night in the Concord jail was not a challenge. The food was decent, and he had slept in far less comfortable quarters on his travels. He wanted to make a point of his resistance—Staples offered to pay his tax for him, but "he said, 'no *sir*; don't you do it.'" Yet the next morning, much to his annoyance, his aunt Maria paid the tax, releasing him.

Emerson thought the whole arrangement a bad idea: "The state tax does not pay the Mexican War. . . . But really a scholar has too humble an opinion of the population, of their possibilities, of their future, to be entitled to go to war with them, as with equals. This prison is one step to suicide." In other words, he would have preferred for Thoreau to try to persuade fellow citizens to abandon slavery—or disunite with the South, as many radical abolitionists including Henry, his mother, and sisters urged—rather than to stage a tax protest. Alcott argued the point, noting that while Emerson found the protest "mean and skulking, and in bad taste," it could be "defended . . . on the grounds of a dignified non-compliance with the injunction of civil powers."

Thoreau managed to turn this minor episode into one of his most famous essays, "On the Duty of Civil Disobedience." Elizabeth Palmer Peabody published it in 1849. It would later be quoted by such champions of nonviolent protest as Mahatma Gandhi and Martin Luther King Jr. Yet Thoreau did not make the case for nonviolence. Indeed, he argued that the combination of slavery and the war with Mexico were justifiable causes for a new American revolution: "when a sixth of the population of a nation which has undertaken to be the refuge of liberty are slaves, and a whole country is unjustly overrun and conquered by a foreign army, and subjected to military law, I think that it is not too soon for honest men to rebel and revolutionize."

In the essay, Thoreau's gift for aphorism rises to his sense of urgency.

If a policy "is of such a nature that it requires you to be the agent of injustice to another, then, I say, break the law." His conclusion is magnificent: "There will never be a really free and enlightened State until the State comes to recognize the individual as a higher and independent power, from which all its own power and authority are derived, and treats him accordingly." He started with objections to slavery and the war, but he went much further, to the existential question of what an individual should do when the state makes him an accomplice to injustice.

The Transcendentalists denounced violence, yet they also came to embrace it. During the final months of the shameful war with Mexico, most of Europe erupted in the "Springtime of the Peoples" of 1848, when monarchies across the continent faced armed citizens demanding constitutional rights. Margaret Fuller celebrated the uprisings. Emerson was more cautious. They each witnessed clashes firsthand.

Ever since the Congress of Vienna of 1814–15, a suite of monarchies had divided and controlled most of the continent. Yet after three decades of peace, tensions were rising. Sicilians and Neapolitans rebelled against King Ferdinand II. In Paris, citizens rioted and barricaded the streets until King Louis Philippe abdicated. Demonstrations broke out in several German states, with a battle on the streets of Berlin. King Ludwig of Bavaria lost his throne. The Habsburg Empire appeared near collapse in Budapest, Prague, Milan, and Venice. Even in Vienna, the Habsburg capital, the streets erupted in violence.

Most of the uprisings were suppressed. Yet in the winter and spring of 1848, democratic hopes soared. Emerson was traveling in England and Scotland in the winter, as the working-class Chartist movement pushed to expand voting rights to all men regardless of wealth. Chartist demonstrators planned a mass march on Parliament in April, to present a petition with their demands. They were outfoxed and outmaneuvered by the Duke of Wellington, who commanded an overwhelming number of troops, and made nervous by a recently passed law threatening death sentences for intimidation of Parliament. The protest fizzled out.

Emerson sympathized with the Chartists' reforms—they sought what most white American males already had—though he disliked the opportunism of the movement's leaders, and he wasn't yet ready to embrace political causes. He was skeptical that England would experience a revolution, believing that at most they might try a "change of forms."

In May he crossed the Channel to visit Paris, where violence threatened the new republic. A provisional government had held elections to the Assembly, with bourgeois candidates significantly outnumbering those from the working class. To radicals, such as Louis Auguste Blanqui—a man who never met a government he didn't hate—the new Assembly was an outrage. On May 15 he led a crowd of several thousand men into the National Assembly, while others advanced on the Hôtel de Ville (city hall) to proclaim yet another new government. The existing government called out the National Guard, and after a chaotic afternoon, the Blanquists surrendered.

Emerson witnessed it firsthand. He wrote to Lidian of "the streets full of bayonets, and the furious driving of the horses dragging cannon towards the National Assembly." He felt no sympathy for an antidemocratic coup. But why had he hesitated to embrace the democratic Chartists? Margaret Fuller, in Rome, did not hesitate to champion the republican cause, even as it became soaked in blood.

Her European sojourn began in 1846. She had been invited by a New York friend, Rebecca Spring, to accompany Spring, her husband Marcus, and their son on a yearlong tour of the continent while serving as a tutor to the nine-year-old boy. Her first dispatch for the *Tribune* made clear that she would focus on intellectual and social movements—she visited two different adult-education institutes, in Manchester and Liverpool, where she was pleased to find lecturers quoting *The Dial.* She sought out leading writers and thinkers, meeting Wordsworth within a few weeks. She soon faced drama on a hike up the 3,200-foot Ben Lomond in the Scottish Highlands in late September, when, after reaching the summit, she lost the trail on the way down. In the dark she had to stop hiking and spend a night on the slopes, exposed and alone, with neither Henry Thoreau's hatchet nor his experience. She was lightly dressed, soaked by rain, and cold. "I thought I should not live through the night. . . . My only chance, however, lay in motion, and my only help in myself, and so convinced was I of this, that I did keep in motion the whole of that long night, imprisoned as I was on such a little perch of that great mountain." In the morning, in a thick mist, she scrambled back up out of her notch and found some shepherds who led her to safety.

She also hoped to meet Nathan. She had written to him about the trip, and finally heard back from him in July, from Hamburg. His tone was warm yet guarded, and he had a favor to ask. He had traveled to Alexandria, Jerusalem, Constantinople, and elsewhere, and he hoped she could help him place some pieces in Greeley's *Tribune*. She had also been taking care of his dog, Joe, who had been causing her some trouble. He suggested that if "you know of no other person that will [adopt the dog], just have him sold at auction or let him run loose." He said he would meet her in London or would leave word for her there.

She reached Liverpool on August 11, the beginning of three months in Great Britain. There was no sign of Nathan in London.

She would meet many people in Europe, but not him. They exchanged two more letters. Hers were bitter. He continued to try to manipulate her. "Miss F., you have judged me without a hearing, you have condemned and insulted me, trampled upon and wounded me, nay! but for the consciousness of my innocence, would have destroyed me! . . . although you seem to wish a cessation of intercourse . . . I might as well bid my heart to cease beating, as to cease feeling for you, a true and tender regard and friendship."

In New York, she had chosen to ignore his mistress. But now she faced an immovable obstacle: He was engaged to marry a German woman. He was done with her. In her journal, she tried to brush him off. "I care not. I am resolved to take such disappointments more lightly than I have."

That fall she traveled to Paris for a few months. She then headed south through Lyons, Marseille, Naples, Florence, and Rome. She had already met with Wordsworth and Thomas Carlyle; now she had the chance to meet Frédéric Chopin and George Sand, the great writer and advocate for women's rights. Sand eclipsed the others in Fuller's recollections: "What fixed my attention was the expression of goodness, nobleness, and power, that pervaded the whole,—the truly human heart and nature that shone in the eyes."

Adam Mickiewicz, a Polish poet and nationalist, became a close companion in Paris. He was married, yet he seemed to pursue her. She was temporarily smitten. As she wrote to Rebecca Spring, "You ask me if I love M. I answer he affected me like music or the richest landscape, my heart beat with joy that he at once felt beauty in me also." There was a romance to his cause of national liberation.

Perhaps the most inspiring meeting of all was with the great Italian revolutionary Giuseppe Mazzini. She met him in London and found him "the most beauteous person I have seen." She meant not only that he had a commanding presence but also that he stood for the highest of ideals. He had served time in prison and then exile, under a death sentence, because he had founded the Young Italy movement, attracting tens of thousands of Italians who wanted to unify the peninsula as a republic. His ideas helped inspire the uprisings of 1848–49. Rome, especially, would become a focus of drama and of his hopes, and Rome was where Fuller would spend her most intense months.

By late 1847, as the independence movement grew, she wanted to extend her trip and write a book about it. She had also fallen in love with a penniless marquis and supporter of independence. They had met in Rome in April. Their relationship resumed when she returned to the Eternal City in October.

She was now no longer writing a tourist's "things and thoughts." She was recording momentous events, a movement to turn "this hollow England . . . this poor France . . . that lost Poland and this Italy bound down by treacherous hands" into new beacons of democracy. Her great hope was that the American ideal, so imperfectly realized at home, could flourish in the old world. That "cause is, indeed, the cause of all mankind at present."

29

Giuseppe Mazzini.

She even changed her mind about abolitionism in America. She had previously shunned the abolitionists because they "were so tedious, often so narrow, always so rabid and exaggerated in their tone." She had been disappointed that the Massachusetts Anti-Slavery Society had insisted on rights only for Blacks, not for women. Now, witnessing a freedom struggle in Italy, she set those high-minded objections aside, realizing that American abolitionists "had a high motive, something eternal in their desire and life . . . God strengthen them and make them wise to achieve their purpose!"

The Italian revolutions of 1848–49 occurred in multiple states under the control of different powers. The Austrian Empire ruled over much of the north, with the exception of Turin and the Savoyard States, ruled by King Charles Albert. The Grand Duchy of Tuscany governed the center of the peninsula. Pope Pius IX ruled the Papal States of Rome and nearby Romagna and Umbria, and King Ferdinand II controlled the Kingdom of the Two Sicilies, based in Naples and Palermo.

Unifying the peninsula as a republic required overthrowing five authoritarians—or at least four, if the pope would agree to help steward a new nation. It was a daunting ambition. Yet in the exciting months of early 1848, it seemed possible.

After the fall of Austria's chancellor, Prince Metternich, and the abdication of France's King Louis Philippe, Fuller had written, "With indescribable rapture these tidings were received in Rome. Men were seen dancing, women weeping with joy along the street." The tricolor flag, a newly powerful symbol, flew everywhere. It was based on the French flag. The colors of the Italian version each carried symbolic meaning: green, for the landscape and human rights; red, for love and the blood of the wars for independence; and white, for faith and the snowy Alps. It would become the official national flag in 1861 when the peninsula finally unified as the Kingdom of Italy.

Initially, Italian liberals were inspired by the pope. In early 1848 he proposed a defensive league, and Tuscany and Naples joined. By April the revolutionaries had taken Milan and Venice and pushed Austrian forces back to a few fortresses. Modena and Parma were in revolt. Liberals hoped that the pope would throw his forces into the battle against Austria.

In earlier centuries, popes had indeed sent armies into battle. Yet during the Napoleonic Wars, the Papal States had been annexed and peeled apart, and French troops had badly defeated the Papal Army. The days of warrior popes were past. Furthermore, Catholics led the Austrian Empire, with whom the pope would never engage in battle. On April 29, Pius issued a statement in which he repudiated "the treacherous advice . . . of those who would have the Roman Pontiff to be the head and to preside over the formation of some sort of novel republic of the whole Italian People."

Austria commanded overwhelming forces. Charles Albert was ready to invade Lombardy. They were ready for a counterrevolution.

Fuller, still in Rome, followed these events closely. She was disappointed but not shocked at the pope's withdrawal from the cause. In her column she dismissed his power, "The work began by Napoleon is finished. There will never more be really a Pope, but only the effigy or simulacrum of one." The fate of Rome's government was not yet decided, yet she was forced to give up her front-row seat and escape to the mountains. The reason was a secret: she was pregnant.

Biographers have long wondered about the man who became her husband. Her friends wondered as well. She had been disappointed in infatuations with highly educated, sparkling men and women, including George Davis and Anna Barker. She had wanted more from Emerson. She had fallen for the duplicitous James Nathan. Each of them, in different ways, had failed her. In Marquis Giovanni Ossoli she found a man different from all of them.

He fought for the republican cause as a captain of the Civil Guard, which she admired. But he seemed to have never read a book in his life. He was quiet. As she wrote to her mother, "He is not in any respect such a person as people in general would expect to find with me. . . . Of all that is contained in books he is absolutely ignorant, and he has no enthusiasm of character. On the other hand, he has excellent practical sense; has been a judicious observer of all that passed before his eyes; has a nice sense of duty . . . a very sweet temper, a great native refinement." To her sister she wrote, "I expect that to many of my friends, Mr Emerson for one, he will be nothing, and they will not understand that I should have life in common with him. But I do not think he will care. . . . I feel great confidence in the permanence of his love. . . . I think he will be an excellent father."

There is no proof that Fuller and Ossoli married, but they likely did wed in a secret ceremony. In the summer of 1848, she relocated to the mountain village of L'Aquila. She lived with a woman who made broths for her and washed her clothes by hand. She wrote to a friend that the locals "say 'Povera, sola, soletta,' poor one, alone, all alone! the saints keep her,' as I pass."

In late July she had to move to an apartment in Rieti, as soldiers were seizing men in the villages around L'Aquila and it was no longer safe for her there. She was low on funds. She wrote to her brother, a

New York friend, and a local banker, begging for loans after promised credit from Horace Greeley failed to appear. By late August she was impatient for the baby to arrive. On September 7, she wrote to Ossoli:

> *Dearest Husband*
>
> *I feel much better than I hoped. The child is doing well too but he still cries a lot, and I hope he will be calmer when you come. . . . Embracing you and kissing you in this dear baby I have in my arms I am Your Affectionate*
>
> *MARGARET*

Angelo Eugene Philip d'Ossoli was born on September 5, 1848. His parents called him Nino.

For the sake of secrecy, she left Nino with a wet nurse and returned to Rome in mid-November. It was wrenching to leave him, and she returned for visits when she could, but the Roman revolution had reached a critical stage and she was determined to witness it, even to lend a hand.

During her seclusion, even as she worked every day on her history of the Italian revolutions, the counterrevolutionaries made gains. Milan fell back into Austrian hands. Mazzini and his men retreated to Switzerland to direct a resistance movement from afar. Mazzini's main ally, Giuseppe Garibaldi, who had fled to Switzerland one week earlier, was forced to admit that the cause of freedom was not yet popular: "For the first time, I saw how little the national cause inspired the local inhabitants of the countryside." He wasn't the only discouraged idealist. Karl Marx and Friedrich Engels published *The Communist Manifesto* in early 1848, with its famous call, "Working men of the world, unite!" Yet the budding Communist League failed to gain followers, and Marx, in Vienna in the late summer, was shouted down at a political meeting. Garibaldi followed Mazzini to Switzerland with a dwindling band of followers.

30

Earliest known photograph of Karl Marx, age forty-three, 1861.

In the south, King Ferdinand crushed the Neapolitan revolution. In Rome, the pope tried various versions of local governments, which failed to please the republicans. Finally, in late September, he appointed Count Pellegrino Rossi, a lawyer, professor, and wily politician, to lead the Roman government. Rossi urged the pope to accept the constitution that had been offered first to Naples and then to Tuscany—but to go no further toward reform: no unification of Italy, no attempt to offer a truly republican government.

Just as Fuller returned to the city, Rossi was assassinated. As he walked into the Chamber of Deputies for the opening of parliament, a group of radicals surrounded him. One struck him on the side. When he stopped and turned, another cut his throat. The conspirators escaped, the murderer hailed as a hero.

Soon mobs began demonstrating outside the pope's palace. Swiss

Guards traded gunshots with the crowd. One of the pope's secretaries was killed. On November 24, a disguised pope slipped out of Rome to take refuge in a fortress in Gaeta, part of Ferdinand's Naples territory.

It was a stunning turn of events. The radicals were now in charge of the city. They dissolved parliament on December 26 and announced elections for a new assembly. The pope promised to excommunicate anyone who participated, but on January 21 the radicals swept the polls, electing (among others) Mazzini and Garibaldi to a new assembly. On February 9, the Constituent Assembly proclaimed Rome a democracy.

Fuller described its first meeting to her *Tribune* readers. A Fundamental Decree was read aloud declaring that the pope had no political authority over the state: "Between each of these expressive sentences the speaker paused; the great bell of the Capitol gave forth its solemn melodies; the cannon answered; while the crowd shouted, *viva la Republica! viva Italia!*"

On March 3, 1849, Fuller wrote to Mazzini, "When I think that only two years ago, you thought of coming into Italy with us in disguise, it seems very glorious, that you are about to enter Republican Rome as a Roman Citizen. It seemed almost the most sublime and poetical fact of history." On March 8 the great man came to see her. They spoke for two hours, discussing recent events and hopes for the future.

The Republic of Rome would not last long. Mazzini led the Constituent Assembly for just one hundred days. France, now under a new Bonaparte, President Louis Napoléon, sent an army to crush the radicals. In April Garibaldi repulsed the French forces, but he was soon distracted by a Neapolitan invasion of the countryside, and the Austrians and Spanish were also marching on Roman territory. From several directions, Catholic authoritarians raced to reestablish the pope.

On June 3 the French again attacked the city, launching a month of bloody shelling and steady losses. Finally, on the thirtieth, the assembly voted to capitulate. Garibaldi led an army of three thousand out of the city. Mazzini remained behind for one week before leaving for yet another exile in Switzerland.

Fuller not only wrote about the French attacks for the *Tribune* but also went to work in a hospital for wounded fighters, serving not only as a bedside nurse but also as the administrator in charge of organizing the schedules of the entire volunteer nursing staff. In early May: "I write you from barricaded Rome. The Mother of Nations is now at bay against them all . . . the soldiers of republican France, firing upon republican Rome!" On May 27: "War near at hand seems to me even more dreadful than I had fancied it. . . . The ruin that ensues, how terrible. I have, for the first time, seen what wounded men suffer." She felt terrible sadness as she watched Garibaldi lead his men out of the city, away from their brief moment of republican power.

In the *Tribune* she etched her political disappointment. Yet she faced a personal challenge that she could not reveal: her husband could no longer safely remain in Italy.

12

Death, Part I

> I have in my pocket a button which I ripped off the coat of the Marquis of Ossoli on the seashore the other day.
>
> —Henry David Thoreau, *Journal*

Fuller, now the marchesa d'Ossoli, moved to Florence with her family in late 1849, where they settled in with a small group of American expats while planning how best to cross the ocean. She needed passports for her husband and son, so she wrote a series of letters to the US chargé d'affaires to the Papal States, Lewis Cass Jr. Next, she needed to secure passage on a ship for the family, accompanied by a nurse for Nino. She settled on a merchant vessel, a small ship that would carry just six passengers along with its crew and cargo, which included heavy slabs of Italian marble. It was the most affordable option. Some friends worried. Fuller wrote that the ship, the *Elizabeth*, was "nearly new, and well kept." Yet "people come daily to dissuade me . . . that the insecurity compared with packet ships or steamers is so great."

She herself worried about shipwrecks, and they happened frequently. In April 1850 she wrote to a friend that "I had intended if I went by way of France to take the packet ship 'Argo' from Havre . . . [but then] I read of the wreck of the *'Argo'* returning from America to France! There were also notices of the wreck of the 'Royal Adelaide,' a fine English steamer, and of the 'John Skiddy' one of the fine American

Packets. Thus it seems safety is not [to] be found in the wisest calculation."

She may have had a premonition of disaster. She wrote in one letter, "I am absurdly fearful and various omens have combined to give me a dark feeling. . . . In case of mishap, however, I shall perish with my husband and my child, and we may be transferred to some happier state."

The voyage was troubled from the start. The departure from Leghorn (Livorno) was delayed by bad weather. After a week, when the ship had crossed the Tyrrhenian Sea to reach Gibraltar, the captain came down with smallpox and died. The crew and its six passengers were held in quarantine while First Mate Henry Bangs took command.

31

Margaret Fuller, pregnant, sat for a portrait by Thomas Hicks in Rome in May 1848, shortly before she left the city.

When the quarantine ended, they set sail on the Atlantic on June 9. Nino became ill the next day. "His eyes were closed, his head and face swollen out of shape, his body covered with eruption." He recovered, however, and the Atlantic crossing proceeded smoothly—until near the end. On July 18 the ship was approaching New York Harbor from the south. That night, pushed by strengthening winds, Captain Bangs overshot his target. In the early-morning hours, in gale-force winds, the *Elizabeth* ran aground. The ship was within sight of Fire Island.

The winds rotated the ship broadside to the shore, and waves crashed onto the deck. The crew cut away the main and mizzen masts, but the marble slabs had punctured the hold. Seawater poured in. William Henry Channing, cousin of Ellery and, like him, a nephew of William Ellery Channing, reconstructed the events from conversations with several survivors, who realized by this point that the ship was doomed.

Apart from the Ossoli party there were just two other passengers, Horace Sumner, a former Brook Farmer and brother to the famous senator Charles, and Catherine Hasty, widow of the ship's late captain. They gathered. Sumner spoke first.

"We must die."

"Let us die calmly, then."

"I hope so, Mrs. Hasty."

One side of the passenger cabin was soon underwater "and furniture, trunks, and fragments of the skylight were floating to and fro." In the early-morning hours, First Mate Charles Davis and a few of the other sailors led the six passengers out of the damaged cabin and up to the forecastle, above the waterline. Even that short journey was harrowing. Davis held one of Hasty's hands as she clutched a railing with the other. "But hardly had they taken three steps, when a sea broke loose her hold, and swept her into the hatchway. 'Let me go,' she cried, 'your life is important to all on board.' But cheerily, and with a smile, he answered, 'Not quite yet'; and, seizing in his teeth her long hair, as it floated past him, he caught with both hands at some near support, and aided by [another] seaman, set her once again upon her feet. A few moments more of struggle brought them safely through."

All six passengers made it to the forecastle, Nino in a canvas bag slung around a seaman's neck. Left behind in the disintegrating cabin was "what, if I live, will be of more value to me than anything," said Fuller—her manuscript.

They still had hope of survival even if not all the passengers could swim (as Fuller could not). They could see people on shore. There was one lifeboat lying distant on the beach. Yet the storm was fierce, and the Fire Islanders were not as focused on rescuing as on scavenging. They watched and waited, preparing to scoop up anything valuable that washed ashore. Eventually, according to a *New-York Tribune* reporter, there would be nearly a thousand people from all parts of coastal Long Island gathered on the beach, "and more than half of them were engaged in secreting and carrying off everything that seemed to be of value."

At nine, at low tide, one sailor with a life preserver braved the water—and made it to shore. Another sailor followed him and made it. Horace Sumner went next. He did not make it.

The crew came up with a desperate option: each remaining adult passenger would cling to a plank with rope handles, while sailors swam and towed them to shore. Catherine Hasty agreed to try. Davis towed her. "Once and again, during their passage, the plank was rolled wholly over, and once and again was righted, with its bearer, by the dauntless steersman; and when, at length, tossed by the surf upon the sands, the half-drowned woman still holding, as in a death-struggle, to the ropes, was about to be swept back by the undertow, he caught her in his arms, and, with the assistance of a bystander, placed her high upon the beach. Thus twice in one day had he perilled his own life to save that of the widow of his captain." The crew then came for Fuller, but she refused to be parted from her husband and son.

By noon the tide had turned. The ship would soon break apart. The commanding officer pleaded again with Fuller to try to escape. Again, she refused to leave her family, but she still hoped for a rescue.

The order was then given for everyone to save themselves. All but four of the crew jumped overboard. Some made it through the waves and the debris. Some did not.

By midafternoon the winds were back at full strength. The Ossolis and their nurse were left with the steward, the carpenter, the cook, and one old sailor "broken down by hardships and sickness." The steward took Nino in his arms, ready to swim for it, "when a sea struck the forecastle, and the foremast fell, carrying with it the deck, and all upon it." The steward and Angelino washed up on the beach, both dead.

The cook and carpenter managed to save themselves. Nino's nurse and the marquis were caught for a moment by the rigging, but only for a moment—they drowned with the next wave. As for Fuller, "Margaret sank at once. When last seen, she had been seated at the foot of the foremast, still clad in her white nightdress, with her hair fallen loose upon her shoulders." Neither her body nor her manuscript were ever found.

When news of the disaster reached Concord, Emerson sent Thoreau to search for Fuller's effects and manuscript. In his journal Waldo lamented that "to the last her country proves inhospitable to her; brave, eloquent, subtle, accomplished, devoted, constant soul!" He considered that the "timorous" would challenge her marriage. "But she had only to open her mouth and a triumphant success awaited her." He wrote several pages about her. He would soon go to work on the *Memoirs of Margaret Fuller Ossoli* with Channing and James Freeman Clarke.

On Fire Island, Thoreau interviewed as many people as he could and inventoried the belongings of the Ossolis that had been found. Only one of their five trunks survived. He wrote to Emerson with some of his initial intelligence.

On the mainland in Patchogue, Thoreau found women who had already altered the gowns of the passengers—presumably including Fuller's—that their husbands and sons had stolen from the beach. On Fire Island the marquis's coat had been found. Thoreau tore off a button as a keepsake.

When he returned to Concord, he delivered a report to Waldo and Lidian. Their daughter Ellen remembered how they listened to Henry read his diary, a sorrow so profound that it shook Lidian's faith.

Emerson devoted several pages in his journals to her loss. He recalled what others had said about Fuller, and what they said about her death. As for himself, "I have lost in her my audience. I hurry now to my work admonished that I have few days left."

Greeley wrote her obituary in the *Tribune*, noting that "America has produced no woman who in mental endowments and acquirements has surpassed Margaret Fuller." He called for a new selection of her writings to be published—her brother Arthur would edit *At Home and Abroad: Or, Things and Thoughts in America and Europe* for publication in 1856. Greeley also called for a memoir, the project that Emerson, Channing, and Clarke produced in 1852.

Greeley took one more step to honor Fuller's memory. He tried to make direct contact with her on the "other side." Spiritualism—speaking to the dead via a medium—was another "ism" that the Greeleys embraced. The fad had been sparked, in part, by the celebrated Fox sisters, thirteen-year-old Kate and seventeen-year-old Maggie. The Fox girls used table-rapping as their ghostly telegraph system. (Under the table, they secretly cracked the joints of their toes to produce the mysterious sound.) They had been staying at the Greeleys' home to try to make contact with the couple's late son.

Now, in late July and early August, the Foxes helped the Greeleys try to contact Fuller. A friend of Emerson's passed along Mary Greeley's report of the séance: "Questions have lately been asked of Margaret through a young [girl], 13 years old, but she [Fuller] is chary of her answers. Mrs. Greeley said perhaps you think this too low a means of communication. Margaret answered, 'Indeed I do Madam.'"

The death of Margaret Fuller Ossoli at age forty ranks as one of the great tragedies in the history of American letters. Yet even with so brief a life, and only a few books published, her reputation should have been secure. In addition to *Summer on the Lakes* (1843) and *Woman in the Nineteenth Century* (1845), she had published a collection of essays, *Papers on Literature and Art* (1846), and had reached tens of thousands of readers with her columns in the *Tribune*. Her professional conversations had helped inspire many women to become active in political causes.

Her views on women's rights inspired and convinced Emerson to embrace the movement. He declined an invitation to speak at the 1850 National Woman's Rights Convention. When he appeared at its 1855 successor, he delivered an address he would later publish as "Woman." He argued for women to have "votes, offices and political equality" with men. He was ten years behind her, and his rhetoric was weaker.

As a critic, too, Fuller's reputation should have been secure. Her reviews of every major American writer were incisive and challenging, not to mention her analysis of much contemporary English literature, and many major Western painters and composers. She did not live long enough to see Hawthorne's famous novels. Yet based on his stories, she knew he had greatness. In September 1846, in a rare bylined essay in the *Tribune* titled "American Literature: Its Position in the Present Time, and Prospects for the Future," she touched on a number of writers including Emerson ("a profound thinker . . . embodied in a style whose melody and subtle fragrance enchant those who stand stupefied before the thoughts themselves"), James Fenimore Cooper, Washington Irving, Ellery Channing, and several others. At the end, she noted that "we have not spoken of Hawthorne, the best writer of the day, in a similar range with Irving, only touching many more points, and discerning far more deeply."

Given her regard for Hawthorne, it is painfully ironic that her reputation suffered a posthumous blow at his hands. In 1857, after Hawthorne had served in a consular position in Liverpool thanks to his friend President Franklin Pierce, he and his family traveled to Italy, reaching Rome in January 1858.

It had been eight years since Fuller's death, but there were many in

Rome who remembered her vividly. Hawthorne met with an American sculptor named Joseph Mozier, whose work he found "not of the finest," but as a man he was "sensible, shrewd, keen, clever . . . very agreeable and lively in his conversation." Mozier spread poison on the reputation of Fuller and her husband:

> He says that Ossoli's family, though technically noble, is really of no rank whatever; the elder brother, with the title of marquis, being at this very time a working bricklayer, and the sisters walking the streets without bonnets—that is, being in the station of peasant girls, in the female populace of Rome. Ossoli himself, to the best of his belief, was Margaret's servant, or had something to do with the care of her apartments. He was the handsomest man whom Mr. Mozier ever saw, but entirely ignorant even of his own language, scarcely able to read at all, destitute of manners; in short, half an idiot, and without any pretensions to be a gentleman.

Hawthorne took this in, and then added his own thoughts in his journal:

> I do not understand what feeling there could have been [from her towards him], except it were purely sensual; as from him towards her, there could hardly have been even this, for she had not the charm of womanhood. . . . She was a great humbug; of course with much talent, and much moral reality, or else she could not have been so great a humbug. . . . There appears to have been a total collapse in poor Margaret, morally and intellectually; and tragic as her catastrophe was, Providence was, after all, kind in putting her, and her clownish husband, and their child, on board that fated ship.

Literary biographers have spent nearly two centuries trying to peer inside the mind of Nathaniel Hawthorne, sometimes on the evidence of his fiction, sometimes by examining biographical facts such as these journal entries. Was he motivated by guilt over his ancestor's persecutions of the Salem witches? Did he have an incestuous relationship with his older sister? Was he unable to handle strong women like Elizabeth Peabody and Margaret Fuller?

At least one scholar has argued that his entire career exhibits an obsession with Fuller. His novels almost all feature versions of strong women, some of whom have a dark side. Many of his stories do the same.

As with any great novelist, it is a mistake to reduce Hawthorne's works to a single motivation or explanation. As disappointing as that journal entry may be, it was at least intended to be kept private. Only after Hawthorne's death did his son Julian go public with it.

Julian was a childhood friend of Louisa May Alcott and a writer who would publish twenty-five books in his long life, including more than one about his father. He would also be convicted of mail fraud, spending a year in prison. In 1884 he published *Nathaniel Hawthorne and His Wife* in two volumes, reproducing letters and other documents by his father—including the Fuller passages from the Italian journals.

It was over three decades since Fuller had died, yet it caused a sensation. Fuller's surviving friends rallied to defend her. James Freeman Clarke, now seventy-four, was among them: "As one of those friends, knowing perfectly that her splendid intellect was no less admirable than her generosity of heart, her heroic devotion to truth, and her aspiration toward everything greatly good, I feel bound to declare the comments false in themselves, and unworthy of the writer." Julian fought back, attacking Fuller in his own words: "Margaret Fuller has at last taken her place with the numberless other dismal frauds who fill the limbo of human pretension and failure."

He helped to cause significant damage to her reputation. By then, the *Memoirs of Margaret Fuller Ossoli* had been in print for over thirty years. Fuller's *Woman in the Nineteenth Century* had been in print for nearly four decades. Two posthumous collections of her works, *At Home and Abroad* and *Life Without and Life Within*, had been in print continuously since the 1850s. Yet Julian Hawthorne's controversial book marked or at least coincided with a turning point, no doubt the result of multiple causes. The *Memoirs* ceased to be reprinted for nearly a century. There would be only one more printing of *Woman in the Nineteenth Century* prior to 1969. It took nearly a century, and the modern resurgence of feminism, for Fuller's reputation to recover.

In 1901, a memorial pavilion to Fuller was erected near the site of the wreck, at Point O'Woods, honoring the "author, editor, orator, poet." Julia Ward Howe composed a tribute for its plaque, ending: "Noble in thought and character / Eloquent of tongue and pen / She was an inspiration to many of her own time / And her uplifting influence abides with us."

As with Fuller herself, the pavilion was destroyed by a storm: Hurricane Sandy, in 2012.

13

The Birth of American Literature

> Great geniuses are parts of the times; they themselves are the times; and possess a correspondent coloring.
>
> —Herman Melville, reviewing Hawthorne's *Mosses from an Old Manse*

On top of the human loss, and the loss of additional books that Fuller might have written, lies a further tragedy: America's greatest literary critic missed the chance to welcome America's first great works of literature.

The 1850s have been called the American Renaissance, the decade when distinctive new voices emerged in prose and poetry. The great works were remarkably concentrated: from *The Scarlet Letter* (1850) to *Moby-Dick* (1851), to *Walden* (1854), to *Leaves of Grass* (1855). In her 1846 essay on American literature in the *Tribune*, Fuller had called on writers "to develop a genius, wide and full as our rivers, flowery, luxuriant and impassioned as our vast prairies, rooted in strength as the rocks on which the Puritan fathers landed. That such a genius is to rise and work in this hemisphere we are confident; equally so that scarce the first faint streaks of that day's dawn are yet visible." That dawn broke just as she vanished into the sea.

Emerson was the wellspring of the Renaissance. Walt Whitman, in 1863, predicted that historians would come to acknowledge Emerson as "the actual beginner of the whole procession" of America's original poets and writers. Today, scholars of American literature often say the same, but that claim has been largely forgotten outside the academy.

The works of the American Renaissance could hardly have been more varied. As the literary critic F. O. Matthiessen described it: "Their tones were sometimes optimistic, sometimes blatantly, even dangerously expansive, sometimes disillusioned, even despairing, but what emerges from the total pattern of their achievement—if we will make the effort to repossess it—is literature for our democracy. In reading the lyric, heroic, and tragic expression of our first great age, we can feel the challenge of our still undiminished resources."

The authors of *The Scarlet Letter*, *Moby-Dick*, *Walden*, and *Leaves of Grass* at times embraced, at times resisted Emerson. What they could not do was ignore him. Hawthorne was drawn to Concord even as he satirized it. Melville, reading Emerson's two essay collections in the 1860s, scribbled a mix of agreement and strong disagreement in their margins.

In the 1850s, all four writers were in their thirties or forties. Each developed a voice, a framing, and a structure that were unique in Anglo-American literature. To be sure, a full accounting of the American Renaissance would include Edgar Allan Poe and Emily Dickinson, two writers who were more distant from Emerson and his circle (though Dickinson did admire his poetry). Poe's works mostly dated from the 1840s, and Dickinson's then-unpublished poems are mostly from the 1860s. Yet it is the four great books of the 1850s that are an outgrowth from and a response to Emerson, with revealing backstories behind their creation.

The Scarlet Letter

Nathaniel Hawthorne, on the evidence of his novels, found it difficult to follow Poe's advice to "cut Mr. Alcott [and] hang (if possible) the editor of *The Dial*." He wrote three novels in quick succession in the early 1850s, two of which feature contemporary reformers. *The Scarlet Letter* is the only one of Hawthorne's mature novels that avoids any hint of the Newness.

Hawthorne was the opposite of Emerson. His tragic worldview clashed with Emerson's idealism, which may explain why he so often wrote stories that undercut the best of reformers' intentions with the flaws of their hearts. In *The Scarlet Letter*, he turned to the seventeenth-century setting of Puritan Boston. Rather than the strange "moral shapes of men" that he satirized elsewhere, the characters in his greatest book face a rigid and restrictive social order. Their flawed hearts thereby become far more dangerous.

When eighteen-year-old Louisa May Alcott noted that she was reading Hawthorne, she commented that "'The Scarlet Letter' is my favorite . . . I fancy 'lurid' things, if true and strong also." Poe's advice may have been wise: by getting Emerson out of his head, Hawthorne freed himself to write his most enduring work.

The story of how he came to write it is its own tale of desperation. His first two story collections had met positive reviews but only modest sales. In the summer of 1849, his situation worsened: He was fired from his Salem Customs House position. The Democratic Party, led by Lewis Cass (father of the chargé d'affaires to Rome), had been defeated by Zachary Taylor and the Whigs. Patronage positions turned over at many levels, including in Salem.

He learned of his termination in June. ("I am turned out of office! There is no use in lamentation.") Sophia had saved up some money but not enough to last long. One friend organized contributions from Hawthorne's admirers and sent a substantial check. Hawthorne wrote in thanks, saying that the letter and check "drew—what my troubles never have—the water to my eyes . . . It is sweet to be remembered and cared for by one's friends. . . . And it is bitter, nevertheless, to need their support. . . . I am ashamed of it, and I ought to be."

In Hawthorne's hour of need, publisher James T. Fields came calling. He was thirty-two years old, the junior partner of William Davis Ticknor who had helped Ticknor and Fields become one of the country's most prestigious imprints. When he heard that Hawthorne had lost his job, he first tried to convince politician friends to find a new position for him, with no success. He recalled one who dismissed the very idea of having a literary man in public office: "Hawthorne is one of them 'ere visionists, and we don't want no such a man as him around."

Next, Fields came to Salem. Fields told Hawthorne he would print two thousand copies "of anything you write." Hawthorne protested that he had nothing to offer. Spying a bureau with drawers that might contain manuscripts, Fields asked again. Finally, he began to leave. "I was hurrying down the stairs when he called after me from the chamber, asking me to stop a moment. Then quickly stepping into the entry with a roll of manuscript in his hands, he said: 'How in Heaven's name did you know this thing was there? . . . It is either very good or very bad,—I don't know which.' On my way up to Boston I read the germ of 'The Scarlet Letter'; before I slept that night I wrote him a note all aglow with admiration of the marvelous story he had put into my hands."

Hawthorne had intended to use a shorter version of the novel as part of a collection of "Old-Time Legends." Fields convinced him to expand it and publish it separately. Hawthorne worried that it would be too "somber." To help lighten it he wrote a lengthy introduction, a framing device of pseudo-nonfiction set in the Custom House. It was a chance for him to satirize his former colleagues ruthlessly. Fields liked the addition, though Hawthorne wondered whether readers would care about his own experiences.

When he finished the novel in February, he reported to a friend that Fields "speaks of it in tremendous terms of approbation; so does Mrs. Hawthorne, to whom I read the conclusion last night. It broke her heart and sent her to bed with a grievous headache—which I look upon as a triumphant success!"

32 

Hawthorne, photographed in London by J. J. E. Mayall, 1860.

The Scarlet Letter was published in March 1850. Its first printing of 2,500 copies sold out quickly. Another 2,500 were printed one month later, and yet another 1,000 five months after that. At last Hawthorne had a commercial success.

Reviews were mostly very favorable. The *Massachusetts Quarterly Review* gushed that "in no work has [Hawthorne] presented so clear and perfect an image of himself, as a speculative philosopher, an ethical thinker, a living man." Some religiously minded reviewers decried the "nauseous" and "debauched" themes and characters. But overall, and over time, *The Scarlet Letter* was accepted as "the most decisive production of the author and one of the remarkable stories of the age." Evert Augustus Duyckinck hailed it as an "entire, perfect creation" and gushed, "Our literature has given to the world no truer product of the American soil, though of a peculiar culture, than Nathaniel Hawthorne."

Nonetheless, the novel's success did not make Hawthorne a rich man. A few months after *The Scarlet Letter* reached stores, a sentimental novel by Susan Warner, *The Wide, Wide World*, became one of America's first true bestsellers. It went through fourteen printings in two years. Louisa's alter ego in *Little Women*, Jo March, spends an afternoon "reading and crying over" it. It was just one of many sentimental novels that would turn at least a few American authors into wealthy women. Hawthorne complained bitterly. "America is now wholly given over to a damned mob of scribbling women, and I should have no chance of success while the public taste is occupied with their trash—and should be ashamed of myself if I did succeed."

He still needed the help of his friends. When one couple offered the Hawthornes use of a cottage on the edge of their property, Tanglewood, in Lenox, Massachusetts, they accepted and moved in March 1850. There Hawthorne would write another success, *The House of the Seven Gables*.

Gables came out in 1851. His Brook Farm–inspired novel, *The Blithedale Romance*, followed in 1852, his third novel in three years, leading some biographers to note that his loss of the Customs House job was a great gift to American literature. By 1852, the Hawthornes were back in Concord. They purchased the Alcotts' Hillside, renaming it the Wayside.

Returning, physically, to the Emerson circle may have been a bad move creatively. Hawthorne would continue to write fiction, including *The Marble Faun*, which he published in 1860, but just as with *The Blithedale Romance*, its contemporary setting and characters were not successful.

Emerson never much liked Hawthorne's fiction. Julian Hawthorne would claim that Emerson "was never able to complete the perusal of any of Hawthorne's stories." In one journal entry, Emerson wrote, "Nathaniel Hawthorne's reputation as a writer is a very pleasing fact, because his writing is not good for anything, and this is a tribute to the man."

Moby-Dick

Another reason to be grateful for Hawthorne's job loss and move to Lenox in 1850 is that he soon met a near neighbor: Herman Melville.

Melville was fifteen years younger than Hawthorne. Yet at the age of thirty-one, after spending five years at sea in his early twenties, he had already published five books. His first, *Typee: A Peep at Polynesian Life* (1846), was supposedly a narrative of four months he spent in the Marquesas Islands in the South Pacific when he jumped ship from a whaling vessel. In truth he had only spent one month there, and he borrowed or plagiarized a good deal of material from other accounts.

It was a bestseller in both America and England. Hawthorne reviewed it for the *Salem Advertiser*, praising its light, vigorous style and its "effective" portrait of island life. While some critics attacked the book for its apparent embrace of voluptuousness, Hawthorne disagreed: Melville "has that freedom of view—it would be too harsh to call it laxity of principle—which renders him tolerant of codes of morals that may be little in accordance with our own; a spirit proper enough to a young and adventurous sailor."

It was an auspicious career start for Melville. Yet during his lifetime

33

Herman Melville, c. 1860.

none of his other eight novels would sell as well. He followed *Typee* with a sequel, *Omoo*, loosely based on a brief stay in Tahiti as well as his voyages on a whaling ship; but even more than with *Typee*, he "altered facts and dates, elaborated events, assimilated foreign materials, invented episodes, and dramatized the printed experiences of others as his own."

Reviews were again positive, though some critics took issue with the book's truthfulness, not to mention its Rabelaisian celebration of alcohol. Horace Greeley hailed Melville as "a born genius, with few superiors either as a narrator, a describer, or a humorist." But he argued that both *Typee* and *Omoo* were immoral books. "Not that you can put your finger on a passage positively offensive; but the *tone* is bad. . . . A *penchant* for bad liquors is everywhere boldly proclaimed, while a hankering after loose company, not always of the masculine order, is but thinly disguised."

In 1849 Melville switched to full-on fiction with a romance about an American sailor who abandons his whaling ship to explore the South Pacific. He began *Mardi: and a Voyage Thither* with an ironic preface:

> Not long ago, having published two narratives of voyages in the Pacific, which, in many quarters, were received with incredulity, the thought occurred to me, of indeed writing a romance of Polynesian adventure, and publishing it as such; to see whether the fiction might not, possibly, be received for a verity: in some degree the reverse of my previous experience.

Mardi is a rambling story, and reviewers were not kind. George Ripley, who had taken Margaret Fuller's position at the *New-York Tribune*, wrote that the "story has no movement, no proportions, no ultimate end; and unless it is a huge allegory—bits of which peep out here and there—winding its unwieldy length along, like some monster of the deep, no significance or point." It did not sell well.

Melville wrote two more sailing novels that blended fiction and nonfiction based on his experiences on a merchant vessel (*Redburn*) and a man-of-war (*White-Jacket*), neither of which succeeded. *White-Jacket* did cause a stir with its discussion of the arbitrary and cruel use of flogging in the US Navy. In four short chapters (out of ninety-three), the book describes an incident of flogging and argues that the captain's unchallenged authority to order it whenever he wishes, but never be subject to it, is antidemocratic and unconstitutional: "You see a human being, stripped like a slave, scourged worse than a hound. And for what? For things not essentially criminal, but only made so by arbitrary laws." Melville's publisher, Harper & Brothers, sent copies to every member of Congress. In September 1850, Congress banned flogging on all US ships.

Melville was a pessimist, and a tragedian. In *Mardi*, a character states that "evil is the chronic malady of the universe." The author of that line was a natural ally of Nathaniel Hawthorne. Their personalities, like their writing styles, were distinct: Melville had bouts of manic energy during which he could not stop talking. Hawthorne was often silent. Yet they connected on a deep level.

When they first met, on a hiking expedition up Monument Mountain in August 1850, they were with James T. Fields, Oliver Wendell Holmes, publisher Evert Duyckinck, and a few others. As Fields recalled, "We scrambled to the top with great spirit, and when we arrived, Melville, I remember, bestrode a peaked rock, which ran out like a bowsprit, and pulled and hauled imaginary ropes for our delectation." After lunching among the rocks and making toasts with "a considerable quantity of Heidsieck" champagne, they took an afternoon hike through the Ice Glen, a ravine with deep ice-filled crevices. "Hawthorne was among the most enterprising of the merry-makers; and being in the dark much of the time, he ventured to call out lustily and pretend that certain destruction was inevitable to all of us." Fields, overweight, wore shoes that slipped on the rocks. Holmes joked, "Ten per cent more to your authors on your next book, and you'll have less fat to complain of."

Three days later Melville visited Hawthorne for more champagne and a walk. Hawthorne invited him to return for a stay of a few days. To prepare, he devoured Melville's three most recent books, writing to Duyckinck in late August, "I have read Melville's works with a progressive appreciation of the author. No writer ever put the reality before his reader more unflinchingly than he does in 'Redburn,' and 'White Jacket.' 'Mardi' is a rich book, with depths here and there that compel a man to swim for his life. It is so good that one scarcely pardons the writer for not having brooded long over it, so as to make it a great deal better."

For his part, Melville published an anonymous two-part rave review of *Mosses from an Old Manse* in Duyckinck's *The Literary World*. He praised Hawthorne's "humor so spiritually gentle, so high, so deep, and yet so richly relishable, that it were hardly inappropriate in an angel." He noted "such a depth of tenderness, such a boundless sympathy with all forms of being, such an omnipresent love, that we must needs say that this Hawthorne is here almost alone in his generation,—at least, in the artistic manifestation of these things." He even compared Hawthorne to Shakespeare: "Now I do not say that Nathaniel of Salem is greater than William of Avon, or as great. But the difference between the two men is by no means immeasurable."

Melville's four-day visit began on September 3. Sophia wrote to her mother that "he has very keen perceptive power, but what astonishes me is, that his eyes are not large & deep—He seems to see every thing very accurately, & how he can do so with his small eyes, I cannot tell.... When conversing, he is full of gesture & force, & loses himself in his subject—There is no grace nor polish."

Melville would visit Lenox at least six more times. Hawthorne and his daughter would reciprocate by visiting him in March 1851. The following August, Hawthorne described a chance meeting as he sat reading:

> While thus engaged, a cavalier on horseback came along the road, and saluted me in Spanish; to which I replied by touching my hat, and went on with the newspaper. But the cavalier renewing his

> salutation, I regarded him more attentively, and saw that it was Herman Melville! . . . We all went homeward together, talking as we went. . . . After supper, I put Julian to bed; and Melville and I had a talk about time and eternity, things of this world and of the next, and books, and publishers, and all possible and impossible matters, that lasted pretty deep into the night.

Throughout these months of visits Melville was struggling with the manuscript of *Moby-Dick*. He was also fretting about his income. He wrote to Hawthorne in June 1851 that "dollars damn me; and the malicious Devil is forever grinning in upon me, holding the door ajar. . . . What I feel most moved to write, that is banned,—it will not pay. Yet, altogether, write the *other* way I cannot. So the product is a final hash, and all my books are botches." Later that month he wrote again: "Shall I send you a fin of the *Whale* by way of a specimen mouthful? The tail is not yet cooked—though the hell-fire in which the whole book is broiled might not unreasonably have cooked it all ere this. This is the book's motto (the secret one),—Ego non baptiso te in nomine [I baptize thee not in the name of the Father, but the Devil]—but make out the rest yourself."

Moby-Dick came out in October 1851 in the United Kingdom, and one month later in the United States. Hawthorne wrote to Melville, praising the novel and apparently offering to review it (that letter has not survived). Melville's response is famous:

> Whence come you, Hawthorne? By what right do you drink from my flagon of life? And when I put it to my lips,—lo, they are yours and not mine. I feel that the Godhead is broken up like the bread at the Supper, and that we are the pieces. Hence this infinite fraternity of feeling. Now, sympathizing with the paper, my angel turns over another page. You did not care a penny for the book. But, now and then as you read, you understood the pervading thought that impelled the book—and that you praised. Was it not so? You were archangel enough to despise the imperfect body, and embrace the soul.

Scholars have long wondered what influence, if any, Hawthorne may have had over Melville's masterpiece. We know that the manuscript-in-progress was sitting on a desk, in plain view, during one of Hawthorne's visits. In Melville's letters to Hawthorne, he speaks several times of wrestling with the book, and the younger man clearly admired the elder. Surely, he would have paid close attention to any advice Hawthorne might have offered. But on this tantalizing question the record is silent.

Given the gulf between the two men's styles—Hawthorne's famous novels are spare and brief, hewing closely to a single theme or question, Melville's novels are extravagant, lengthy journeys through oceans and subcultures—it is hard to imagine what Hawthorne might have said to Melville that would have changed the course of *Moby-Dick*. Melville's book includes lengthy digressions on the typology of whales; the symbolic significance of white; the existing paintings and etchings of whales; and the history of fatal encounters with whales, among other topics. (With tongue in cheek, he defends including that history in order to prove that *Moby-Dick* is no "monstrous fable, or still worse and more detestable, a hideous and intolerable allegory.") Would Hawthorne have advised him to trim these side branches?

We will never know. Yet there is one intriguing sign built into *Moby-Dick* at its start—the book is dedicated to Hawthorne: "In token of my admiration for his genius." Hawthorne discovered this compliment at a private dinner with Melville at a hotel in Lenox. The two men dined at a table alone, lingering long after all other diners had dispersed. Melville handed Hawthorne an inscribed copy. It moved him profoundly.

The two men's masterworks have a commonality: They are both tragedies built around the power of a symbol—the scarlet *A* and the great white whale—that marry allegory to drama. Lewis Mumford, writing about the American Renaissance in *The Golden Day*, goes so far as to say that "at heart, the American novelists were all transcendental. The scene was a symbol: they scarcely had the patience to describe it: they were interested in it only because it pointed to something more important." Melville admired Emerson as "more than a brilliant fellow" but insisted that he did not "oscillate in Emerson's rainbow." Neither he nor Hawthorne subscribed to Transcendentalism as a movement. Still, Mumford rightly notes that their famous books are churning with deep meaning beneath their surface symbols. Their characters are trapped—Hawthorne's by the strict codes of Calvinism, Melville's by Captain Ahab's tyranny—but they long for liberation. These are tragic novels about trapped individuals, craving freedom.

Hawthorne admired his friend's new novel. In December, from his temporary home in West Newton, Massachusetts, he wrote to Duyckinck, "What a book Melville has written! It gives me an idea of much greater power than his preceding ones."

The initial reviewers did not agree. *The Athenaeum* (London) called it "an ill-compounded mixture of romance and matter-of-fact." That review was widely circulated and quoted in America. Duyckinck himself reviewed the novel in *The Literary World* in November. Even he offered a very mixed assessment of his friend's "bulky and multifarious volume," calling it an "intellectual chowder of romance, philosophy, natural history, fine writing, good feeling, bad sayings," and noting that the characters and setting are "idealized throughout."

There were some positive notices, including by Horace Greeley in the *New-York Tribune*: "We think it the best production which has yet come from that seething brain, and in spite of its lawless flights, which put all regular criticism at defiance, it gives us a higher opinion of the author's originality and power than even the favorite and fragrant first-fruits of his genius, the never-to-be-forgotten Typee."

Melville was discouraged. He would continue to write in different genres, including poetry and short stories (most famously, "Bartleby the Scrivener"), but he would never enjoy commercial success. *Moby-Dick* initially sold fewer than four thousand copies, of which six hundred were in the United Kingdom. It was out of print by the time Melville died, in 1891.

One British review of *Moby-Dick*, reprinted in *Harper's New Monthly Magazine*, captured the ultimate significance of the novel:

> Want of originality has long been the just and standing reproach to American literature; the best of its writers were but second-hand Englishmen. Of late some have given evidence of originality; not *absolute* originality, but such genuine outcoming of the American intellect as can be safely called national. Edgar Poe, Nathaniel Hawthorne, Herman Melville are assuredly no British off-shoots; nor is Emerson, the *German* American that he is! . . . What romance writer can be named with HAWTHORNE? Who knows the horrors of the seas like HERMAN MELVILLE?

The reviewer was right. Yet two more original and singular American writers of that decade were still to come.

Walden

In the summer of 1845, just days before Henry Thoreau moved into his cabin on Walden Pond, Nathaniel Hawthorne wrote to his publisher friend Evert Duyckinck with some advice. Duyckinck, the son of a New York bookseller, was the editor of Wiley & Putnam's Library of American Books, a series of books by American authors that would include Edgar Allan Poe (*The Raven and Other Poems*), Hawthorne himself (*Mosses from an Old Manse*), Herman Melville (*Typee*), and Margaret Fuller (*Papers on Literature and Art*). Duyckinck had declined Thoreau's *A Week on the Concord and Merrimack Rivers*. Hawthorne had asked Emerson if he would like to contribute, "but he seems to think it preferable to publish on his own account." He added:

> As for Thoreau, there is one chance in a thousand that he might write a most excellent and readable book; but I should be sorry to take the responsibility, either towards you or him, of stirring him up to write anything for the series. He is the most unmalleable fellow alive—the most tedious, tiresome, and intolerable—the narrowest and most notional—and yet, true as all this is, he has great qualities of intellect and character. The only way, however, in which he

34

Henry David Thoreau, portrait by Benjamin Maxham, 1856.

> could ever approach the popular mind, would be by writing a book of simple observation of nature.

By 1849, Thoreau's publishing record was sparse. He had published seven essays and a few poems in *The Dial* in the early 1840s. He had published "Resistance to Civil Government," "A Walk to Wachusett," and "Katahdin" (or, as he spelled it, "Ktaadn") in various magazines. For a man in his early thirties, his reputation was not promising.

Thoreau was still digging out of the financial hole created by his first book. From 1849 to late 1853, when he purchased the unsold stock, he gave some twenty-five lectures in Massachusetts and Maine. He spoke of his excursions to Cape Cold and Canada, his love of walking, and his life in the woods. Throughout those years he also worked on *Walden*.

He had initially discussed a two-book deal with James Munroe, and that firm announced *Walden* in the back pages of *A Week*. But the failure of *Concord and Merrimack* put an end to the plan. Instead, Thoreau expanded and revised his original draft, which had begun as a series of answers to questions that his lecture audiences posed to him.

Walden went through no fewer than six revisions. The result includes material from his journals from as early as 1839 and especially from 1850 to 1854. It is more than double the length of the first draft. It is not so much a record of his experience on the pond as it is a re-creation of it—"a completer & truer account," as he put it.

In *A Week* he had incorporated previously written poetry and essays, creating an awkward mélange that did not easily fit together. *Walden* also includes many side trips, but they are much more closely tied to the experience of living "deliberately" in the woods. His revisions were not just expansions, they were also careful polishings. He was obsessed with accuracy, checking and correcting the prices of items down to the penny. He was also obsessed with the rhythm of his sentences, trimming and altering them for the ideal flow. He cut passages even if they were vivid examples of satire when they distracted from his larger points.

The result is a true American original—a memoir-based essay on the beauty of the natural world and a commentary on the failings of human society, where "the mass of men lead lives of quiet desperation." It does not matter that he structures it falsely as a single year, despite residing twice as long at the cabin. It does not matter that he incorporates experiences from many other years. It does not matter that he paints a misleading picture of his isolation, only briefly mentioning visitors or his trips to town. What matters is the value of his observations and commentary, which have made the book a classic.

The Thoreau in *Walden* is still a Transcendentalist, but one who is transitioning from mystical idealism toward a more purely deductive natural science. In his later revisions he changed the title of a central chapter from "Animal Food" to "Higher Laws," and it is certainly idealist—he argues that everyone who wants to preserve his or her "higher faculties" should abstain from eating meat, and even from eating more than is absolutely necessary. He also explores the idea that there are natural laws of leaves and crystals that operate beyond actual leaves and crystals—in a famous climactic passage, he is inspired by the details of sandbanks to rhapsodize that as "the earth expresses itself outwardly in leaves, it so labors with the idea inwardly. The atoms have already learned this law, and are pregnant by it. . . . The feathers and wings of birds are still drier and thinner leaves. Thus, also, you pass from the lumpish grub in the earth to the airy and fluttering butterfly." Yet even this talk of inner laws is tethered to observation and surface detail. His turn toward natural science and away from transcendental spiritualism has been much discussed by scholars; it is hardly a stark, simple change. Yet unlike Bronson Alcott, he was deeply interested in unlocking the mechanics of nature.

As for human nature, Thoreau remains a skeptic, and a satirist. He is still a romantic when it comes to freedom, but he is also a stern moralist—"There is never an instant's truce between virtue and vice," and "from exertion come wisdom and purity; from sloth ignorance and sensuality."

In the end, *Walden* is an inspirational book. In its concluding chapter are some of his most famous aphorisms:

> "If a man does not keep pace with his companions,
> perhaps it is because he hears a different drummer."

> "However mean your life is, meet it and live it; do not shun
> it and call it hard names. It is not so bad as you are."

> "Rather than love, than money, than fame, give me truth."

The launch of *Walden* proved more successful than *A Week*. Ticknor and Fields generated more attention and sales. Still, it took five years to sell their first printing of two thousand copies. One year after its release, Ticknor sent Thoreau a check for $51.60, writing, "We regret, for your sake as well as ours, that a larger number of Walden has not been sold." Like *Moby-Dick*, it would be out of print before its author's death (as of 1859), but unlike Melville's novel, it was brought back immediately, and it has remained in print ever since.

At least the reviews were widespread and favorable. "All American kind are delighted with 'Walden' as far as they have dared say," wrote Emerson to a friend in late August, three weeks after publication. James T. Fields had sent many copies to reviewers. Some, including Horace Greeley, called it "curious," but others hailed its originality and wisdom, calling it "remarkable" despite or because of Thoreau's eccentricity. The *Boston Daily Bee* called it "an original book, this, and from an original man—from a very eccentric man . . . Get the book. You will like it. It is original and refreshing; and from the brain of a *live* man."

Once again, a London reviewer was the one who grasped its larger significance, calling it "a brave book, one in a million, an honour to America, a gift to men."

One year later would come one final American voice of the 1850s with another brave masterpiece.

Leaves of Grass

Emerson's second set of essays had begun with "The Poet," including this famous passage: "We have yet had no genius in America, with tyrannous eye, which knew the value of our incomparable materials, and saw, in the barbarism and materialism of the times, another carnival of the same gods whose picture he so much admires in Homer. . . . Yet America is a poem in our eyes; its ample geography dazzles the imagination, and it will not wait long for metres."

Like each of his Newness followers, Emerson wrote poetry and thought of himself as a poet. Yet neither he nor his followers were most famous for their poetry. Emerson's essays, Fuller's essays and books, Hawthorne's fiction, and Thoreau's essays and books were pioneering in ways that their poetry was not. In their poems they relied on conventional rhyme schemes and classic forms. They could be elegiac, they could be stirring, and they were certainly American in their topics. But none of them answered Emerson's call for a carnival of the gods, an all-encompassing transformation of America's "incomparable materials." In 1855, that poet arrived in the person of Walt Whitman.

He was thirty-five. Born in rural Long Island, he was raised there and in Brooklyn, which at the time was a small but fast-growing city, full of immigrants and known as the City of Churches of "virtually all denominations." He attended two different Sunday schools and sampled many different Sunday services. Thanks to an apprenticeship at the Long Island *Patriot* and work at a Brooklyn printer, followed by a job as a compositor at the *Long-Island Star*, he learned the craft of printing amid the fierce partisanship of antebellum journalism. His experience was the opposite of Thoreau's small-town, nature-loving, solitary contemplation.

Whitman had worked as a schoolteacher. Much like Margaret Fuller, Henry Thoreau, and Louisa May Alcott, he disliked the long hours and low pay. Also like them, he followed Bronson Alcott's footsteps with a liberal, conversational approach to education. Teaching in Southold on Long Island in 1840, where he roomed at the homes of his students to save money, he may have faced a crisis. According to some sources, he was denounced by a Presbyterian minister for his "behavior to the children, and his goings-on."

It was a charge of sodomy. The outraged parishioners chased him down and tarred and feathered him. Biographers disagree on the merits of this story. The evidence comes from local inhabitants' lore, shared nearly a century after the fact. In any event, by 1841 Whitman had stopped teaching.

His career in journalism and printing was a checkered one. He founded the *Long-Islander* in 1838 and sold it after less than a year. He worked briefly at the *Long Island Democrat*, the *New World*, the *Aurora*, and a slew of Manhattan papers before returning to Brooklyn for two years at the *Brooklyn Eagle*. All the while he devoured New York opera and theater and wrote essays, journalism, and conventional poems. Also, as Louisa May Alcott would do, he wrote short fiction in popular genres. One novel, *Franklin Evans, or, The Inebriate* (1842), was a temperance story, a then-popular genre in which the evils of drinking were painted in lurid detail. Though he later dismissed it as "damned rot—rot of the worst sort" and claimed that he wrote it in just three days "with the help of a bottle of port or what not," during his lifetime it sold better than anything else he wrote. He needed the cash. The publishers paid him $75 up front and $50 more when it proved a success.

Unlike Emerson, Thoreau, or Bronson Alcott, Whitman was engaged in the hurly-burly of politics and metropolitan life. Yet his poems up until the early 1850s were mostly unremarkable, conventionally rhymed, sentimental, and often didactic. The final stanza of "The Love That Is Hereafter," a poem about "weak, proud, and erring man," serves as an example:

For vainly through this world below
We seek affection. Nought but wo[e]
Is with our earthly journey wove;
And so the heart must look above,
Or die in dull despair.

What was it that caused the author of pulp fiction and traditional poems to change into the author of *Leaves of Grass*, a radically original work of poetry? *Leaves* first came out in 1855 and became his life's work, evolving through multiple editions up to a "Deathbed Edition" in 1891–92. It turned Whitman into a beloved national icon. So what changed for him in the early 1850s?

The simple answers are politics and ambition. The longer answer involves Ralph Waldo Emerson and Margaret Fuller.

Whitman and Greeley were in the audience one day in 1842 when Emerson delivered his lecture on "The Poet." Whitman wrote a review of it for the *Aurora*, hailing it as "one of the richest and most beautiful compositions, both for its matter and style, we have ever heard anywhere, at any time." He also took a jab at Greeley, noting that he "was in ecstasies whenever any thing particularly good was said . . . he would flounce about like a fish out of water, or a tickled girl—look around, to see those behind him and at his side; all of which very plainly told those both far and near, that he knew a thing or two more about these matters than other men." Later, he would tell a friend that "my ideas . . . were simmering and simmering, and Emerson brought them to a boil."

He was also impressed by Margaret Fuller's 1846 essay in the *Tribune* on American literature, which he reread multiple times. Between Emerson's and Fuller's essays lay a challenge: Where is America's original poetry?

As a newspaperman in the days of the partisan press, Whitman was a political animal. He was opposed to slavery in the 1840s and much of the 1850s—though, like Lincoln, he cared about preserving the Union above all. His abolitionism cost him his job at the *Brooklyn Eagle*, which led to a brief position at the New Orleans *Daily Crescent*, his only early chance to travel through much of the country. When he returned to New York he gave political speeches and became a delegate to the 1848 convention of the Free Soil Party. That branch of the old Democratic Party together with other liberal Northerners opposed allowing slavery in any new state or territory. They recruited Martin Van Buren as their candidate. They failed miserably in the election.

Whitman's final poems before *Leaves of Grass* were published in 1850. They were all political. Like the Emerson circle in Concord, he was appalled by that year's congressional compromise which allowed new states and territories (New Mexico, Utah) to make their own decisions about slavery. He wrote two satires: "Song for Certain Congressmen," about politicians who cave to pressure, and "The House of Friends," accusing Northern politicians of being even worse than their Southern brethren. Finally, when Daniel Webster spoke in favor of the hated compromise, Whitman wrote "Blood-Money," a free-verse howl. After recalling Judas's selling out of Christ, it concludes:

Witness of Anguish—Brother of Slaves,
Not with thy price closed the price of thine image;
And still Iscariot plies his trade.

He would rarely use conventional rhymes again. He would also express disgust with American politics, or at least its politicians. In an 1856 essay that he withdrew from publication, "The Eighteenth Presidency!," he wrote that "of all the persons in public office in These States, not one in a thousand has been chosen by any spontaneous movement of the people, nor is attending to the interests of the people; all have been nominated and put through by great or small caucuses of the politicians . . . and all consign themselves to personal and party interests." He dismissed Buchanan and Fillmore as "galvanized old men . . . relics [of] resentments of a past age," and dismissed the political parties as "too small." He called for working men to join together to "abolish slavery, or it will abolish you."

His ambition for the first edition of *Leaves of Grass* stretched absurdly far. He believed America needed a poet who could not only embrace the entire country but also help keep it from fracturing. He didn't just want to offer a new and bold voice. He wanted to save the United States of America.

The first edition announced his hopes in a nine-page preface: "The United States themselves are essentially the greatest poem . . . not merely a nation but a teeming nation of nations . . . the genius of the United States is . . . always most in the common people."

As for his role: "Of them a bard is to be commensurate with a people. . . . His spirit responds to his country's spirit." That meant all of America's peoples: women and men, Northerners and Southerners, including "slavery and the tremulous spreading of hands to protect it, and the stern opposition to it which shall never cease till it ceases. . . . For such the expression of the American poet is to be transcendant [*sic*] and new."

What followed were just twelve untitled poems. The first one, which would eventually become "Song of Myself," ran for forty-three pages. The remaining eleven spanned only thirty-eight more. He wrote in the first person, but his "I" is not simply "Walt Whitman." It is both himself and his nation, celebrating America's length and breadth and its many appetites of body and spirit. Near the start, he challenges his readers:

Have you reckoned a thousand acres much? Have you reckoned the
earth much?
Have you practiced so long to learn to read?
Have you felt so proud to get at the meaning of poems?

Some of his most famous passages can be read as sexual or spiritual, or both. As Thoreau would write to a friend about the second edition: "As for its sensuality,—& it may turn out to be less sensual than it appears—I do not so much wish that those parts were not written, as that men & women were so pure that they could read them without harm."

35

Walt Whitman, engraving from a daguerreotype, used as the frontispiece to *Leaves of Grass*.

In part because of its sensuality, in part because of its unconventional, free-form voice, Whitman could not convince a publishing house to take *Leaves* on. So he self-published it, overseeing the layout, and printing eight hundred copies in three versions with different prices. He did not put his name on the title page, but he did include a frontispiece illustration of himself, in plain, open-necked clothing, a democratic "rough" rather than a patrician. He was identified as "Walter Whitman" on the copyright page. The opening poem includes this stanza:

> *Walt Whitman, an American, one of the roughs, a kosmos,*
> *Disorderly, fleshy and sensual . . . eating drinking and breeding.*
> *No sentimentalist . . . no stander above men and women or apart from them . . . no more modest than immodest.*

There had never been a voice quite like his. He was not the first poet to use free verse, but he was the first to try to embrace his entire world. He filled the first editions of *Leaves of Grass* with catalogues celebrating "my dinner, dress, associates, looks, business, compliments, dues" not to mention leaves, ants, scabs, stones, modes of transportation, animal varieties, vocations, and Americans from every region—the lists pile up and up. He celebrates them all. As he explains, "I hear and behold God in every object . . . I see something of God each hour of the twenty-four."

A self-promoter, he wrote three anonymous reviews of his own book and convinced friendly editors to publish them in the *Brooklyn Daily Eagle*, the *United States Review*, and the *American Phrenological Journal*. Today, this would cause a scandal, but at the time it was a popular ploy. Whitman's self-praise was almost as exuberant as the poems themselves:

> An American bard at last! . . . No skulker or tea-drinking poet is Walt Whitman. He will bring poems to fill the days and nights—fit for men and women with the attributes of throbbing blood and flesh.

In one of his three self-reviews, after commenting on Tennyson and the state of Anglo-American poetry, he quotes *Leaves* and comments, "It is indeed a strange voice! . . . If this is poetry, where must its foregoers stand?"

The few others who reviewed the book were mostly negative. Charles A. Dana, in the *New-York Daily Tribune*, granted that the poems "are certainly original in their external form" but complained that the language is "reckless and indecent." Charles Eliot Norton called it a "curious and lawless" collection, "a compound of the New England transcendentalist and New York rowdy." From London came outrage and contempt: "The depth of [Whitman's] indecencies will be the grave of his fame, or ought to be if all proper feeling is not extinct" (the *Critic*). Ditto from Boston: "We can conceive no better reward than the lash for such a violation of decency as we have before us" (the *Boston Intelligencer*).

Whitman had mailed a copy to Emerson. The letter that came back from Concord would become one of the most famous in American literary history:

> *Dear Sir,*
>
> *I am not blind to the worth of the wonderful gift of "Leaves of Grass." I find it the most extraordinary piece of wit and wisdom that America has yet contributed. I am very happy in reading it, as great power makes us happy. It meets the demand I am always making of what seemed the sterile & stingy nature, as if too much handiwork, or too much lymph in the temperament, were making our Western wits fat and mean. I give you joy of your free and brave thought. I have great joy in it. I find incomparable things said incomparably well, as they must be. I find the courage of treatment which so delights us, & which large perception only can inspire.*
>
> *I greet you at the beginning of a great career, which yet must have had a long foreground somewhere, for such a start. I rubbed my eyes a little, to see if this sunbeam were no illusion; but the solid*

sense of the book is a sober certainty. It has the best merits, namely, of fortifying & encouraging.

I did not know until I, last night, saw the book advertised in a newspaper, that I could trust the name as real & available for a post-office. I wish to see my benefactor, & have felt much like striking my tasks, & visiting New York to pay you my respects.

R. W. Emerson

Whitman shared the letter with Charles Dana and allowed him to publish it in the *Tribune*. The following spring he planned a second edition of *Leaves*, adding twenty new poems, giving them titles (the future "Song of Myself" was now "Poem of Walt Whitman, an American"), and appending a "Correspondence" section with Emerson's letter and his own lengthy open letter in response. It was full of chutzpah: "A few years, and the average annual call for my Poems is ten or twenty thousand copies—more, quite likely." As a coup de grâce, he stamped "I greet you at the beginning of a great career" with Emerson's name, in gold, on the spine.

He hadn't asked Emerson for permission. Waldo was irked, telling a friend he would have qualified his praise if he knew it would be published. "'There are parts of the book,' he said, 'where I hold my nose as I read.'"

The second edition, as with the first, did not sell well. Yet Whitman gained another Concord champion when he gave a copy to Henry Thoreau. They met in person thanks to Bronson Alcott, who had arranged for Thoreau to do some surveying work for a failed utopian community in Raritan, New Jersey. Alcott had already met Whitman and been deeply impressed. He felt uncomfortable observing the two men on his second visit: They were "like two beasts, each wondering what the other would do, whether to snap or run; and it came to no more than cold compliments between them."

Nonetheless, Thoreau came away impressed, if somewhat perplexed, writing to a friend that he and Alcott "were much interested and provoked. He [Whitman] is apparently the greatest democrat the world has seen. Kings and Aristocracy go by the board at once, as they have long deserved to. A remarkably strong though coarse nature, of a sweet disposition, and much prized by his friends. Though peculiar and rough in his exterior . . . he is essentially a gentleman. I am still somewhat in a quandary about him,—feel that he is essentially strange to me, at any rate; but I am surprised by the sight of him."

When Thoreau proceeded to read the book, he was smitten:

> *That Walt Whitman, of whom I wrote to you, is the most interesting fact to me at present. I have just read his 2nd edition (which he gave me) and it has done me more good than any reading for a long time. . . . There are 2 or 3 pieces in the book which are disagreeable to say the least, simply sensual. He does not celebrate love at all—It is as if the beasts spoke. . . . But even on this side, he has spoken more truth than any American or modern that I know. I have found his poem exhilarating [and] encouraging.*

Through the rest of his life, Whitman would continue to expand and reorganize and reissue the book. The third edition, in 1860, added 146 new poems and landed with a Boston publisher, Thayer and Eldridge, who sold more copies than either of the first two editions had achieved. The exact number is unknown, but it was in the thousands.

This edition grouped the poems into clusters, including "Calamus" and "Enfans d'Adam," groupings that would continue in later editions, the latter anglicized as "Children of Adam." Even on the brink of the Civil War, Whitman still held out hope that the Union could be saved. He prefaced the edition with a poem he called "Proto-Leaf," including these lines:

> *I will make a song for These States, that no one*
> *State may under any circumstances be subjected*
> *to another State,*
> *And I will make a song that there shall be comity by*

> *day and by night between all The States, and*
> *between any two of them . . .*

The controversy over Whitman's sensuality would never abate. The "Enfans d'Adam" poems, in particular, bothered Emerson. They rhapsodized about "Limitless limpid jets of love hot and enormous, / quivering jelly of love, white-blow and delirious juice." Emerson feared a backlash.

On a visit to Boston in 1860, the two men took a walk. Emerson tried to convince the poet to remove those poems. As Whitman later recalled:

> During those two hours he was the talker and I the listener. It was an argument-statement, reconnoitring [*sic*], review, attack, and pressing home . . . of all that could be said against that part (and the main part) in the construction of my poems, "Children of Adam." More precious than gold to me that dissertation. . . . Each point of E.'s statement was unanswerable, no judge's charge ever more complete or convincing, I could never hear the points better put—and then I felt down in my soul the clear and unmistakable conviction to disobey all, and pursue my own way.

Later he would revise and soften or remove some of his poems. After the Civil War, he shifted his goals and his voice, no longer writing poems with the first person standing in for the nation. His fame would grow. He would give lectures on Abraham Lincoln, his beloved redeemer president, that included his conventional "O Captain! My Captain!" poem, and he would be praised far and wide, including by Andrew Carnegie, who loved his poems celebrating capitalism. Whitman managed his public image right up to the design of his grave site. The poet who was initially dismissed as pornographic or unreadable would end his life as a beloved national celebrity. The so-called Deathbed Edition of *Leaves* in 1892, the ninth and final version, had swollen to almost four hundred poems. Readers have been reading it ever since.

36

Walt Whitman helped design this grand tomb at Camden's Harleigh Cemetery, using over seventy-two tons of granite. Whitman, his parents, siblings, and sister-in-law are interred under his name.

• • •

From Hawthorne to Melville to Thoreau to Whitman in just a few short years: American literature had its true birth in the 1850s. Margaret Fuller had predicted it, Emerson had inspired it, and the results were as varied and exciting as the young nation itself. Emerson had helped inspire the utopian excitement of the 1840s, and he had directly or indirectly inspired the literary eruption of the 1850s. Whether pushing back against his idealism (Hawthorne, Melville), celebrating individual perfection (Thoreau), or celebrating the boisterous clamor of democratic voices (Whitman), a new literature had been unleashed. It is impossible to imagine these books coming from any other nation.

Of course, the extraordinary hopes of Whitman for *Leaves of Grass*—to save the Union—couldn't be accomplished by a book or lecture. America was tearing apart in the 1850s. The crisis brought the Emerson circle onto a political stage that would upend every part of American life. The Newness was just one of the many victims of the violence.

Book II

The Crisis

14

The Great Cause

> What should concern Massachusetts is not the Nebraska Bill, nor the Fugitive Slave Bill, but her own slaveholding and servility. Let the State dissolve her union with the slaveholder. . . . She can find no respectable law or precedent which sanctions the continuance of such a Union for an instant.
>
> —Henry David Thoreau

The abolitionists were on the right side of history, and the Emerson circle were abolitionists. Those statements are true, yet they obscure more than they illuminate. The story behind the Concord abolitionists is a complicated tale of racial prejudice, philosophical temperament, and courage.

It took bravery to join the abolitionist cause in the 1830s. It grew easier as time went on. It also took bravery to support abolitionism with deeds rather than just words. Thousands of rioters ransacked the churches and homes of white abolitionist leaders and Black citizens in New York City in the summer of 1834; the so-called Anti-Abolitionist Riots lasted nearly a week. Abolitionist newspapermen were often under physical threat. A crowd seized William Lloyd Garrison, the Boston-based editor of *The Liberator*, and dragged him through the streets in 1835, threatening his life. A mob shot and killed Elijah Lovejoy, editor of the *Observer*, in Alton, Illinois, in November 1837.

Even attending an antislavery meeting could be dangerous. In May 1838, the Anti-Slavery Convention of American Women gathered at Pennsylvania Hall in Philadelphia. A mob outside smashed the windows, forcing the women to flee, and then burned the building.

Bravery aside, most abolitionists held deep prejudices against Black people—they detested slavery but did not believe in racial equality. Almost all whites in antebellum America were racist. It was a rare white man or woman who believed that Blacks were equal to whites, fully capable of political and economic achievement.

The members of the Emerson circle came to embrace abolitionism at different times and in different ways. They held differing, and in some cases repugnant, views of Black people. And they did not all agree on the best path to destroy the institution of slavery. Yet in the end they united on the moral necessity of doing so, including by direct action.

The first to embrace the cause among them were the women, including Abba Alcott and Lidian Emerson, followed by one man, Bronson Alcott. Bronson heard Garrison speak twice in Boston in October 1830, but he did not immediately convert to the cause. On the fifteenth, he wrote that Garrison "was full of truth and power." But one day later he equivocated. "There is sometimes a want of discrimination, perhaps, between the slave-holder who keeps his slaves from motives of expediency and the one whose principles are in favor of slavery." Abba needed no convincing. Her brother Samuel May had converted to the cause and become an important ally of Garrison, and she agreed with him; when the Alcotts were living in Philadelphia, she helped found the local Female Anti-Slavery Society in December 1833, just days after Samuel had done the same for the American Anti-Slavery Society. Soon, Bronson came around. When the mob dragged Garrison through the streets, local police rescued him and placed him in protective custody for one night. Abba was able to convince Bronson that they should keep him company.

Many women in Emerson's life were early converts. His aunt Mary attended a meeting of the Middlesex County Anti-Slavery Society in

1835 and started lobbying Waldo on the issue. Lidian, together with Henry Thoreau's mother and aunts, helped found the Concord Female Anti-Slavery Society in 1837, soon after Lidian heard the Grimké sisters speak in Concord, which converted Lidian to the cause. In general, women outnumbered men when it came antebellum reform movements. As one scholar describes, "In the 1830s and early 1840s social reform was a job not for the famous Transcendentalists of Concord, but for their female kin—their mothers and aunts, sisters and wives." According to Abba, Louisa May "was an abolitionist at the age of three."

Notwithstanding Bronson's early conversion, he held ugly views on skin color. As someone who believed that external appearances reflected internal, spiritual truths, he was convinced of a melanin-based hierarchy of spirituality: Whites were on top, followed by yellow, olive, and copper-skinned people, with dark complexions at the bottom. Within the white tier, fair-haired and blue-eyed features—like his own—were superior to dark-haired and brown-eyed ones, like Louisa May's.

Emerson's views on racial hierarchies were not as detailed as Alcott's, yet Emerson believed that the Black "race" would fade away while the white race would dominate the world. In 1838 he wrote, "The Whole History of the negro is tragedy. By what accursed violation did they first exist that they should suffer always? . . . I think they are more pitiable when rich than when poor. Of what use are riches to them? They never go out without being insulted. Yesterday I saw a family of negroes riding in a coach. How pathetic!"

He believed the Black race was destined to perish, as were American Indians. He never gave up thinking that races—by which he meant nationalities, not just skin-color groups—held intrinsic traits that could be ranked hierarchically. In 1854, he made a note in his journals that "it is race, is it not, that puts the 100,000,000 of British India under the absolute dominion of a remote island in the north of Europe?" He would repeat that line in *English Traits*, his 1856 book drawn from his visits to England and Scotland.

Yet he could be inconsistent. In a more optimistic mood, he once wrote that "in this continent,—asylum of all nations,—the energy of Irish, Germans, Swedes, Poles, and Cossacks, and all the European tribes,—of the Africans, and of the Polynesians,—will construct a new race, a new religion, a new state, a new literature, which will be as vigorous as the new Europe which came out of the smelting-pot of the Dark Ages."

Still, for the most part, Emerson and Alcott stuck to their view that the white "race" was destined to dominate the earth. And they were willing to consider extreme measures to encourage that presumed course of history. In one 1854 conversation, according to Emerson, Alcott "compassionately thought that if necessary to bring them [Blacks] sooner to an end, polygamy might be introduced [among whites] & these made the eunuchs."

In other words, sterilize Black men while encouraging white men to have as many children as possible. Of all the millions of words in Emerson's published and unpublished writings, that "compassionately" is the single most painful to read.

How did Emerson become a staunch abolitionist? At first, he hoped that moral suasion would be sufficient to end the institution. As a Transcendentalist, he believed it was up to individuals to understand and do the right thing. But not only was he surrounded by abolitionists in the family—not just his wife and aunt but also his brother Charles, who gave a speech in Concord in 1835 advocating immediate emancipation, and his step-grandfather, Ezra Ripley—he was forced to confront historical facts. When Lovejoy was murdered in 1837, he wrote in his journal, "When a zealot comes to me & represents the importance of this Temperance Reform my hands drop—I have no excuse—I honor him with shame at my own inaction. Then a friend of the slaves shows me the horrors of Southern slavery—I cry guilty, guilty."

Lovejoy's killing pushed him to speak out. He gave a speech at the Second Church in Concord—the text does not survive, but one account of it does—which was not exactly fire and brimstone, but which denounced that abolitionist speeches were banned in most churches and "almost all the public halls in Boston." If he was not yet ready to insist that slavery be abolished, he was at least ready to let others say so: "If the motto on all palace-gates is 'Hush,' the honorable ensign to our town-halls should be 'Proclaim.'" It would take seven more years before he would give his own abolitionist proclamation.

Henry Thoreau preceded him to the cause. He served as curator of the Concord Lyceum in 1842, when Frederick Douglass spoke there. It was four years since Douglass had escaped slavery and three years before he would publish his first famous memoir. He was an energetic and highly accomplished speaker—as part of this first solo tour, he spoke in some forty-two towns in eastern and central Massachusetts. Two months later, in December, the firebrand Wendell Phillips gave an antislavery speech at the invitation of the Concord Female Anti-Slavery Society. When Phillips appeared again in March 1845, Thoreau wrote a review of the speech for *The Liberator*, praising his eloquence.

Throughout the 1840s and 1850s the Thoreau home was an important stop on the Underground Railroad, as was the Alcotts' Hillside for the years they lived there. It is impossible to know how many fugitives they sheltered, as the need for secrecy discouraged record-keeping, but Bronson wrote about one escapee named John in 1847:

> Our friend the fugitive, who has shared now a week's hospitalities with us, sawing and piling my wood, feels this new taste of freedom yet unsafe here in New England, and so has left us for Canada. We supplied him with the means of journeying, and bade him a good god-speed to a freer land. . . . He has many of the elements of the hero. His stay with us has given image and a name to the dire entity of slavery, and was an impressive lesson to my children, bringing before them the wrongs of the black man and his tale of woes.

Louisa later recalled that "fugitive slaves were sheltered under our roof, and my first pupil was a very black George Washington whom I taught to write on the hearth with charcoal, his big fingers finding pen and pencil unmanageable."

During Henry's two years at Walden Pond, witnesses recalled him sheltering escapees during the day before bringing them to his mother's house after dark. One Concord resident, Ann Bigelow, named the Thoreau home as one of three major refuges in Concord, saying that "nearly every week some fugitive would be forwarded with the utmost secrecy to Concord." Henry often escorted them to the northbound train, buying their tickets and ensuring they had money.

Thanks to various accounts, we know of one case in which Thoreau borrowed Emerson's carriage and drove a fugitive named "Lockwood" (not his real name), a man with a $500 bounty on his head, from his family's house to the train station in South Acton early one morning. The fugitive was paranoid and at one point jumped out, but Thoreau managed to reassure him, and soon "Lockwood" was bound for Montreal.

Henry did not leave records about these clandestine activities, but he did write about one fugitive in 1851. His journal account reveals the tangled layers of relationships, genetic and financial, that were not uncommon under slavery:

> Just put a fugitive slave, who has taken the name of Henry Williams, into the cars for Canada. He escaped from Stafford County, Virginia, to Boston last October . . . had been corresponding through an agent with his master, *who is his father* [emphasis added], about buying himself, his master asking $600, but he having been able to raise only $500. . . . Intended to dispatch him at noon through to Burlington, but when I went to buy his ticket, saw one at the depot who looked and behaved so much like a Boston policeman that I did not venture that time.

Emerson did not offer his home as a way station, but he did loan his carriage to Thoreau for the many occasions when Henry needed to bring a fugitive to the railroad station. It was typical of Emerson: he would lend money, he would lend support, but he stopped short of direct action.

Finally, on August 1, 1844, in a ten-thousand-word speech in Concord, Emerson came out as an abolitionist of a kind. He was invited to speak by the Middlesex County Anti-Slavery Society on the topic of "Emancipation in the British West Indies," a keynote address alongside talks by Frederick Douglass and several others. Yet on that morning, there was no venue open to them—the local ministers had refused use of their meetinghouses, and town officials had refused use of the schoolhouse and courthouse. A crowd in front of the courthouse finally forced its way inside, but nobody proved willing to ring the meetinghouse bell to invite other attendees. Finally, Thoreau stepped up and rang it himself.

The speech was a far cry from Emerson's typically judicious, weigh-all-sides rhetoric, though it featured his typically extensive research. It would stand as the most comprehensive statement he would ever make on the topic. He began by describing the evils of slavery in no uncertain terms:

> For the negro, was the slave-ship to begin with, in whose filthy hold he sat in irons, unable to lie down; bad food, and insufficiency of that; disfranchisement; no property in the rags that covered him; no marriage, no right in the poor black woman that cherished him in her bosom, no right to the children of his body; no security from the humors, none from the crimes, none from the appetites of his master; toil, famine, insult and flogging; and, when he sank in the furrow, no winds of good fame blew over him, no priest of salvation visited him with glad tidings: but he went down to death.

And then: "The blood is moral: the blood is anti-slavery: it runs cold in the veins: the stomach rises with disgust, and curses slavery."

Yet the speech left some radical abolitionists dissatisfied. Emerson put the burden of abolition on Black people rather than all of society. In his journals, he continued to resist political activism and denigrate antislavery speakers. During the entire decade of the 1840s, he gave only four talks on slavery, and he continued to argue that Southern whites would eventually come to understand that the institution is immoral—an argument for gradualism that his family and key friends all rejected.

At least the Concord Transcendentalists were aligned on the aim of abolitionism. In the next decade the issue erupted throughout the North, and the Emerson circle found its great cause. As Thomas Wentworth Higginson wrote about the Newness many years later, "It is possible that those seemingly vague and dreamy times might have communicated to those reared in them too passive and negative a character but for the perpetual tonic of the anti-slavery movement." Put another way, abolitionism brought the Transcendentalists into the political arena.

For more than thirty years, Congress had tried to avoid or at least defer tension between the North and South via a series of compromises. The Missouri Compromise (a set of acts passed in 1820 and 1821) had banned slavery north of the thirty-six-degree, thirty-minute parallel, except in Missouri. With the Gag Rule (1836 through 1844) Congress had censored itself, refusing to consider petitions that would have limited or abolished slavery in states and territories.

Then came the Compromise of 1850. It was a wide-ranging bill with a number of provisions—repealing the Missouri Compromise and admitting California as a free state and New Mexico as a slave territory, among others. Yet it failed to achieve any actual compromise, as it enflamed the North. The measure that drove the abolitionists wild with fury was its Fugitive Slave Act. It made Underground Railroad–supporting whites subject to federal prosecution—anyone attempting to aid a fugitive was subject to a $2,000 penalty and six months of imprisonment—and it made federal and local governments responsible for returning captured fugitives to their enslavers. Worse yet, it denied alleged runaways the right to state their case before a jury. If an enslaver could claim ownership of a fugitive, he was allowed to seize that person off the streets of Boston and elsewhere.

The act inspired both Emerson and Thoreau to imitate Jonathan Swift's "modest proposal" with satires of their own. Emerson, in his journal, imagined a law that might be inspired by "the too great increase of blacks[,] that every fifth manchild should be boiled in hot water" and that "any fifth child so selected, having escaped into Boston . . . will not the mayor & alderman boil him? Is there the smallest moral distinction between such a law & the one now enacted?"

Thoreau, drafting a speech in his own journal, wrote:

> If I were seriously to propose to Congress to make mankind into sausages, I have no doubt that most would smile at my proposition and if any believed me to be in earnest they would think that I proposed something much worse than Congress had ever done. But gentlemen if any of you will tell me that to make a man into a sausage would be much worse (would be any worse), than to make him into a slave—than it was then to enact the fugitive-slave law—I shall here accuse him of foolishness—of intellectual incapacity—of making a distinction without a difference.

The threat of capturing and returning fugitives to the South was not new. Boston's small Black community had long concealed and aided fugitives, and even rescued them when they were caught. In 1836, Eliza Small and Polly Ann Bates were brought before a judge who could order them to be returned to their enslaver. They were rescued by a coordinated strike:

"On a given signal, a group of black women rushed into the courtroom, whisked the runaways out of the building to a waiting carriage, and escaped the city. In this action a key role was played by a black cleaning woman 'of great size,' who subdued an officer of the court long enough for the rescue to be effected." The incident came to be known as the Abolition Riot.

In 1842, when fugitive George Latimer was arrested in Boston, a group of Blacks tried but failed to rescue him. Black and white abolitionists collected funds to purchase his freedom. Afterward, they pressed the state legislature to pass the 1843 Personal Liberty Act, forbidding state officials and facilities from being used to apprehend fugitive slaves. Black abolitionists also formed the Freedom Association to provide fugitives with food, clothing, shelter, and other aid.

Now, thanks to the Fugitive Slave Act, not only were Boston authorities obligated to enforce the federal law, but free Blacks faced new threats of false claims or outright kidnappings. The effect of the act was dramatic. Within a month, some two thousand free Blacks and fugitive slaves fled Northern states; within six months, some one hundred Blacks fled Boston. Over the next decade several hundred Northern Blacks would be dragged to the South and into slavery. Many thousands more would flee to Canada, Mexico, and the Caribbean.

The Fugitive Slave Act inspired Boston abolitionists to revive a "vigilance committee" of over two hundred men who were committed to aiding fugitive slaves. Emerson helped fund the group; Alcott joined it. Between 1850 and 1858 the Vigilance Committee would aid over four hundred fugitives, harass slave catchers, and cause them to be arrested for defamation for labeling their targets "slaves."

They would also, on occasion, resort to force. In one case in 1851 the Vigilance Committee stormed a courthouse to liberate the first fugitive arrested in New England under the new law. Shadrach Minkins had been working as a waiter at the Cornhill Coffee House when he was caught and imprisoned at the courthouse. A group of committee members overpowered his captors and rushed him to a safe house in Cambridge, and then to Concord for a night before moving him on to Leominster, then Vermont, and finally to Quebec.

Twice, however, the committee failed in its efforts.

In the wake of the courthouse storming, the authorities beefed up security for the next case: Thomas Sims, a seventeen-year-old fugitive from Georgia who stowed away on a boat and reached Boston in April. Once captured, he was placed under heavy guard.

The Vigilance Committee considered several rescue plans. Sims was held in a room on a high floor, but the windows were unbarred, and he was free to walk about the room—so the committee planned to set out mattresses at a prearranged time, allowing him to leap safely to the street. Yet by the morning, the windows had been newly barred.

Then the committee debated a sea-born raid of his ship as it left Boston Harbor to return him to Georgia. They gave up those plans "not because it was piracy, but because there was no absolute certainty that the fugitive would be sent South in that precise way." As one member noted, "It left me with the strongest impressions of the great want of preparation, on our part, for this revolutionary work. Brought up as we have all been, it takes the whole experience of one such case to educate the mind to the attitude of revolution."

Louisa May Alcott, age eighteen, was ready to man the barricades. "I felt ready to do anything,—fight or work, hoot or cry,—and laid plans to free Simms [*sic*]. I shall be horribly ashamed of my country if this thing happens, and the slave is taken back."

Sims was put aboard a ship and returned to the South, where he was publicly whipped and then sold to a new owner in Mississippi. He would remain a slave until 1863, when he finally managed to escape to the Union lines during the Civil War.

The Sims case inspired Bronson Alcott to action. As he wrote, "The question 'What has the North to do with slavery?' is visibly answered. Here it is in the Capital and the State has opened its Court of Justice (so called) not to protect and free, but to convict and remand the fugitive, who sought its protection and sympathy, to slavery and all its horrors." The day after Sims's arrest the Vigilance Committee met and elected Bronson as a new member. He patrolled the city until after midnight.

The second failure of the Vigilance Committee came in 1854. It almost cost Alcott his life.

Anthony Burns, a young slave in Richmond, Virginia, escaped by boat to Boston in February. He had learned how to read and write and had become a Baptist preacher. He would preach to small groups of slaves, even though such gatherings could seem threatening to whites. Occasionally "the door would be suddenly burst open by a throng of profane officials, each with cord in hand, bent on securing as many victims as possible." The worshippers would extinguish their lanterns and rush to escape through any possible exit. Anyone caught would be whipped.

Burns stowed away with the help of a sympathetic sailor. His voyage lasted a brutal few weeks. He hid in a small, dark space. His accomplice brought him bread and water only every third day. The temperatures dropped as they moved north. When the ship finally reached Boston, it took him a full week to recover.

His literacy proved his undoing. He wrote a letter to his brother in Richmond, revealing his whereabouts. It was intercepted by his brother's enslaver. Once notified, Burns's enslaver obtained a warrant for his arrest under the Fugitive Slave Act. On May 24, 1854, Burns was arrested as he walked back to his boardinghouse from a day job at a clothing store. Law enforcement agents hustled him to the courthouse, locking him in the same room that had held Thomas Sims.

At first neither the local press nor the Vigilance Committee were aware of the arrest, and the authorities hoped to hurry the legal proceedings before word spread. But the next day, the attorney Richard Henry Dana Jr. happened to pass by the courthouse and hear about Burns. He pushed inside, advocated for the prisoner, and convinced the judge to delay the trial until May 29. That gave the Vigilance Committee a window of a few days.

They met right away. Bronson had been preparing to travel to Worcester to host a conversation, and the committee had key supporters there, including Thomas Wentworth Higginson. A Harvard-educated Unitarian minister, Higginson had been forced to resign from the pulpit of a liberal church in Newburyport in 1849 when his abolitionist views became too radical for his congregation. Ever since then he had devoted himself to the cause by giving speeches. On the night of the twenty-fifth, Alcott and Higginson stayed up late discussing the case. The next day, they returned to Boston together.

An antislavery meeting had been scheduled at Faneuil Hall that evening. As Higginson recalled, the committee came up with a ruse to try to fire up the audience to rush out and mob the courthouse. Since the authorities might suspect trouble when the meeting was finishing, the committee planned to interrupt it. They would station key members near the courthouse and then send someone into Faneuil Hall to shout about a "mob of negroes" already attacking the jailers, at which point the meeting's speaker would send everyone over to Court Square.

Higginson arranged to have a box of axes at hand. He positioned himself near the courthouse and waited. Lewis Hayden, a leading Black abolitionist, had recruited ten men to join the attack, and colleagues of Higginson had recruited white allies.

Events went wrong immediately. The Faneuil Hall crowd was overflowing, but there were many non-abolitionists in attendance. Higginson recalled, "I waited for the trap to be sprung, and for the mob of people to appear from Faneuil Hall. The moments seemed endless. Would our friends never arrive? Presently a rush of running figures, like the sweep of a wave, came round the corner of Court Square, and I watched it with such breathless anxiety as I have experienced only twice or thrice in life. . . . A single glance brought the conviction of failure and disappointment. We had the froth and scum of the meeting, the fringe of idlers on its edge. The men on the platform, the real nucleus of that great gathering, were far in the rear."

The courthouse authorities locked the doors. Higginson, Hayden, and a dozen-odd men, Black and white, including "a stout negro," used a beam as a battering ram on the building's southwest door. They broke a hinge and created a narrow opening.

"There was room for but one to pass in. I glanced instinctively at my black ally. He did not even look at me, but sprang in first, I following. . . . We found ourselves inside, face to face with six or eight policemen, who laid about them with their clubs, driving us to the wall and hammering away at our heads." Someone in the crowd fired a shot, killing a marshal's deputy inside, as the deputies fought back furiously and forced the attackers back. Hayden and another attacker had each fired a shot to cover the retreat—it was never clear who had killed the deputy.

A standoff ensued.

A witness recalled what happened next:

> After a moment of tense, nerve-racking, silence there emerged from the crowd, deliberately and with an attitude of great peace in his venerable manner, Amos Bronson Alcott, philosopher, poet, writer, dreamer. As he ascended the steps alone, his familiar cane tapping the stone with a startlingly clear and leisurely sound, he paused. Turning to one of the ejected rescuers, he asked calmly, "Why are we not within?"
>
> "Because," came the answer, "these people will not stand by us."
>
> Without a word Mr. Alcott placidly continued his ascent, still slowly tapping his cane from step to step. A revolver shot was heard within, the bullet speeding past him without injury or in any sense affecting his motion. But just ere entering the door he paused again, turned, and without in the slightest manner accentuating or retarding his pace, retraced his steps.

Alcott's serene self-confidence, the trait that had handicapped his career for so long, became a source of moral courage under fire.

The raid failed. The police arrested nine members of the crowd (four Black, five white) on various charges, including "riotous conduct."

One week later, on June 2, a contingent of state militia lined the streets as marines and infantry marched Burns to the waterfront and put him aboard a cutter to return him to Virginia.

The Burns case made national headlines. It inspired Walt Whitman to write "A Boston Ballad" as part of *Leaves of Grass*. The poem doesn't mention Burns by name, but it is a wicked satire of the armed forces that ensured his return to Virginia. Whitman imagines the ghosts of Revolutionary War soldiers watching the spectacle:

Here gape your great grand-sons—their wives gaze at
them from the windows,
See how well dress'd—see how orderly they conduct themselves.

Worse and worse! Can't you stand it? Are you retreating?
Is this hour with the living too dead for you?

Burns spent four months in prison in Richmond before he was sold to a North Carolina enslaver for $905. The following February, that new owner agreed to sell him to a prominent Boston abolitionist for $1,300. Finally, Burns was a free man.

Enthusiastic crowds greeted Burns in New York and Boston. When his former Virginia church excommunicated him for disobeying "the laws of God and man," his response was eloquent: "That law which God wrote on the table of my heart, inspiring the love of freedom, and impelling me to seek it at every hazard, I obeyed; and, by the good hand of my God upon me, I walked out of the house of bondage. . . . You charge me with disobeying the *laws of men*. I utterly deny that those things which outrage all right are laws. To be real laws, they must be founded in equity."

In the aftermath of the Burns case, Abba's brother Samuel Joseph May and her uncle and cousin, Sam May and Sam Jr., helped organize a new secret society: the Anti-Man-Hunting League. It grew to eighty members in Boston and over four hundred across the state. Bronson joined in January 1855. Their plan: to kidnap any future slave hunters and slaveholders who came to Boston.

They developed an elaborate scheme for their kidnappings that they rehearsed repeatedly. It was simple: as soon as they learned that a slave hunter was staying in a local hotel, members of the league would take up every other available room. They would pretend to be there on business and would take care not to discuss the fugitive's case openly. When they spotted their quarry in the lobby, they would first try to negotiate a price for the fugitive's freedom. If that failed, a team of six

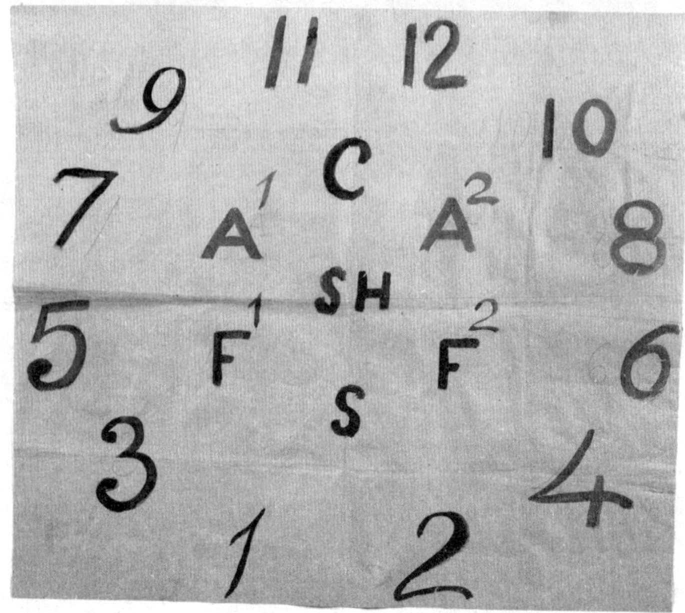

Diagram of the Anti-Man-Hunting League, showing how to abduct a slave hunter (SH) with men carrying his arms, legs, and head, led by a chief of the committee, surrounded by twelve men for protection.

men would seize him by the arms, legs, and head, wrestle him to the ground, and then carry him to a waiting carriage, with a second group of twelve men in a circle around them for protection. They would drive him out of town to a safe house. If need be, they would transfer him to multiple safe houses in something of a reverse Underground Railroad.

That Alcott would join an organization committed to kidnapping shows how far he had traveled from his earlier idealism. Back in the late 1830s he had joined a different organization: the New England Non-Resistance Society. Founded by William Lloyd Garrison, that society condemned the use of force even in self-defense, while seeking a peaceful end of slavery or, at least, disunion with the slave states. Now he endorsed the use of force.

The league members took turns playing the role of the resisting slave hunter. They kept coded records—the minutes of each meeting referred to members only by a unique number. Yet they never had the chance to try a real kidnapping. One member believed that the Burns affair and its national coverage frightened off all other would-be slave hunters.

The Burns case inspired Henry Thoreau to draft one of his greatest polemics. He interrupted his usual journal entries to write pages of outrage in May and June. On the Fourth of July, he spoke at an abolitionist gathering in South Framingham, along with Sojourner Truth and William Lloyd Garrison. Garrison opened the meeting by burning a copy of the Constitution.

Thoreau's lecture was titled "Slavery in Massachusetts." It would soon be printed in *The Liberator* (twice) and the *New-York Tribune*.

> The whole military force of the State is at the service of . . . a slaveholder from Virginia, to enable him to catch a man whom he calls his property; but not a soldier is offered to save a citizen of Massachusetts from being kidnapped! Is this what all these soldiers, all this *training* has been for these seventy-nine years past? Have they been trained merely to rob Mexico, and carry back fugitive slaves to their masters? . . .
>
> A government which deliberately enacts injustice, and persists in it, will at length ever become the laughing-stock of the world. . . .
>
> But it has been left to the courts of justice, so-called—to the Supreme Court of the land—and, as you all know, recognizing no authority but the Constitution, it has been decided that the three millions are, and shall continue to be, slaves. Such judges as these are merely the inspectors of a pick-lock and murderer's tools, to tell him whether they are in working order or not.

What should be done? Nothing less than dissolve the union:

"What should concern Massachusetts is . . . her own slaveholding and servility. Let the State dissolve her union with the slaveholder. She may wriggle and hesitate, and ask leave to read the Constitution once more; but she can find no respectable law or precedent which sanctions the continuance of such a Union for an instant." There were only a few times in Thoreau's life when he became so exercised about a political issue that he stopped his nature journaling and instead devoted pages to drafts of polemical speeches. When he did so, his writing was as sharp and powerful as anyone's.

The Concord radicals had a new purpose. The youngest of them, Louisa May Alcott, was fired up. Yet she first had to fight her own circumstances before she could join a larger struggle.

15

The Trials of Louisa May

> Being willful, I said, "I won't teach, and I can write, and I'll prove it."
> —Louisa May Alcott, 1862 journal entry

Louisa was at war with the world, and with poverty.

It was not easy to be a daughter of Bronson Alcott. When she was young, the family moved constantly as he cycled through teaching jobs, followed by the Fruitlands failure. When she was a teenager, after a few happy years in Concord, she faced more moves and precious little income. Abba had to take any employment she could, and bring in boarders. In 1848, after three years in Concord, Abba applied to be a matron at a new "idiot asylum" in South Boston, but she didn't get the job. She blamed the rejection on prejudice against Bronson.

A group of Abba's friends contributed $30 per month for her to run a mission for the poor in Boston, making her one of the first full-time social workers in the city. The family left Concord and returned to Boston. There, Bronson hosted a series of conversations—Elizabeth Peabody sold tickets at her West Street bookstore—that proved a modest success. His topic was "Man: His History, Resources, and Expectations." He would host seven more series over the next four years.

The family struggled with poverty. They could only afford a basement apartment, three rooms plus a kitchen, in a cheerless neighborhood—the first of three successive apartments, each one worse than the last. Abba took it hard, but Bronson kept faith in his righteousness. In April 1850, he described "Further talk with my desponding wife on family affairs. Embarrassed on every side, with no possible means of relief. . . . It is a small matter, this of sympathy, support, and success, as far as I am concerned, since time and purpose overtake and avail themselves of the solitary and so-called visionary thinker's ideas at last, to compensate him for long neglect."

The older girls did what they could to help. Anna taught a group of twenty girls before moving to Lenox to serve as a governess; Louisa, age seventeen, took over Anna's class. Louisa wrote that it is "hard to be cheerful when I think how poor we are, how much worry it is to live, and how many things I long to do I never can. . . . I'm so tired I don't want to live, only it's cowardly to die till you have done something."

In 1851 both girls started work as governesses. Lizzie became a housekeeper. Louisa commented that they were "poor as rats." When a well-to-do lawyer came to Abba's mission seeking live-in help for his invalid sister, Louisa volunteered.

It was not what she hoped. In her journal, she wrote only this: "I go to Dedham as a servant & try it for a month, but get starved & frozen & give it up."

"How I Went Out to Service," a story she wrote at the time but did not publish for many years, recounts her seven weeks in James Richardson's home. It has been accepted by some biographers as factual, though Louisa embellished the truth for the sake of the narrative. The tale is grim. Richardson's sister, Louisa's supposed responsibility, was "a very nervous little woman, with a small button of pale hair on the outside of her head and the vaguest notions of work inside." She had no apparent interest in Louisa—but her brother did. He talked endlessly, presented her with a rose, and secretly stared at her. Once, when she caught him and tried to exit the room, he held her back, saying, "It refreshes my eye to see something tasteful, young, and womanly about me." In the evenings, he insisted she listen to him read from his writings. They struck her as "rubbish."

She tried to avoid him. He left notes under her door. When she confronted him, protesting that she had been hired to care for his sister and not to listen to his monologues, he retaliated by giving her menial tasks. She quit. In the story, when the Louisa character opens an envelope with her wages and discovers only $4, she and her outraged parents mail the money back to him—a gesture that in reality they could not afford.

She amused herself in two ways during these years of intense penury: acting in family plays, which she wrote, and writing poems and stories. She and Anna loved to act, and as fans of *Little Women* know, they could be creative with improvised costumes. A few of Louisa's plays survive, with such romantic titles as *Captive of Castile; or, The Moorish Maiden's Vow* and *Norna; or, The Witch's Curse*. They are pure escapism and quite fun, with lines such as " 'Tis my lord returning from the court. Fly, Louis, fly! Thou are lost if he discover thee." Louisa liked to play the male leads while Anna played the maidens.

Louisa also wrote stories in several genres. Her first publication was a poem titled "Sunlight," in 1851; her second was a short story, "The Rival Painters: A Tale of Rome," published anonymously in 1852 in the *Boston Olive Branch*. As she recorded in her journal, "My first story was printed, and $5 was paid for it. It was written in Concord when I was sixteen. Great rubbish!"

She had also written children's stories for Ellen Tucker Emerson when they were Concord neighbors. Those stories became her first published book, *Flower Fables*, in 1855, full of faeries and elves.

"How I Went Out to Service" bears the seeds of her eventual success with autobiographical fiction. She had a great eye for details and satisfying endings. Even in her journal, in 1854, she embellished a story about Bronson and Abba. It concerned Bronson's return from a conversation tour out West:

> In February Father came home. Paid his way, but no more. A dramatic scene when he arrived in the night. We were waked by hearing the bell. Mother flew down, crying "My husband!" We rushed after,

> and five white figures embraced the half-frozen wanderer who came in hungry, tired, cold, and disappointed, but smiling bravely and as serene as ever. We fed and warmed and brooded over him, longing to ask if he had made any money, but no one did till little May said, after he had told all the pleasant things, "Well, did people pay you?" Then, with a queer look, he opened his pocket-book and showed one dollar, saying with a smile that made our eyes fill, "Only that! My overcoat was stolen, and I had to buy a shawl. Many promises were not kept, and travelling is costly, but I have opened the way, and another year shall do better."
>
> I shall never forget how beautifully Mother answered him, though the dear, hopeful soul had built much on his success, but with a beaming face she kissed him, saying, "I call that doing *very well.* Since you are safely home, dear, we don't ask anything more."

He actually had sent $180 home from the road, and his oldest daughter, Anna, accompanied him on the final journey home—but it's a good story.

The 1850s were full of hard work and paltry rewards for Louisa. She tried to sell another set of children's stories titled *Christmas Elves*, but publishers declined it. She moved to Boston and started selling stories to the *Saturday Evening Gazette*. She wrote a play that generated some interest at one theater, but it was never produced. She took on sewing and teaching jobs. In her journal, she recorded her income for the winter of 1855: $50 from teaching, $50 from sewing, $20 from her stories.

In 1856 the *Gazette* published seven of her stories for $10 each, with three more the following year. Some were sensational, some sentimental, some realistic, and some domestic. She had not settled into her mature style; she was testing several genres. It proved to be valuable experience. It was also a hard lesson in economics. Years later, she would offer advice to aspiring writers, in a column in the *Saturday Evening Gazette*:

38

Louisa May Alcott, age twenty-six.

> Now that women have made a place for themselves in journalism and literature, it is wise for them to cultivate, not only their intellectual faculties, but their practical ones also and understand the business details of their craft. The ignorance and helplessness of women writers is amazing, and only disastrous experience teaches them what they should have learned before.

After the family moved to Walpole, New Hampshire, both Lizzie and May came down with scarlet fever. May recovered quickly, Lizzie did not. Louisa returned home from Boston and found her sister seriously ill. Louisa nursed her for months and took over the housework, still managing to write stories in her scant spare time. Lizzie did not succumb to the disease that year, but she was weakened by it and would not live much longer.

In 1857 the family moved back to Concord again, and soon after, into the home that would be their anchor for two decades. It was next

39

Orchard House, the Alcotts' long-lasting Concord home, which Louisa called "Apple Slump."

door to their former home, now Hawthorne's, in Concord. The property included an apple orchard that Bronson loved. He christened their new home "Orchard House." Louisa called it "Apple Slump."

She continued to divide her time between Boston and this new home, while writing stories and dreaming of success. After reading a biography of Charlotte Bronte, she wrote, "Wonder if I shall ever be famous enough for people to care to read my story and struggles. I can't be a C.B., but I may do a little something yet."

The next year brought her to the edge of despair. In January she noted that "Lizzie much worse, Dr. G. says there is no hope . . . I pray she may go soon." Louisa described the end, two months later:

> A curious thing happened, and I will tell it here, for Dr. G said it was a fact. A few moments after the last breath came, as Mother and I sat silently watching the shadow fall on the dear little face, I saw a light

mist rise up from the body, and float up and vanish in the air. Mother's eyes followed mine, and when I said, 'What did you see?' she described the same light mist. Dr. G said it was the life departing visibly.

Emerson and Thoreau were among the pallbearers at Lizzie's funeral. Louisa wrote that she no longer feared death. It seemed "friendly and wonderful."

Soon after Lizzie died, Anna became engaged to John Pratt. To Louisa, it was almost like losing a second sister. She returned that fall to Boston to take on more work, noting that she was the family's sole breadwinner. She hit her nadir in October. She even contemplated suicide. She walked to Boston's Mill Dam and stared at the water below. As she described it to her family, "My courage almost gave out, for every one was so busy, & cared so little whether I got work or jumped into the river that I thought seriously of doing the latter. . . . But it seemed so mean to turn & run away before the battle was over that I went home, set my teeth & vowed I'd *make* things work in spite of the world, the flesh & the devil."

For many years she would work on a semiautobiographical novel eventually published as *Work: A Story of Experience*. The protagonist, Christie Devon, is an orphan who leaves the home of her aunt and uncle to try a series of occupations: from housekeeper, to actress, to governess, to private nurse, to seamstress. Falling into debt and battling illness, she reaches a low point:

> The world looked very dark to her, life seemed an utter failure, God a delusion, and the long, lonely years before her too hard to be endured. . . . A flight of steps close by led to a lumber wharf, and, scarcely knowing why, she went down there, with a vague desire to sit still somewhere. . . . She knew it was no place for her, yet no one waited for her, no one would care if she staid [*sic*] for ever, and, yielding to the perilous fascination that drew her there, she lingered with a heavy throbbing in her temples, and a troop of wild fancies

> whirling through her brain . . . she began to wonder how a human body would look floating through the night.

There is reason to believe that Louisa was describing her own feelings at the Mill Dam in 1858. In an 1873 letter responding to five sisters who had commented on this scene in the novel, she wrote, "*I* did not like the suicide in 'Work,' but as much of that chapter was true I let it stand as a warning to several people who need it to my knowledge, & to many whom I do not know. I have already had letters from strangers thanking me for it, so I am not sorry it went in. One must have both the dark & the light side to paint life truly."

In the late 1850s and early 1860s Louisa sold many stories—some quite lurid—to a variety of newspapers and magazines, under pseudonyms or anonymously. Just as Walt Whitman had done, she tried melodramas and "blood and thunder" thrillers, along with romances. She wrote more than twice as many of them as Whitman did, including several novels.

Because she used a variety of pseudonyms, or no name at all, scholars have worked for decades to follow her footsteps and locate her stories. Even recently, new candidates have been proposed for the list. Her journals mention some that have not yet been found. All in all, she built a substantial body of work. None of it made her wealthy.

She had a partial breakthrough in 1860 when *The Atlantic Monthly* accepted two of her stories and published them under her own name: "Love and Self Love," a tragic romance in the vein of Jane Austen, and "A Modern Cinderella: or The Little Old Shoe." The latter exhibits her trademark humor, and pokes fun at her famous Concord neighbor. One of the Cinderella character's sisters plunges into a period of nonstop reading of Carlyle, Goethe, and Schiller. "A mild attack of Emerson followed, during which she was lost in a fog, and her sisters rejoiced inwardly when she emerged."

She exulted when she sold "Love and Self Love," writing that "my fifty dollars will be very happy money . . . Success has gone to my head . . . Twenty-seven years old, and very happy."

When seized with inspiration she disappeared into what she called a "vortex" of manic productivity. In 1860 she began working on *Moods*, a novel for adults that would turn into a years-long project, with two published versions. As she worked, "Genius burned so fiercely that for four weeks I wrote all day and planned nearly all night, being quite possessed by my work." In February 1861 she worked on a second draft in another frenzy. Her mother brought tea up to her attic writing space and worried that Louisa wasn't eating enough. Finally, she had to stop: "my head was dizzy, my legs shaky, and no sleep would come."

When she read the new draft aloud to the family, Bronson asked, "Where did you get your metaphysics?" He always preferred philosophy to literature, never having much use even for Shakespeare. By now he had a small but steady income, as superintendent of Concord's schools, for $100 per year. It was his first opportunity to teach in two decades, and he worked hard at it for six years.

Despite her first publications in *The Atlantic Monthly*, that magazine was not easy for her to crack. She had more success with popular outlets that didn't pay as well. By 1862 she went back to teaching a group of girls, sponsored by *The Atlantic*'s editor, James T. Fields. In February she wrote that she was "very tired of this wandering life and distasteful work, but kept my word and tugged on."

She showed some of her work to Fields, including "How I Went Out to Service." He rejected it, saying, "Stick to your teaching; you can't write." (Years later, he would acknowledge the error.) In the summer, when she sold two stories to the editor of *Frank Leslie's Illustrated Newspaper*, she received a more encouraging response. As she wrote, "Mr. L. says my tales are so 'dramatic, vivid, and full of plot,' they are just what he wants."

Her genre experience taught her a great deal about the craft of writing. Later, in a letter written to an aspiring writer, she advised, "Mind grammar, spelling, and punctuation, use short words, and express as briefly as you can your meaning. Young people use too many adjectives to try to 'write fine.' The strongest, simplest words are best, and no *foreign* ones if it can be helped."

If only Bronson had learned that lesson. In a P.S. she added, "The lines you send me are better than many I see, but boys of nineteen cannot know much about hearts, and had better write of things they understand. Sentiment is apt to become sentimentality, and sense is always safer, as well as better drill, for young fancies and feelings. Read Ralph Waldo Emerson, and see what good prose is, and some of the best poetry we have."

She would soon gain a very different kind of experience, full of tragedy. In the fall of 1859, she had witnessed a state encampment of soldiers in Concord and commented, "I like a camp, and long for a war, to see how it all seems. I can't fight, but I can nurse." When the Civil War began in 1861, she spent many hours sewing uniforms for the Union troops. The early war news was bad for the Union, and she wished she could do more, writing, "I like the stir in the air, and long for battle like a warhorse when he smells powder. The blood of the Mays is up!" Finally, in late 1862, when she turned thirty and became eligible, she signed up for a three-month stint as a nurse.

Before she left, she entered a story in a contest sponsored by Frank Leslie for his illustrated newspaper. The winner would be published there and receive $100, a sum greater than any she had yet received for a story. She couldn't resist the challenge.

16

War, Part II

> A man of rare common-sense and directness of speech, as of action; a transcendentalist above all, a man of ideas and principles,—that was what distinguished [John Brown].
>
> —Henry David Thoreau, "A Plea for Captain John Brown"

The Civil War began with a dress rehearsal, in the 1850s. It would end in 1865 with two of Emerson's famous neighbors no longer alive. Emerson would be at the start of a long mental decline. The war would also leave a permanent stamp on the health and lives of Louisa May Alcott and Walt Whitman. Of the Emerson circle, only Bronson Alcott would sail through it with his Transcendentalism and health intact.

The rehearsal was sparked by yet another congressional compromise: the Kansas–Nebraska Act of 1854. The act created two new territories that would make their own decisions about the legality of slavery, based on popular vote. The result was a classic case of unintended consequences. In May 1854, when the act passed, fewer than eight hundred white settlers lived in Kansas. Nine months later there were over eight thousand, half of whom were from Missouri, a slave state. The Missourians did not want a free territory on their border. Conversely, abolitionists from the East raised funds and urged their followers to move westward to swell the antislavery population in Kansas. That act was even less successful than any of Congress's attempts to forestall a crisis.

In November 1854 Kansas voted to choose a delegate to Congress, and a proslavery candidate won easily. Not only were proslavery settlers in the majority, but so-called border ruffians flooded in from Missouri to stuff ballot boxes. In March 1855, when Kansas voted to create a legislature, it happened again.

Free-soilers, who wanted to ban slavery in the territory, disputed the Kansas elections. Soon the territory divided into two camps, with two capitals, two constitutions, and militias conducting raids, battles, and murders. There were dozens of political killings between 1854 and 1859.

"Bleeding Kansas" made headlines and spurred activists across the country. In 1856 a Boston publisher issued *The Reign of Terror in Kanzas* [*sic*], a collection of firsthand reports and secondhand anecdotes of murder, tarring-and-feathering, scalping, and pitched gun battles. Emerson obtained a copy. Kansas Committees sprang up throughout the North, raising money and sending Sharps rifles to the free-soilers. The famous New York preacher Henry Ward Beecher helped raise some of that money, stating that the rifles would have more moral power "than in a hundred Bibles." Sharps rifles became known as "Beecher Bibles."

Antislavery settlers swarmed into Kansas from Massachusetts and Ohio. Eventually, they would outnumber proslavery Kansans. In the short term, they faced significant armed resistance. The Massachusetts (later New England) Emigrant Aid Company increased its efforts to reinforce and support them.

In Concord, Ellen Tucker Emerson reported that the organization raised $1,360 in May 1856, and that the women and girls of the town were sewing clothing and raising more money for Kansas Territory abolitionists. Her father gave a speech in September before a Cambridge relief meeting: "We hear the screams of hunted wives and children answered by the howl of the butchers. . . . In the free states, we give a snivelling [*sic*] support to slavery. The judges give cowardly interpretations to the law, in direct opposition to the known foundation of all law, that *every immoral statute is void*." He called for a new "revolution of the nineteenth century" that would be more difficult than the first American Revolution.

Others went beyond rhetoric to direct action. Thomas Wentworth Higginson became "the first transcendentalist in arms" when he went to Kansas in 1856 and was commissioned as a general in the Kansas Army. He described it as "precisely like waking up some morning and stepping out on the Battle of Bunker Hill."

The most controversial man who took up arms became a cause célèbre for the Emerson circle: John Brown.

Brown was born and raised in Connecticut and Ohio by strict Calvinist and abolitionist parents. His father operated a tannery, where Brown learned that trade. He initially wanted to become a clergyman, studying at seminaries in Massachusetts and Connecticut, until he ran out of money and suffered eyesight problems, and returned to Ohio in 1817. He set up his own tannery and worked hard at it. Three years later he married and started a family. Soon he had three sons, and he ruled his home "with a rod in one hand and the Bible in the other." Brown would eventually have twenty children by two wives.

Business failures and multiple moves marked his early career. In 1826 the family moved to the Pennsylvania wilderness. John launched

John Brown, 1857.

and built a new tannery while also establishing a post office and opening the township of Richmond's first school. He occasionally preached at the Calvinist Congregational Society, which he had organized. Like his father, he opposed slavery.

In 1835, he and the family moved back to Ohio so he could form a tanning partnership with a wealthy local businessman in the eastern part of the state, not far from his father's tannery in Hudson. That project fell through. Brown tried real estate next, convincing some local citizens to form the Franklin Land Company, borrowing heavily, and speculating in land purchases all around the township.

The Panic of 1837 crushed those plans. His creditors foreclosed on their loans. They dragged him into court over repayments he could not afford. By 1842 he was bankrupt.

He would never really succeed as a businessman, and he would continue to face lawsuits by future partners and customers. In some ways, he was a Calvinist Bronson Alcott. He failed at multiple ventures. He was obsessed with religion the way Alcott was obsessed with transcendentalism. They were both ardent abolitionists. Apart from Christianity, however, they differed in one other core belief: Brown was the rare antebellum white person who believed Blacks to be fully equal to whites.

At some point he hatched the idea that slavery would never be eradicated unless Northerners crossed into the South and encouraged a slave rebellion. It was hardly a new idea, though previous revolts had been led by free or enslaved Blacks rather than would-be white saviors. Slave rebellions had struck terror into Southerners for decades: Gabriel Prosser planned a rebellion in Virginia in 1800 before the authorities discovered his plans, and twenty-six men were executed. The German Coast uprising in Louisiana in 1811 involved some five hundred insurgent slaves. Denmark Vesey was convicted and executed for planning a massive revolt in South Carolina in 1822—a conspiracy that is still debated by historians, but at the time inspired the city of Charleston to construct an arsenal to defend against future uprisings. Nat Turner's rebellion in Virginia in 1831 succeeded in killing dozens of people, until whites violently suppressed him and his followers. Fifty-six were executed.

It was also not new for Brown himself to advocate violence. In 1851 in Springfield, Massachusetts, he had convened a meeting of forty-four Blacks, some of whom were fugitives passing through the city. He urged them to arm themselves, to learn how to use their weapons, and to be ready to attack any slave catcher who might come after them. His plan: They would swiftly kill anyone who posed a threat and then retreat to the homes of white supporters. He called his new organization the League of Gileadites, after the biblical Mount Gilead, where Gideon led the Israelites to freedom.

Perhaps it was inevitable that such a man would be swept up in the Kansas crisis. In 1855 five of Brown's sons moved into the eastern part of the territory. John Jr. wrote to him about the border ruffians who were organizing into "Annoyance Associations" to terrorize free-state settlements. They were armed and receiving men and money from supporters in the South. John Jr. told his father that he and his brothers were prepared to fight, but they needed weapons.

Brown traveled to Ohio and Illinois on his way to join his sons, soliciting money and weapons and loading everything into a small wagon for the final journey to his sons' settlement in Osawatomie, Kansas, near Pottawatomie Creek. He arrived in October 1855.

That fall, as violent skirmishes broke out in Lawrence, a force of over two thousand Missourians and Kansas militia prepared to burn that abolitionist town. Brown and four of his sons drove a wagon full of weapons to Lawrence, where they found armed settlers drilling and erecting earthworks. On the spot, local authorities commissioned John Brown as a captain in the First Brigade of Kansas Volunteers.

The Lawrence siege ended with a peaceful negotiation. The Missourians retreated across the border. Brown considered it a major victory—but the territory's war was just beginning. In January, after Kansas voted for an abolitionist legislature and a governor amid yet more violence at the polls, the federal government stepped in. President Franklin Pierce had already appointed a proslavery governor, and

Pierce did not accept the abolitionists' choice. He jailed him. Pierce spoke to Congress to denounce the free-staters as treasonous.

Pierce's position outraged Emerson's friends. Only Hawthorne continued to stand by his college friend.

New wagon trains began rolling in from free states. In April, fearing an invasion from Missouri, a group of free-staters organized the Pottawatomie Rifles as a defense company. They elected John Jr. as captain. His brother Jason joined as a member.

In May, a proslavery judge charged a grand jury to indict the entire Free State government in Topeka for treason. A proslavery armed mob overran Lawrence, destroying the printing presses and offices of two Free State newspapers, along with the Free State Hotel. To Brown, it appeared as if a full-scale war had been launched.

Three days later, Brown led four of his sons and two other men to an encampment on Pottawatomie Creek, near three homes of militant proslavery men. Late in the evening they called on the first of them, James Doyle. They ordered Doyle and his two adult sons to go with them as prisoners. Outside, Brown's sons Owen and Frederick stabbed and hacked them to death. Brown fired one shot into Doyle's head.

They proceeded to Allen Wilkinson's home, ordering him outside and slashing him to death. Across the river, after midnight, they entered the home of James Harris, who had three houseguests. After interrogating Harris and two of his guests, they took William Sherman outside and hacked him to death.

The news of the Pottawatomie massacre spread. On May 31, Greeley's *Tribune* noted a letter in *The St. Louis Republican* about "eight" proslavery settlers killed. Brown's name was not mentioned, and Greeley's item ran under a skeptical headline about "Pro-Slavery Falsehoods." On June 3, the paper ran a brief correction to confirm the truth of the massacre, noting that the "victims were most horribly mutilated. In some instances after their throats had been cut, their legs and arms had been chopped off and their eyes gouged out." Yet Brown's name went unmentioned, and the *Tribune* and other abolitionist papers generally buried the story amid accounts of proslavery violence, both factual and invented.

Still, a report to Congress that summer identified Brown as the likely leader, and a warrant was issued for his arrest. A major question still lingers: Did Emerson and his friends know about the massacre?

Franklin Sanborn, a Concord schoolmaster and a staunch abolitionist, became one of Brown's key supporters. Sanborn had traveled to Kansas and returned to report on the horrors. In the winter of 1857 he took a leave to work full-time as the secretary of the Massachusetts State Kansas Committee. In early January 1857, he met Brown for the first time at his Boston office.

Sanborn would later write that Brown's "fame was wonderfully increased by the bloody deed of Pottawatomie, which rumor instantly ascribed to him." Yet when he brought the massacres up in conversation, Brown denied any involvement, and Sanborn chose to believe him. Meanwhile, the Northern press was paying far more attention to the dramatic caning of Senator Charles Sumner by Representative Preston Brooks, in the Senate, on May 22, 1856, so its coverage of the massacre was scant.

Neither Emerson nor Thoreau ever wrote specifically about Brown's massacre, and many scholars have assumed that they were unaware of it. But this ignorance seems unlikely, given the story's sensationalism. It seems more likely that the Concord Transcendentalists were abandoning their long-held opposition to capital punishment amid the crisis over slavery.

Brown's deeds after Pottawatomie were more defensible. Southeastern Kansas had erupted in guerilla warfare, with Brown leading his armed band in gun battles. On June 2 his men defeated a Missouri militia at the Battle of Black Jack. At the end of August he was defeated by a much larger Missouri militia, but escaped capture. With federal troops seeking to arrest him, he decided to head east to try to raise funds.

To many, Brown was a hero—a freedom fighter who knew that slavery could only be ended with bloodshed. Firebrand abolitionist Wendell Phillips would declare in 1859 that "John Brown of Osawatomie . . . makes the whole crystallize into right and wrong, and marshal themselves on one side or the other."

• • •

As a sign of just how far the Transcendentalists had evolved from the Over-Soul to realpolitik, Brown's strongest supporters included Emerson, Thoreau, and Alcott. Sanborn first introduced Brown to them. Sanborn's eventual attitude about the massacre, written long after the fact, was telling: "Such a deed must not be judged by the every-day rules of conduct. . . . The cause here was a public one; the crisis was momentous, and yet invisible to all but the eyes divinely appointed to see it and to foresee its consequences." The end justified the means.

When Sanborn met Brown for the first time, Brown explained that he wanted to raise $30,000 and obtain two hundred Sharps rifles to supply home guard units in Kansas. Sanborn agreed to help. He introduced Brown to Theodore Parker, the prominent Boston Unitarian and abolitionist, who in turn connected Brown with William Lloyd Garrison. Soon, Brown met with most of the leading abolitionists in Boston. The National Kansas Committee agreed to give him one hundred rifles and some funding. In February 1857 Brown appeared before the Massachusetts legislature to appeal for additional funds, although none were forthcoming. He began giving speeches throughout New England and New York.

Emerson heard him speak in February. He wrote that Brown "gave a good account of himself" and that "the first man who went into Kansas from Missouri to interfere in the elections . . . 'had a perfect right to be shot.'" In March Sanborn brought Brown to Concord, taking him to Thoreau's house for lunch. Emerson dropped by and stayed for much of the afternoon. Thoreau and Emerson each invited Brown to spend a night with them. That night Brown spoke at a town meeting, arguing that the border ruffians "had a perfect right to be hung," as Thoreau remembered.

For the rest of 1857 and 1858, Brown continued to travel, raise money, and hint at a new, bold plan: to take a few dozen armed men into Virginia to generate a slave rebellion. He continued to lead abolitionist militias in Kansas. In December 1858 he raided the homes of two planters in Missouri and liberated eleven slaves. In January 1859 he led them past an ambush to freedom. Yet Kansas was quieting. The free-staters had prevailed, and their constitution would soon be adopted.

Brown beseeched his six closest Boston supporters, including Sanborn, for money to support "BY FAR the most *important* undertaking of my whole life." Those men would become known as the "Secret Six."

In May 1859 he came again to Concord and gave a talk. Alcott, Emerson, and Thoreau attended. To Alcott, Brown spoke "with surpassing simplicity and sense, impressing us all deeply by his courage and religious earnestness . . . an idealist in thought and affairs of state." Sanborn likely knew of Brown's plans, but to Alcott and many others, Brown was evasive.

On October 16 Brown finally launched his grand scheme: He led sixteen white and five Black men in a raid on the federal armory at Harpers Ferry, Virginia. They seized it and took a number of hostages. He hoped it would trigger a slave revolt; it did not. Instead, a combination of military companies and later US Marines under the command of Robert E. Lee defeated Brown. Ten of Brown's men were killed. Seven, including Brown, were captured. Only five escaped.

Aside from Sanborn and the other members of the Secret Six, few knew of Brown's plans. One who did was Frederick Douglass, a supporter who had hosted "Old Brown" on multiple occasions in his Rochester home. There, Brown had drafted a "provisional constitution" for an interim Virginia government, in case his invasion succeeded. Douglass noted that Brown was obsessed with the document, "till I confess it began to be something of a bore to me."

Yet Douglass did not support the raid. He saw it as suicidal. In late August, in Pennsylvania, he spent two days trying to dissuade Brown, telling him "Virginia would blow him and his hostages sky-high." Brown tried hard to persuade Douglass to join him, to no avail.

During the remaining six weeks of Brown's life, from his capture to his execution on December 2, he spoke to reporters and wrote hundreds of letters. He rejected proposals by Sanborn and others for a jailbreak, stating, "I am worth inconceivably more to *hang* than for any other purpose." Though many people considered him insane, he seemed to know what he was doing. To others, he was a saint, the two chief interpretations at the time.

In Concord, the Emerson circle was in the latter camp. Louisa wrote to a friend, "What are your ideas on the Harpers Ferry matter? If you are [like me] you are full of admiration for old Brow[n]'s courage & pity for his probable end. We are boiling over with excitement here for many of our people (anti Slavery I mean) are concerned in it." In a November lecture on courage in Boston, Emerson went so far as to say of Brown that his "martyrdom, if he shall suffer, will make the gallows as glorious as the cross." At least, that's how it was reported in the press. Some believe he said the gallows would be "glorious, like a cross."

On October 30 Thoreau delivered "A Plea for Captain John Brown" in Concord, a speech he would repeat in Boston to over 2,500 people, and again in Worcester. It would soon be printed in newspapers across the country. In his lifetime, it was his single most widely read essay. It was an eloquent defense of Brown's cause and looming martyrdom. He called Brown "a transcendentalist above all, a man of ideas and principles." He added, "No man in America has ever stood up so persistently and effectively for the dignity of human nature, knowing himself for a man, and the equal of any and all governments. In that sense he was the most American of us all."

On the hour and day of Brown's execution, church bells tolled throughout the North, churches held commemorative services and public prayers, and banks and businesses closed. In the town hall in Concord, Thoreau gave a variation on his plea, adding, "Some eighteen hundred years ago Christ was crucified; this morning, perchance, Captain Brown was hung. These are the two ends of a chain which is not without its links. He is not Old Brown any longer; he is an angel of light."

Yet even in Concord, some felt differently. That same day, local anti-abolitionists hung Brown in effigy. They left a mock "Last Will and Testament of Old John Brown" at the scene, naming six of Brown's

Concord supporters as his heirs, including Thoreau and Emerson: "I bequeath to H.D. Thoreau, Esq., my body and soul, he having eulogized my character and actions at Harper's Ferry above the Saints in Heaven. . . . I bequeath to Ralph Waldo Emerson all my personal property, and my executions cap, which contains nearly all the brains I ever had."

Thoreau was not quite done with the Brown affair. One of Brown's surviving followers, Francis Jackson Merriam, had returned to Boston from the safety of Canada when Brown was hanged. He wanted to plan a second raid, but Sanborn and a few others persuaded him to return to Canada by train. Sanborn found him to be out of his senses. Merriam took the wrong train, winding up in Concord, where he spent a night at Sanborn's house. Sanborn stayed away, for his own safety; Henry Thoreau guarded Merriam. Thoreau knew him only by the recurring alias "Lockwood." In the morning Thoreau borrowed Emerson's carriage to drive him to the railroad station in South Acton. He made it to Montreal.

Four months later, five federal marshals came to Franklin Sanborn's home and handcuffed him. They had orders to take him to Washington to answer questions before a hostile Senate committee. He resisted as best he could while his sister rushed around to neighboring houses to sound the alarm. He recalled what happened next:

> My hands were powerless, but as they approached the door I braced my feet against the posts and delayed them. I did the same at the posts of the veranda, and it was some minutes before they got me on the gravel walk at the foot of my stone steps. Meanwhile, the church bells were ringing a fire alarm, and the people were gathering by tens. At the stone posts of the gateway I checked their progress once more, and again, when the four rascals lifted to insert me, feet foremost, in their carriage (a covered hack with a driver on the box), I braced myself against the sides of the carriage door and broke them in.

When one of the marshals grabbed his feet, his sister yanked the man's beard so hard that he dropped them. A neighbor named Anne Whiting climbed up next to the driver "and assured him that she was going as far as he and his horses went." Her father beat on some of the marshals with his cane. Finally, the local deputy sheriff organized a posse of twenty men who manhandled Sanborn away from his captors, while twenty or thirty others pursued the marshals in their broken carriage all the way to Lexington. It wasn't just a matter of force; Sanborn's lawyer, John Shepard Keyes, quickly secured a writ of habeas corpus from a sympathetic Concord judge, Ebenezer Rockwood Hoar, to present to the marshals. The town lined up to support its fellow citizen.

Seven months later, Abraham Lincoln was elected to the presidency. It was the first time Bronson Alcott voted in a presidential election—finally, the philosopher fully engaged in politics. The Sanborn arrest and rescue may have played a part in the election. It made headlines "from Bangor to New Orleans" just three weeks before the Democratic Party's convention in April. There, the party split between Southern and Northern factions, with the Southerners appalled at Sanborn and other abolitionists who ascribed their "illegal behavior to a higher purpose." At a subsequent convention in June, when the two factions could not agree on a platform plank about protecting slavery, the Southerners walked out. Neither faction could seriously challenge Lincoln's campaign.

In December, South Carolina seceded from the Union, followed quickly by Mississippi, Florida, Alabama, Georgia, Louisiana, and Texas, all before Lincoln's March inauguration. When the South Carolina militia bombarded US troops at Fort Sumter in Charleston's harbor, in April 1861, the Civil War had arrived.

Emerson welcomed it with a speech: "We are wafted into a revolution which, though at first sight a calamity of the human race, finds all men in good heart, in courage, in a generosity of mutual and patriotic support. We have been very homeless, some of us, for some years past,—say since 1850; but now we have a country again." He later said that "it was God's doing, and is marvellous [*sic*] in our eyes."

• • •

Only two members of Emerson's circle would play a direct role in the war, both as nurses: Louisa May Alcott and Walt Whitman. Whitman, on the cusp of forty-two, was too old to serve in battle. His brother George was ten years younger, and he enlisted one week after the attack on Fort Sumter. Considering the casualty rates for Union troops throughout the conflict—some 360,000 killed in battle, or by disease, or as prisoners of war—George proved to be resilient. He fought in twenty-one engagements, including costly battles at the Second Battle of Bull Run, the Wilderness, Spotsylvania, Cold Harbor, Antietam, and Fredericksburg. He was lightly wounded only once. His letters home, and his wounding at the Battle of Fredericksburg, had a major impact on Walt.

A year and a half after Fort Sumter, Louisa wrote "War news bad" in her journal. It had been bad from the start, beginning with the Union's defeat at Manassas. One visitor to Concord wrote that "optimism had fled even from the home of Emerson . . . Thoreau, sadly out of health, was the only cheerful man in Concordia; he was in a state of exaltation about the moral regeneration of the nation."

By late 1862 the news was worse. Despite overwhelming superiority in numbers and industrial might, the Union's Army of the Potomac under General George McClellan had repeatedly lost to Robert E. Lee's Army of Northern Virginia. Lee had taken command on June 1, 1862. He fought seven battles over seven days at the end of the month, pushing McClellan's army into a retreat down the Virginia peninsula. In September, Lee invaded the North for the first time, culminating in the bloodiest day of battle in American history, at Antietam.

It was a tactical draw but, finally, a strategic win for the North. It ended Lee's plans north of Virginia, at least for a time. Yet when McClellan failed to pursue Lee's army after that battle, Lincoln lost confidence in his general and removed McClellan from command.

Nathaniel Hawthorne had visited Washington earlier in the year and written "Chiefly About War Matters, By a Peaceable Man" for *The*

Atlantic Monthly. He was no abolitionist, and he enjoyed being a contrarian to Emersonian radicals—or, for that matter, to readers of the magazine. In his essay he managed both to attack John Brown ("Nobody was ever more justly hanged") and to defend McClellan against accusations of "sloth, imbecility, cowardice, [and] treasonable purposes." He recognized that most Union soldiers liked their general. He agreed with them, based on just one meeting. He even wrote an insulting depiction of President Lincoln, with whom he also met. His horrified editor, James T. Fields, removed it. Hawthorne's final sentence suggested that it might be acceptable to separate North from South permanently. Ever the satirist, he then added a false editor's note: "We regret the innuendo in the concluding sentence. The war can never be allowed to terminate, except in the complete triumph of Northern principles."

Louisa turned thirty on November 29, 1862. Finally, she could serve as a nurse—Dorothea Dix, who oversaw the Union nursing program, insisted on the age minimum in order to keep young women away from the young soldiers. Louisa left on December 11 for what was intended as a three-month nursing stint at the Union Hotel Hospital in Georgetown. The whole family "broke down" at the moment of her departure, and as she hugged her mother she wondered if she would "ever see that dear old face again?" She spent the twelfth running around Boston, taking care of final errands. She reached Georgetown the next evening. "A solemn time, but I'm glad to live in it, and am sure it will do me good whether I come out alive or dead."

Her travel and first few days at the hospital coincided with one of the largest and deadliest battles of the war. McClellan's replacement, Ambrose E. Burnside, was a West Point graduate with mutton-chop facial hair and solid military experience. Burnside knew Lincoln wanted him to push the Army of the Potomac to Richmond, ahead of Lee, and to move with the speed that McClellan had never achieved. If his army could cross the Rappahannock River quickly, it could block Lee's approach to the Confederate capital.

In mid-November his army marched thirty-five miles in two days, reaching Falmouth, across the river from the port town of

Fredericksburg. Burnside had ordered pontoon bridges to be sent ahead of his troops, but the Washington bureaucracy bungled the request. The bridges didn't start arriving until November 25. Not until December 11 could engineers assemble them.

That three-week delay proved a fatal pause. It gave Lee time to bring his army together and fortify high positions around the town. George Whitman wrote to his mother on December 8, "I hardly think there will be a fight here at Fredericksburg, as we have orders to fix up our tents as though we were expected to stay here some time."

When Burnside attacked on December 11, he could take the lightly guarded town itself but he could not reach the higher-ground positions of the Confederates. For three days Burnside threw wave after wave of men against Lee's army. Each was repulsed. On December 15 Burnside admitted defeat and retreated. His army suffered over twelve thousand killed, wounded, or captured, more than double the Confederate numbers.

George Whitman was among the wounded. When Walt saw his name on a casualty list on December 16—not knowing that it was just a light scratch on the side of George's jaw—he rushed to Virginia to find his brother. He lost his wallet to a Philadelphia pickpocket en route.

At Louisa's hospital, just days after her arrival, the wounded began pouring in. She was about to experience the full horrors of Civil War medicine.

Amputees filled military hospitals in that era. No one understood the need for sterilization, so wounded limbs often became infected and were removed. Walt Whitman saw this firsthand when he spent three days trying to find his brother, starting at a field hospital near the battle. "Out doors, at the foot of a tree, within ten yards of the front of the house [hospital], I notice a heap of amputated feet, legs, arms, hands, &c., a full load for a one-horse cart." When he found George, he was relieved. Nevertheless, those days of hospital visits moved him profoundly. He relocated to Washington, obtained work with the government, and visited Washington hospitals nearly every day for the rest of the war.

41

Civil War hospital in Fredericksburg, Virginia.

Louisa's nursing stint was much briefer, yet it affected her profoundly. She lightly fictionalized it in *Hospital Sketches* and wrote several related short stories, touching on rape (by enslavers) and justifying violence (by the enslaved), among other topics. In her journal, she described a typical day:

> Up at six, dress by gas light, run through my ward & fling up the windows though the men grumble & shiver, but the air is bad enough to breed a pestilence & as no notice is taken of our frequent appeals for better ventilation I must do what I can. Poke up the fire, add blankets, joke, coax, & command, but continue to open doors & windows as if life depended on it, mine does, & doubtless many another. . . . I go to breakfast with what appetite I may. . . . Till noon I trot, trot, giving out rations, cutting up food for helpless "boys," washing faces, teaching my attendants how beds are made or floors swept, dressing

> wounds, taking Dr. Fitz Patrick's orders, (privately wishing all the time that he would be more gentle with my big babies), dusting tables, sewing bandages, keeping my tray tidy, rushing up & down after pillows, bed linen, sponges, books & directions, till it seems as if I would joyfully pay down all I possess for fifteen minutes' rest.

The afternoon was more of the same, along with writing letters for some of the men. Her shift finally ended at nine p.m.

One of the doctors, John Winslow, took her around the capital and out to dinner, apparently interested in a romantic relationship. She spurned his advances.

In *Hospital Sketches* she describes the aftermath of Fredericksburg. Forty ambulances arrived at the hospital, eighty beds were prepared and ready, and in came the wounded "so riddled with shot and shell, so torn and shattered, [they] have borne suffering for which we have no name, with an uncomplaining fortitude, which made one glad to cherish each as a brother." Many could not be saved. Her sketch includes one man named John whom every patient came to love and admire, as did she. He died in her arms.

In September 1862, Abraham Lincoln had signed the preliminary Emancipation Proclamation, announcing that on January 1, 1863 "all persons held as slaves within any State, or designated part of a State, the people whereof shall then be in rebellion against the United States, shall be then, thenceforward, and forever free." The proclamation was more symbolic than pragmatic. The Union could not enforce it since it only applied to the Confederacy. For some critics, it did not go far enough, leaving slavery alone in the border states. Some also complained that Lincoln had waited so long. The president had wanted it to follow a victory—the strategic win at Antietam—so it would not appear to be an act of desperation. Yet the symbolic importance of the proclamation was huge. And when the Union armies started winning battles and taking territory, it became more than just a symbol.

Emerson, for one, hailed the proclamation without qualification, writing an essay in *The Atlantic Monthly* that compared it to the Declaration of Independence: "these are acts of great scope, working on a long future, and on permanent interests, and honoring alike those who initiate and those who receive them. . . . Forget all that we thought shortcomings, every mistake, every delay . . . call these endurance, wisdom, magnanimity, illuminated, as they now are, by this dazzling success." As one historian notes, the essay marks his "complete conversion from the celestial politics of moral reform to the earthly politics of President Lincoln." Put another way, Emerson was embracing a prime example of the conclusion of his "Experience" essay, "the transformation of genius into practical power."

To the Black community, the proclamation was a torch of freedom. Louisa witnessed local Black citizens celebrating in the streets. In *Hospital Sketches* she describes waiting for New Year's Day "with more eagerness than I had ever known before, and though it brought me no gift, I felt rich in the act of justice so tardily performed toward some of those about me. As the bells rang midnight, I electrified my roommate by dancing out of bed, throwing up the window, and flapping my handkerchief with a feeble cheer in answer to the shout of a group of colored men in the street below."

In Boston, a Jubilee Concert was arranged to celebrate emancipation. Emerson participated by reciting a new poem, "Boston Hymn." He repeated it at a reception that evening. Julia Ward Howe also recited her "Battle Hymn of the Republic," set to the music of "John Brown's Body."

Louisa would not last much longer in Georgetown. She fell dangerously ill with typhoid pneumonia. She was confined to her room and treated with calomel. On January 8, Bronson described a lively letter from his "active, interested" daughter. Less than a week later the hospital sent a telegram informing the family that Louisa could not continue on the job. Bronson left Concord, reaching Georgetown on the morning of the sixteenth. It took several days before Louisa's doctors allowed her to travel. By the twenty-fourth, father and daughter were back in Concord.

Louisa remained feverish and suffering from hallucinations. In one, "I had married a stout, handsome Spaniard, dressed in black velvet with very soft hands & a voice that was continually saying, 'Lie still, my dear.' This was mother, I suspect." When she recovered from the delirium she learned she had almost died. Only after two months was she able to leave her room.

She would suffer bouts of illness for the rest of her life: headaches, rheumatism, musculoskeletal pain, and rashes. Several years after the war's end she wrote to her parents that a doctor told her that it stemmed from the treatments she had received at the hospital. Calomel contains mercury, and massive doses of it can cause serious problems to the nervous system. She believed this for the rest of her life.

Walt Whitman, too, suffered ill health during the war, including a bad infection after his arm was cut with a gangrene-exposed scalpel. He too was treated with calomel. After the war he faced recurring bouts of dizziness, eventually suffering a paralytic stroke. A few months before Louisa's letter to her parents, he wrote about his dizzy spells that "the doctor says it is all from that hospital malaria, hospital poison absorbed in the system years ago."

Health aside, both writers were enormously productive in the wake of their war service. Their war-inspired stories and poems achieved wide fame. Whitman published his *Drum Taps* poems after the war ended, and he wrote about his wartime years at great length in his prose. Louisa returned to the pages of *The Atlantic Monthly* with two stories in 1863, one set in a war hospital. Her *Hospital Sketches* became a successful book.

Both writers would achieve even greater success in the years ahead. But for most of the rest of the Emerson circle, the war marked the end of their major works. Two of them did not even survive it.

17

Death, Part II

It is time to be old,
To take in sail:—
The god of bounds,
Who sets to seas a shore,
Came to me in his fatal rounds,
And said: "No more!"

—Ralph Waldo Emerson, "Terminus"

In August 1860, Henry Thoreau invited Ellery Channing to take a trip to Mount Monadnock in New Hampshire, Thoreau's fourth visit to the mountain. They climbed to the summit in a rainstorm and found the spot where he had made camp two years earlier. Thoreau used his hatchet to build a "substantial" shelter out of scrub spruce. They dried themselves by a campfire and enjoyed being alone on the popular mountain. The next day would bring back its usual crowds.

They spent six days there. Thoreau noted that at least five hundred people reached the summit during that week, but not one discovered their camp. He rose at four o'clock every morning. He took extensive notes on the nature he observed. He mapped the summit, studied the bogs and river drainages, and sketched the clouds. He created one of the most thorough catalogs of the Monadnock biosphere ever recorded.

He was forty-three and brimming with energy. He soon plunged into a new writing project, pondering Darwin's theory and applying it to the evolution of seeds and plants. He wrote "The Succession of Forest Trees," a speech for the Middlesex Agricultural Society's gathering in Concord, in September. Greeley printed it in his *New-York Tribune* and became excited when Thoreau told him he planned to expand it into a book. How are seeds carried by wind, water, and animals? Why do hardwoods often replace a cut-down pine grove, only to be reconquered by pines over time? Henry had theories to offer and more work to do. He had already compiled many pages of "Notes on Fruits," and he may have been aiming for a broad natural history of Concord. It would have been his most scientific book of all, even as he continued to leaven empiricism with poetry.

On November 29 Bronson Alcott dropped by to plan the upcoming commemoration of John Brown's death. Alcott wasn't feeling well, and soon was bedridden with a fever, sore throat, and cough. Four days after their meeting, Thoreau also came down with a cold. Except it wasn't just a cold. He had climbed his last mountain.

Thoreau's family had a history of tuberculosis, the great scourge of that era. Families like his and Emerson's were said to be "consumptive." Henry's grandfather had died of the disease in 1801. His father's death in 1859 was consistent with its symptoms. His brother had it, though tetanus killed him before consumption could. Now Henry had it, too.

He continued to give talks despite a bad cough. He worked on the book he was now calling *The Dispersion of Seeds*. Curiously, after all he had written and spoken about John Brown a year earlier, his journals contain nothing about the election of Abraham Lincoln and little about the secession of Southern states. Only in one letter in early 1861 did he contemptuously repeat his desire for disunion: "A nation of 20 millions of freemen will be far more respectable & powerful, than if 10 millions of slaves & slave holders were added to them." Apparently, the individual action of John Brown was heroic and inspirational, while the collective politics of union and disunion were barely worth mentioning.

Illness forced him to spend time resting at home. Alcott, Channing, and Emerson visited. In the spring his doctor urged him to leave New England for purifying air elsewhere, anywhere that would be better for his lungs. He chose Minnesota, a popular destination for consumptives.

The journey to St. Anthony by train and riverboat took two weeks. He was accompanied by Horace Mann Jr., son of the famous educator and Mary Peabody Mann. They would only stay for a few weeks. Before returning to Concord, they traveled up the Minnesota River to a gathering of thousands of Sioux Indians (now known as Dakota). By June 11 they were home. The trip did nothing to improve Henry's condition.

He made it through one more winter. He knew the end was coming. In February he agreed to publish essays in *The Atlantic Monthly*, now under James T. Fields rather than the hated James Russell Lowell, with whom he had fought over a deleted sentence. His sister Sophia helped him approve each page, sometimes reading them aloud. "Autumnal Tints," "Higher Laws," "Life Without Principle," "Walking, or The Wild," and "Wild Apples" were published just before and then after he died on May 6. On May 4, Bronson Alcott stopped by and kissed his brow.

"Life Without Principle," in the October 1863 issue of the magazine, is a fitting final statement of his philosophy. He urged his readers to "Read not the Times. Read the Eternities." Even as the Civil War raged, he looked beyond it: "America is said to be the arena on which the battle of freedom is to be fought; but surely it cannot be freedom in a merely political sense that is meant. Even if we grant that the American has freed himself from a political tyrant, he is still the slave of an economical and moral tyrant."

In the months and years to come, much of his writing would be published for the first time, including the bulk of *Excursions*, *The Maine Woods*, *Cape Cod*, and *A Yankee in Canada*, thanks to careful curation by Sophia. The wide readership that had eluded Henry during his lifetime materialized, as Bronson Alcott predicted, over many decades.

His death brought great grief to Concord, even for those who might have agreed with neighbor Elizabeth Hoar, who once said, "I love Henry, but do not like him; and as for taking his arm, I should as soon take the arm of an elm tree."

Bronson Alcott planned the funeral at First Parish Church, basing it on the memorial for John Brown that Thoreau had organized a few years earlier. He ordered Concord's teachers to dismiss classes early that day. The church bell tolled forty-four times, for Thoreau's age, as the mourners processed inside and filled the pews. Henry lay in state, covered in wildflowers and boughs, some placed there by Louisa. As she commented, "A party of great people from Boston came up, the church was full & though he wasn't made much of while living, he was honored at his death."

Emerson gave the eulogy. It was a lengthy appreciation and one of the last extended original essays he was able to write. His mental faculties were declining.

42

THE

MAINE WOODS.

BY

HENRY D. THOREAU,

AUTHOR OF "A WEEK ON THE CONCORD AND MERRIMACK RIVERS," "WALDEN," "EXCURSIONS," ETC., ETC

BOSTON:

TICKNOR AND FIELDS.

1864.

Title page of *The Maine Woods*, published posthumously in 1864.

Emerson's speech would be published in *The Atlantic Monthly* in August 1862.

> He was a born protestant. He declined to give up his large ambition of knowledge and action for any narrow craft or profession, aiming at a much more comprehensive calling, the art of living well. . . . He was bred to no profession; he never married; he lived alone; he never went to church; he never voted; he refused to pay a tax to the State; he ate no flesh, drank no wine, he never knew the use of tobacco; and, though a naturalist, he used neither trap nor gun. . . . It cost him nothing to say No; indeed, he found it much easier than to say Yes. It seemed as if his first instinct on hearing a proposition was to controvert it, so impatient was he of the limitations of our daily thought.

In the course of his long speech Emerson touched on several criticisms: Thoreau wasn't a good poet; he could be hard to like; some of his prose is hard to understand; his virtues ran to extremes; he lacked ambition.

The attack on his friend's lack of ambition was especially harsh: "I so much regret the loss of his rare powers of action, that I cannot help counting it a fault in him that he had no ambition. Wanting this, instead of engineering for all America, he was the captain of a huckleberry-party." Louisa thought the speech good, but inappropriate to the occasion.

Thoreau, in his journals, had written a ready response to Emerson's criticism: "Better for me, says my genius, to go cranberrying . . . to get but a pocketful and learn its peculiar flavor, aye, and the flavor of Gowing's Swamp and of *life* in New England, than to go consul to Liverpool [like Hawthorne] and get I don't know how many thousand dollars for it, with no such flavor. Many of our days should be spent, not in vain expectations and lying on our oars, but in carrying out deliberately and faithfully the hundred little purposes which every man's genius must have suggested to him."

Emerson did capture many of Thoreau's signal qualities. "He knew the country like a fox or a bird, and passed through it as freely by paths of his own. . . . The depths of his perception found likeness of law throughout Nature, and I know not any genius who so swiftly inferred universal law from the single fact."

He had the good sense to finish the essay with some epigrams by its subject, including:

"The bluebird carries the sky on his back."

"The tanager flies through the green foliage
as if it would ignite the leaves."

Louisa wrote her own tribute in the form of a poem, "Thoreau's Flute." She wrote it in her notebook while working at the wartime hospital. She didn't plan to do anything with it. Bronson discovered it while she was recovering from typhoid fever. He showed it to Hawthorne, who sent it around to several friends, including James T. Fields. When Fields's wife wrote to Louisa with a gentle suggestion or two, she replied, "Poetry is not my forte & the lines were never meant to go beyond my scrap book." Yet on the spot, she came up with a revision to the line that Annie Fields had questioned. In September 1863, *The Atlantic Monthly* published "Thoreau's Flute":

We, sighing, said, "Our Pan is dead;
His pipe hangs mute beside the river;—
Around it wistful sunbeams quiver,
But Music's airy voice is fled.
Spring mourns as for untimely frost;
The bluebird chants a requiem;
The willow-blossom waits for him;—
The Genius of the wood is lost."

Then from the flute, untouched by hands,
There came a low, harmonious breath:

"For such as he there is no death;—
His life the eternal life commands;
Above man's aims his nature rose:
The wisdom of a just content
Made one small spot a continent,
And tuned to poetry Life's prose.

"Haunting the hills, the stream, the wild,
Swallow and aster, lake and pine,
To him grew human or divine,—
Fit mates for this large-hearted child.
Such homage Nature ne'er forgets,
And yearly on the coverlid
'Neath which her darling lieth hid
Will write his name in violets.

"To him no vain regrets belong,
Whose soul, that finer instrument,
Gave to the world no poor lament,
But wood-notes ever sweet and strong.
O lonely friend! he still will be
A potent presence, though unseen,—
Steadfast, sagacious, and serene:
Seek not for him,—he is with thee."

Walden, which had fallen out of print, was reprinted the year of Thoreau's death. It has never been out of print since. Its global impact has been enormous. It is one of the most widely translated of all American books. There are thirteen different versions in Japanese alone.

The other wartime loss to the Emerson circle inspired more ambivalent reactions among his neighbors. Nathaniel Hawthorne and his family had returned from their European travels in 1860, moving back into the Wayside, next to the Alcotts. Bronson would later describe his awkward neighbor: "During all the time he lived near me, our estates being separated only by a gate and shaded avenue, I seldom caught sight of him; and when I did it was but to lose it the moment he suspected he was visible; oftenest seen on his hill-top screened behind the shrubbery and disappearing like a hare into the bush when surprised."

Though Hawthorne rarely visited his neighbors, the families were on good terms. At one point, Hawthorne wrote light verse about Bronson to amuse the girls:

There dwelt a Sage at Apple-Slump
Whose dinner never made him plump.
Give him carrots, potatoes, squash, parsnips, and peas,
And some boiled macaroni, without any cheese,
And a plate of raw apples, to hold on his knees,
And a glass of sweet cider, to wash down all these,—
And he'd prate of the Spirit as long as you'd please.
This airy Sage of Apple-Slump.

Hawthorne continued to write. His final complete novel, *The Marble Faun*, was published in 1860. He took frequent walks and received occasional visits from James T. Fields. He told Fields about his plan for *The Dolliver Romance*, which the publisher thought "would have been the greatest of his books." Hawthorne managed to write three chapters, but he couldn't finish it. He edited some of his English notebooks into *Our Old Home* (1863), but he was no longer capable of new, original work.

He dedicated *Our Old Home* to Franklin Pierce, though Pierce's reputation was in tatters after the Bleeding Kansas crisis. Fields tried to talk him out of the dedication ("To Franklin Pierce, as a slight memorial of a college friendship, prolonged through manhood, and retaining all its vitality in our autumnal years"). So did Hawthorne's sister-in-law, Elizabeth Peabody, much to his irritation. The book sold well. Emerson cut the dedication out of his copy.

Hawthorne's health deteriorated through 1863 and into early 1864. He managed to take a short trip with William Ticknor, Fields's partner, but Ticknor was also in poor health. When they reached Philadelphia, Ticknor died in his hotel bed, shaking Hawthorne. When he returned to Concord Sophia found him "so haggard, so white, so deeply scored with pain and fatigue was the face, so much more ill than I ever saw him before."

In May 1864 Franklin Pierce visited and found Hawthorne ailing badly. Pierce proposed a carriage trip to New Hampshire in hopes that it might revive his friend. They left on May 12. Six days later, in Plymouth, they took adjoining hotel rooms. They left the connecting door open, and Pierce checked on his friend soon after midnight. Hawthorne was sleeping peacefully. Two hours later, Pierce woke and checked again. Hawthorne was dead.

At the funeral in Concord on May 23, Fields placed the unfinished manuscript of *The Dolliver Romance* on Hawthorne's coffin. Emerson and Alcott were among the pallbearers. Prominent attendees included Ellery Channing, Henry Wadsworth Longfellow, Oliver Wendell Holmes, John Greenleaf Whittier, and James Russell Lowell. And, of course, Franklin Pierce.

The Emerson circle held complicated feelings about their neighbor. Louisa wrote that he was "a beautiful soul in prison, trying to reach his fellow beings through the bars." Emerson wrote in his journal of "the painful solitude of the man, which, I suppose, could not longer be endured, and he died of it. . . . I thought him a greater man than any of his works betray." He recalled past conversations and the long trek they once took to visit the Shaker community in Harvard, Massachusetts, wishing that they could have developed a better friendship.

Emerson would continue to give lectures and write in his journals, but his mind and energy declined. The Concord torch now passed to the circle's youngest member.

18

A Child Shall Lead

> My dear—dearest Miss Alcott! At such a juncture! You got my letter? No? No matter! Nothing to parallel it has occurred in my experience! All else put aside—street blocked—country aroused—overwhelmed—paralyzed! *Uncle Tom's Cabin* backed off the stage! Two thousand more copies ordered this very day from Chicago alone! But that's a fleabite—tens of thousands—why, dearest girl, it's the triumph of the century!
>
> —Thomas Niles, publisher of *Little Women*, to Louisa May Alcott when she arrived at his office (according to Julian Hawthorne).

When Louisa May recovered from typhoid fever in 1863, she returned to her writing desk. Health problems would plague her for the rest of her life. Yet the family was destitute, despite Bronson's annual salary, and she needed to sell stories. And she knew how to please her audience: The story she had submitted to Frank Leslie's contest had beaten some two hundred other entrants. Now that she was home Leslie sent her the $100 prize (roughly $2,500 in today's dollars), equal to Bronson's yearly wages.

"Pauline's Passion and Punishment" was introduced on the front page of *Leslie's Illustrated Newspaper* on December 27, 1862. It appeared in the following two installments, with illustrations. Pauline, a jilted lover, marries her former lover's companion and shows him off to her ex, who has married a rich woman. When they meet again, he insists he can prove she still loves him, a "challenge to the tournament so often held between man and woman—a tournament where the keen tongue is the lance, pride the shield, passion the fiery steed, and the hardest heart the winner of the prize, which seldom fails to prove a barren honor, ending in remorse."

Leslie called it "a story of exceeding power, brilliant in description, thrilling in incident and unexceptionable in its moral." He identified Louisa only as "a lady of Massachusetts," which suited her. She continued to use pseudonyms for her genre fiction.

The line between highbrow and lowbrow was not clearly drawn in the nineteenth century, if it ever can be. It often depends more on the observer's eye than the writer's forehead. Still, there was a gulf between *The Atlantic Monthly* and *Frank Leslie's Illustrated Newspaper*. Leslie devoted many pages to war news, with full-page illustrations, mixing in serialized fiction, scraps of humor, and ads aimed at his female readership—for sewing machines, wedding cards, clothes wringers, and cures for "nervous sufferers." In contrast, the November 1863 issue of *The Atlantic Monthly*, which carried a new Civil War story of Louisa's, ran for over ninety pages of text with no illustrations. Her story, "The Brothers," appeared alongside a lengthy historical essay by Francis Parkman, a natural history of glaciers by Louis Agassiz, poetry by Longfellow, and an essay by Thoreau. There were no ads in the back, only a review of academic George Ticknor's three-volume *History of Spanish Literature*. (The audience for the first edition "was small at home, and not numerous anywhere.")

Louisa would feel torn between these literary worlds—the former demanding lurid or sentimental plots, the latter avoiding romances, dashing aristocrats, and mummy's curses. She could write thrillers and romances quickly, and she could disguise her name under pseudonyms. Yet they would never make her rich. It was writing from direct experience that would do that.

When *Hospital Sketches* ran in Franklin Sanborn's *The Common-*

wealth (Boston) under the pseudonym Tribulation Periwinkle, it was well received, and this time, the identity of the author was no mystery. Henry James Sr. wrote a note to Bronson praising the book. Bronson wrote in his journal, "I see nothing in the way of a good appreciation of Louisa's merits as a woman and a writer. Nothing could be more surprising to her or agreeable to us." There were two offers to publish the sketches as a book. She accepted James Redpath's, and dropped the pseudonym. Favorable reviews appeared in the *Liberator*, the *Boston Evening Transcript*, and the *Waterbury American*, among other outlets, to Louisa's "surprise & delight." The first edition of one thousand copies sold out. Another was ordered. She earned a nickel on each copy.

This success inspired Redpath to bring out *On Picket Duty, and Other Tales*, a ninety-six-page collection of four stories, along with a portion of *Hospital Sketches*. Louisa then returned to her adult novel *Moods* for a third time in the summer and fall of 1863—between selling "The Brothers" to *The Atlantic Monthly* and sending more stories to Frank Leslie. Redpath expressed interest in publishing this novel as well, but only if she cut it in half.

She refused. Ticknor and Fields rejected it as well. Publisher A. K. Loring agreed to take it on, yet he, too, insisted on some cuts and other specific changes, with which she wrestled. Finally, one night in October:

> A way to shorten & arrange "Moods" came into my head. The whole plan laid itself smoothly out before me & I slept no more that night but worked on it as busily as if mind & body had nothing to do with one another. Up early & began to write it all over again. The fit was on strong & for a fortnight I hardly ate slept or stirred but wrote, wrote like a thinking machine in full operation. When it was all rewritten, without copying, I found it much improved though I'd taken out ten chapters & sacrificed many of my favorite things, but being resolved to make it simple, strong & short I let everything else go & hoped the book would be better for it.

It was finally scheduled for publication in late 1864.

The story centers on a love triangle between the protagonist, Sylvia, and two male friends—one modeled on Emerson, the other on Thoreau. Louisa wove in many Concord references, including Thoreau's boat and Emerson's library, but the heart of the story asks a controversial question that transcends its setting: Should a woman remain in a marriage if she doesn't love her husband?

Sylvia loves the Thoreau character but agrees to marry the Emerson man when she thinks her true love is unavailable. Yet she cannot bring herself to love him. She and the Thoreau character reconnect and confess their mutual love, which drives her husband away to Europe. Eventually, the Thoreau character says to her, "Unhappy marriages are the tragedies of our day, and will be, till we learn that there are truer laws to be obeyed than those custom sanctions, other obstacles than inequalities of fortune, rank, and age."

Moods was important to Louisa. Initially it sold well, prompting a reprint, and Louisa wrote that "for a week wherever I went I saw, heard, & talked about 'Moods,' found people laughing or crying over it, & was continually told how well it was going, how much it was liked, how fine a thing I'd done." The early reviews that she saw were "mostly favorable & gave quite as much praise as was good for me."

Unfortunately, many reviewers felt differently. *The Commonwealth* called it "artless." Several outlets attacked the novel's depiction of marriage as a nonbinding agreement. The *Providence Daily Journal* dismissed it as "one of the foolish novels. A story about married life, written evidently by one who knows nothing about it."

Henry James Jr., in a lengthy assessment in the *North American Review*, took issue with most of her characters and their decisions: "The two most striking facts with regards to 'Moods' are the author's ignorance of human nature, and her self-confidence in spite of this ignorance." He condescendingly closed by saying "there is no reason why Miss Alcott should not write a very good novel, provided she will be satisfied to describe only that which she has seen." When Louisa had the chance to dine at the James's home in Boston, she met him and found him friendly and companionable. He was twenty-two, eleven years her junior, and many years away from writing *Daisy Miller*, *Washington Square*, and *The Portrait of a Lady*.

She continued to work on the novel that would become *Work*, but she also published short stories in the *Saturday Evening Gazette*, *Flag of Our Union*, *The Commonwealth*, and elsewhere. One of her 1864 stories, "V.V., or, Plots and Counterplots," is an early experiment in detective fiction. She needed the money, and she also enjoyed the fun of it.

In her journal she recorded earnings of $745 for that year, the equivalent of just under $15,000 in current dollars. It was by far the main source of income for the Alcotts—Bronson lost his position as superintendent of Concord's schools in the spring. He worried about Louisa's "paling spirits" as she was "a good deal worn with literary labor." In the spring of 1865, she received a welcome offer from the wealthy Boston shipping magnate William Fletcher Weld to travel to Europe with his family and serve as a nurse and companion to his daughter, Anna. It was her first chance to see England, Germany, France, and Italy. The trip would last a year. They departed in July.

Her charge, Anna, was a burden. She wrote in her journal that she tried her "best to suit & serve her but don't think I did so very well . . . hers is a very hard case to manage & needs the patience and wisdom of an angel."

Still, the opportunity to see Westminster Abbey, the Rhine River, Goethe's birthplace, the cathedrals and churches in Cologne and Freiburg, and the "tall, white, spectral" Alps, was irresistible. After weeks of travel Louisa and Anna settled into the Pension Victoria in Vevey, Switzerland, on Lake Geneva, in late September. They would stay there until the end of the year.

Louisa wrote about this period in "Life in a Pension" for *The Independent*, describing the "motley collection of lodgers from all quarters of the world: a Russian baron, page to the Czar; an English colonel and family; an Irish lady, daughter, and governess; a consumptive young Pole; two Scotch sisters; one fat Frenchman; a cosmopolitan lady and daughter; a retired English physician, wife, and friend; a family of rebels from South Carolina; and two young ladies from Boston." The essay is full of her characteristic humor, yet it skirts around the most important connection she made in Vevey. That consumptive Pole was the person who came closest to capturing Louisa's heart.

Ladislas Wisniewski had joined a failed Polish student uprising against Russia's Tsar Alexander II, for whom Poland was a vassal state. The uprising landed Wisniewski in prison. There, he contracted tuberculosis. He spoke little English, and Louisa struggled with her French. Nonetheless they formed an immediate connection. In her sketch, Louisa joked that "two hiccups and a sneeze will give [his] last name better than letters . . . Altogether captivating and romantic was the boy, in his blue and white university suit, with his charming manners, many accomplishments, and the fatal malady, of which he seldom spoke." He was twelve years younger than she.

He was an accomplished pianist who entertained the pension guests in the evenings. As an ill veteran of conflict, he reminded her of her Civil War patients: "the memory of certain dear lads at home made my heart open to this lonely boy. . . . He constituted himself my escort, errand-boy, French teacher, and private musician, making those weeks infinitely pleasant by his winning ways." In a month she helped him conquer English. She called him "Laddie." He brought her flowers every evening and left notes under her door.

In her journal she described the relationship as "a little romance," but she later went back and scratched out the words that followed. It marked the only instance in her entire journal that she destroyed a passage. At some point later she inserted two words: "Couldn't be."

Finally, in December, it was time for Louisa and Anna to depart for Nice. Laddie said to her, "*Bon voyage*, dear and good little mamma. I do not say adieu, but *au revoir*." It was a tearful parting.

Five months later, after a long stay in Nice, Louisa went to Paris on her own, "feeling as happy as a freed bird." When she arrived at the train station, "tired, bewildered, and homesick," she "suddenly saw a blue and white cap wave wildly in the air, then Laddie's beaming face appeared, and Laddie's eager hands grasped mine so cordially that I began to laugh at once, and felt that Paris was almost as good as home." They would enjoy two final weeks together. As she explained to her readers, "My twelve years' seniority made our adventures quite proper, and I fearlessly went anywhere on the arm of my big son."

Now they said goodbye for good. He gave her a bottle of cologne. She kissed him "tenderly," worrying that she might never see him again. She was correct, though Laddie recovered from consumption and they wrote letters for five more years.

Long after she had become the famous author of *Little Women*, whose readers wanted to know every detail about the models for its male protagonist, she noted that "it is hardly necessary to add, for the satisfaction of inquisitive little women, that Laddie was the original of Laurie, as far as a pale pen and ink sketch could embody a living, loving boy."

She returned home in July 1866. She found her mother looking old, and feeling sick and tired, while her father was as "placid as ever." The family was deeper in debt. She had not earned much money during her travels.

She plunged back into a writing frenzy, producing twelve stories in less than three months. She sold two long ones to Frank Leslie for $200 and sold a shorter one along with a poem to *Flag of Our Union*. The editor of *Flag* asked her for a longer story and she produced 185 pages in two weeks.

It was an astonishing output that included several multi-installment stories. When she added up her year's earnings it came to over $1,100 (nearly $22,000 in current dollars). Some of the stories were more lurid than ever, with ghosts, suicides, and kidnappings. She also created some strong and unconventional female characters. In "Behind a Mask, or, A Woman's Power," a scheming, manipulative woman of low background enters a wealthy home as a governess, disguising her advanced age and flirting with the two nephews of the owner until they each fall in love with her. She spurns them by winning over the aging uncle, who proposes, making her an aristocrat just before her schemes are revealed. She is a triumphant antihero, quite unlike the popular protagonists of sentimental fiction.

Louisa's burst of productivity kept the creditors at bay. It also brought her to a physical low by the winter of 1867. She could barely write anything in her journal, making only brief monthly entries starting in January: "Sick from too hard work . . ." February: "Ditto ditto . . ." March: "Ditto ditto . . ." April: "Slowly mending . . ." May: "Still gaining, but all feeble." Finally, in June, she got back to work.

Her mother's health was bad, with rheumatic fever and an eye operation that left her unable to read. Only Bronson was able to get anything done. He was working on a new book called *Tablets*, consisting of essays on gardening, recreation, fellowship, friendship, and culture, among other topics. He was no longer using archaic verb forms or leaping straight into abstractions. At age sixty-seven, he was drawing on many years of practical experience in his garden and living room—still a philosopher, but now one who could offer practical advice and genuine wisdom.

In September Louisa received the offer that would change her life. "Niles, partner of Roberts, asked me to write a girls book. Said I'd try." She was also offered a job as the editor of *Merry's Museum*, a children's magazine, for $500 per year. She agreed to that, too, and "began at once on both new jobs, but didn't like either." She moved to Boston in October.

Louisa's health was much better in the winter of 1868. In Boston she could often visit her sister Anna. Her younger sister May was giving art lessons and helping with the family's finances. Louisa kept writing short stories and she prepared a new edition of *Hospital Sketches* for Roberts Brothers. In four months in Boston, she wrote "eight long tales, ten short ones, [and] read stacks of manuscripts, and [did] editorial work."

She also did some acting for charity. She gave repeated performances of the title character in *Mrs. Jarley's Far-Famed Collection of Waxworks*, a play based on Charles Dickens's *The Old Curiosity Shop* by Concord resident G. B. Bartlett, which was performed throughout the country for charitable purposes. She loved to act. One writer noted that "One does not half know Miss Alcott who has not seen her—as Mrs. Jarley—display her 'wax-works.' I think it is quite the best bit of broad comedy that I can remember."

For $100, she agreed to write an essay much closer to Margaret Fuller's work than anything she had previously done. *The New York Ledger* asked her to give advice to young women. The result was "Happy Women," a feminist defense of "superior women who, from various causes, remain single, and devote themselves to some earnest work; espousing philanthropy, art, literature, music, medicine, or whatever task taste, necessity, or chance suggests, and remaining as faithful to and as happy in their choice as married women with husbands and homes." The essay sketches four anonymous examples: L., a rich man's daughter who becomes a physician; M., a brilliant, talented, yet poor girl who spurns a suitor she does not love, becoming a music teacher; S., a "poor, plain, ungifted, and ordinary" woman who lives to serve others and becomes a missionary; and finally, "A.," a self-portrait. "A." is "a strongly individual type, who in the course of an unusually varied experience has seen so much of what a wise man has called 'the tragedy of modern married life,' that she is afraid to try it." Literature is her life. She does not have a husband, but she does have parents, siblings, friends, and babies in her circle. She is content.

Louisa concluded the essay by saying, "If love comes as it should come, accept it in God's name. . . . If it never comes, then in God's name reject the shadow of it, for that can never satisfy a hungry heart." It was the theme of *Moods*. It would be a theme of *Little Women* as well.

At the end of February Bronson took Louisa to a meeting of the Radical Club, a new group he had joined; he called it the New Radical Religious Club. Louisa dismissed it as a "curious jumble of fools and philosophers." He spent the night at her apartment. The next day, before returning to Concord, Bronson called on Roberts Brothers to discuss his *Tablets* manuscript. He wrote to Louisa with good news: they were prepared to publish it. He added, "I spoke of 'The Story for the Girls' which R. & Bs. asked you to write. And find that they expect it and would like to have it ready by September at longest. . . . Niles, the literary partner, spoke in terms of admiration of your literary ability, thinking most highly of your rising fame and prospects. He obviously wishes to to [*sic*] become *your* publisher and *mine*." Bronson wanted Louisa to come home to Concord to finish the book for girls.

She returned home on February 29 yet avoided working on the "girls' book." She asked her father to pitch a "fairy book" to Niles instead, but Niles said no, he wanted the book for girls. "So I plod away, though I don't enjoy this sort of thing. Never liked girls or knew many, except my sisters, but our queer plays and experiences may prove interesting, though I doubt it."

In June she had twelve chapters ready for Niles. "He thought it *dull*, so did I." Still, she pressed on and had the complete manuscript ready in mid-July. In August, Roberts Brothers negotiated a deal for it, with

 43

Orchard House in 1865, with the Alcotts in front.

Niles urging her to keep the copyright. Reviewing the page proofs in late August she wrote that "it reads better than I expected. Not a bit sensational, but simple and true, for we really lived most of it . . . Mr. N. likes it better now, and says some girls who have read the manuscripts say it is 'splendid!'" Niles asked her to add a teaser at the end, to point toward a sequel.

In early September Bronson's *Tablets* arrived in stores. For the first time in his life, the sixty-eight-year-old philosopher met with success. The first printing sold out quickly. A second was ordered. It was his first book since *Conversations with Children on the Gospels*, thirty-two years earlier.

Tablets includes some of Alcott's abstruse arguments, but they are largely relegated to its final quarter, "Book II.—Speculative." As Franklin Sanborn would note, this section "caused much perplexity, for the reason that it requires a peculiar alertness on the part of the reader in the art of reading between the lines."

It is the first three-quarters, "Book I.—Practical," that attracted readers and critics. *Tablets* is a celebration of rural life. As Bronson put it, "I may be scholarly inclined, and my tasks indoors delightful, yet my garden claims me, monopolizing all my morning hours. . . . My garden waits; is the civiller [*sic*] host, the better entertainer."

Tablets is filled with lengthy quotations from Homer and many others, and even book one has its share of Alcott's hierarchies, ranking fruits above grains, herbs, and roots, successively. Yet Bronson wrote it with an appealing simplicity and quaintness. At a time when the American economy was shifting toward manufacturing and urbanization, the self-reliant homesteader that he celebrated was on the decline. His message: count your blessings.

> Life, when hospitably taken, is a simple affair. Very little suffices to enrich us. Being, a fountain and fireside, a web of cloth, a garden, a few friends, and good books, a chosen task, health and peace of mind—these are a competent estate, embracing all we need.

Tablets also includes paeans to good fellowship and conversation, to books, to women's "constancy, fidelity, fortitude, kindness, gratitude, grace, courtesy, discretion, taste, conversation, [and] the adornments of life," and to families and children. Alcott makes a new plea for his style of education through dialogue. He also exhibits a new gift for aphorism: "Good books, like good friends, are few and chosen; the more select the more enjoyable."

Favorable reviews appeared in newspapers and periodicals throughout the country, which Bronson clipped and preserved. Everyone found the book charming. The *Boston Daily Advertiser* said that "*Tablets* are like windows through which the busy worker, pausing for a minute in the rush and distraction of his ten thousand little cares and duties, may look out into great spaces and draw a deep full breath, may look far into the past, far forward into the future, and far up into the heavens."

Profiles of Bronson appeared in several papers, including *The Republican*, the *New-York Tribune*, and the *Buffalo Daily Courier*. A lengthy three-part review of *Tablets* in *The Republican* was especially gratifying. After noting the reasons why critics might attack the book, the reviewer defends it, and Alcott's entire career, in detail, stating that Alcott's "whole life and utterances have been one unceasing effort toward the emancipation of spiritual self-consciousness."

In his seventh decade he was celebrated and praised as never before. He continued to host conversations in towns and cities, to positive notices.

He also continued to engage with political issues, especially the growing push for women's suffrage. Louisa was an enthusiast, and Abba was ahead of them both—as early as 1853 she had petitioned the state legislature to amend the Massachusetts Constitution to extend "all civil rights" to women. Now, in November 1869, Bronson attended the first American Women's Suffrage Convention in Cleveland, along with such luminaries as Susan B. Anthony, Julia Ward Howe, and Henry Ward Beecher, who would be appointed as the group's first president. Bronson spoke up to say that "this was the initiation of one of the most magnificent revolutions known in history."

Abba, in another petition to the state legislature, was more articulate. Women "must help make the Laws, be educated as Jurists, Drs. Divine, Artists, Bankers. It will occupy and give dignity to their minds and lives."

Ten years later, after the Massachusetts Legislature had made it legal for women to vote in school committee elections, Louisa would be the first woman in Concord to register to vote. On March 29, 1880, at the Concord Town Meeting, she was the first of twenty women to cast a vote. Bronson had requested that the women be allowed to vote first, and as soon as they did, a motion passed to close the vote—making this the first women-only election in Concord history. She noted in her journal, with emphasis, "*We* elected a good school committee. Quiet time, no fuss."

Louisa's life beginning in the late 1860s changed. On September 30, 1868, *Little Women*—the first volume—arrived in bookstores. Its success was immediate. The first printing of 2,000 copies sold out within days. Another 4,500 were in print by the end of the year. By October 30 Niles was able to tell her that a London edition was coming soon, and he asked for part two by the spring. On November 1, she began writing. "I can do a chapter a day, and in a month I mean to be done." Soon, "I am so full of my work, I can't stop to eat or sleep, or for anything but a daily run."

Years later, Julian Hawthorne told a fanciful version of part one's success. In his telling—which he claimed was Louisa's own "amusing exaggeration"—three months after she had delivered her draft to Niles, with no news from him, she went to Boston to demand the return of the manuscript. The sidewalk outside his office was "cluttered up with packing cases, which truckmen were loading onto drays. . . . Inside it was worse; she had to edge her way along narrow crevices, colliding with impatient shopmen and porters; she feared the establishment was being seized for debt; probably her manuscript would be in the rubbish heap in the back yard." Finally, she reached Niles's office. He was hunched over his desk, "riding the whirlwind and directing the storm." She dared to speak up:

"'I've come to ask you—'

"Without looking up he waved her away. 'Go away. I've given orders—most important. How did you get in here?'

"Louisa's ire rose. 'I want my manuscript!'"

Niles looked up, saw that it was Louisa, and "vaulted over the desk and landed at her feet, leaving his spectacles in mid-air. He grasped her frenziedly by both elbows; she thought he was going to hit her, and recoiled; the man was plainly mad."

Finally, Niles manages to speak. "My dear—dearest Miss Alcott! At such a juncture! You got my letter? No? No matter! Nothing to parallel it has occurred in my experience! . . . Why, dearest girl, it's the triumph of the century!"

Little Women was drawn from the Alcotts' lives—so closely that its fans often wonder about the facts behind every character and scene. It tells of the March family and its four daughters, whose personalities correspond to the four Alcott girls. Their mother, like Abba, is called "Marmee" by the girls. The oldest daughter, Meg, like Anna Alcott, is meek and well-behaved, loves to act in plays that Jo (Louisa) writes, and marries an honest local man named John. The third daughter, Beth, like Lizzie Alcott, dies of scarlet fever. The youngest, Amy, like May, loves to paint.

Yet Louisa changed and invented many aspects of the story. She moved the girls' father off-stage for most of part one. The March household is a woman's world. Louisa dreamed up a wealthy, crotchety Aunt March. The crucial male companion of the girls, their neighbor Laurie, was another invention. Louisa insisted that he was based partly on Laddie Wisniewski and partly on Alf Whitman, a younger friend from Kansas who had attended school in Concord. Yet Laurie is an original.

Despite these inventions, she was writing and dramatizing life as she knew it—just what Henry James had urged her to do. And she was exploring the possibilities for women's happiness. Mail from readers poured in. They clamored for part two.

Many readers were desperate for Jo to marry Laurie. As Louisa wrote to an acquaintance, "'Jo' should have remained a literary spinster but so many enthusiastic young ladies wrote to me clamorously demanding that she should marry Laurie, or somebody." As *Little Women* fans know, Louisa married Laurie to the youngest March sister, Amy, and invented a new character, the kindly Professor Bhaer, to be Jo's surprising spouse.

Some readers wanted different pairings. They weren't afraid to say so:

> *Dear Miss Alcott,—I have read the first part of "Little Women," and cried quarts over Beth's sickness. If you don't have her marry Laurie in the second part, I shall never forgive you, and none of the girls in our school will ever read any more of your books. Do! Do! have her, please.*

44

Louisa May Alcott at the height of her success, in 1870. Portrait by George Healy.

Part two was a huge success. Translations soon appeared in French, Dutch, and German. Bronson tracked the sales of part one in his journals through a fifth printing in late December 1868. For part two he recorded "the 19th 000 [thousand]" in July 1869 and "the 48th 000" in April 1870. Sales would never slow down, reaching one million copies during Louisa's lifetime.

Reviewers praised part one as "fresh, sparkling, natural, and full of soul." There were many notices, uniformly positive, which Bronson avidly tracked in his journals. For part two there were even more. Some reviewers realized that the book had become more than "just" a book for girls. "'Little Women' is the very best of books to reach the hearts of the young of any age from six to sixty, though its merits will be most appreciated by those who have reached the contemplative period of life," wrote *Eclectic Magazine*. Louisa had set out to write a "girls' book." She succeeded in writing a book that would be beloved by women of all ages.

Finally, she could pay off the family's remaining debts. She couldn't shake her health challenges, but she could enter a new phase of life as a famous and successful writer who reached more readers than the rest of the Emerson circle combined.

19

We Are in Life

In the midst of death, we are in life.

—Henry David Thoreau

As early as 1866, when Waldo Emerson wrote "Terminus," he was aware of his own decline. He shared the poem with his son Edward when they met in New York that December. It is a meditation on aging, and the need to accept it. The final lines are these:

I trim myself to the storm of time,
I man the rudder, reef the sail,
Obey the voice at eve obeyed at prime:
"Lowly faithful, banish fear,
Right onward drive unharmed;
The port, well worth the cruise, is near,
And every wave is charmed."

Edward recalled that "it almost startled me. No thought of his ageing had ever come to me, and there he sat, with no apparent abatement of bodily vigor, and young in spirit, recognizing with serene acquiescence his failing forces; I think he smiled as he read."

Waldo's career was not over, but his original thinking and writing lay behind him. For a while, he continued to lecture at a vigorous pace.

He gave eighty talks in 1867. He continued at a lower rate through 1872 before tailing off to just a few per year through the rest of the decade. His daughter Ellen accompanied him, ready to step in when a word escaped him or to help keep the pages of his scripts in order.

The 1870s belonged to Bronson and Louisa. In 1869, the year her finances started to improve, Louisa published a huge range of stories, some for as little as $10. Not all have survived. We know she wrote twenty-four for the *Youth's Companion*, of which some have been located. All are morality tales.

Louisa serialized the chapters of *An Old-Fashioned Girl* in *Merry's Museum* before Roberts Brothers issued it as a successful book. Meanwhile, she wrote her final blood-and-thunder stories in *Frank Leslie's Lady's Magazine*, *Putnam's Magazine*, *Frank Leslie's Chimney Corner*, and *New World*. One of these, "Lost in a Pyramid, or, A Mummy's Curse," reads like an elevator pitch for a modern Hollywood blockbuster.

She did all this despite fighting illness. In her journal, she said she "wrote nothing but little tales" in the winter, and did "little all summer, Poorly" and felt "very poorly" in October.

Her health issues would vary in intensity for the rest of her life, but her writing output remained prodigious. From 1870 to 1880 she published eight novels: *An Old-Fashioned Girl* (1870 in book form, after serialization) and *Little Men* (1871) were followed by *Work: A Story of Experience* (1873), *Eight Cousins* (1875), *Rose in Bloom* (1876), *A Modern Mephistopheles* (1877), *Under the Lilacs* (1878), and *Jack and Jill* (1880). Henry James weighed in one more time, on *Eight Cousins*, comparing her to a Thackeray or Trollope for the world of children: "She is a satirist. She is extremely clever. . . . [The novel] is evidently written in very good faith." But those were the only kind words he had to say. Overall, he found the novel "unfortunate not only in its details, but in its general tone." It is "poor entertainment and poor instruction." It became one of the top sellers of the year.

All but one of those novels were domestic fiction, as were her many short-story collections: six volumes of *Aunt Jo's Scrap-Bag* (1872–82), *Proverb Stories* (1882), *Spinning-Wheel Stories* (1884), three volumes of *Lulu's Library* (1886–89), and *A Garland for Girls* (1887).

The one exception, *A Modern Mephistopheles*, was a rewritten version of a novel she had first crafted in 1866 that had been rejected by a publisher at the time who found it too sensational. Now, Roberts Brothers was launching a "No Name" series of anonymously published novels by famous authors, provoking readers to guess who had written each one. Thomas Niles urged her to give it a shot, so Louisa spent two weeks rewriting her Faust-like story. Along with everyone else in the Emerson circle, she admired Goethe. She once wrote that "E[merson] gave me Goethe's works at fifteen, and they have been my delight ever since. My library consists of Goethe, Emerson, Shakespeare, Carlyle, Margaret Fuller, and George Sand."

A Modern Mephistopheles is the story of a writer who publishes two bestselling books under his own name, though they had been secretly written by his Mephistophelian sponsor, a man heavy-handedly named Jasper Helwyze. The secret fraud torments the writer even as he loves, marries, and impregnates a pure-hearted woman. Helwyze tries seducing his wife, tries drugging her, and then tries sowing doubt about her husband's faithfulness. She resists it all. Yet when she delivers her baby, both mother and child perish. The writer blames himself. Helwyze repents but becomes paralyzed. The writer survives and resolves to make an honest living.

Louisa had always enjoyed her lurid stories, and this tale of devilry, seduction, and hashish was as lurid as any of them. She wrote in her diary that the idea "had been simmering ever since I read Faust last year. Enjoyed doing it, being tired of providing moral pap for the young." When Thomas Niles read the manuscript in February 1877, he wrote to her that "it does not seem to me to be so much sensational as weird & unearthly; as I think of it now I seem to see the curtain going down on a scene of hell fire & brimstone with Faust in the middle. . . . It is intensely interesting & I think some of your best work is in it."

Reviewers enjoyed it too. It was the sixth volume in the No Name series. Several reviewers deemed it the best of them. Franklin Sanborn, in *The Republican*, guessed that it was "probably by Mrs. [Harriet] Prescott Spofford, but there are many parts of the book which sound like Miss Alcott, while some things in it recall Julian Hawthorne." *The Woman's Journal* wrote that "we are satisfied that the book is the work of Miss Alcott" and *The Literary World* reviewer "hovers between Miss Alcott and Mrs. Spofford." The vast majority settled on Spofford, the author of "The Amber Gods" and other sensational stories.

Only after Louisa died did Roberts Brothers reissue *Mephistopheles* along with "A Whisper in the Dark" under Louisa's name. Since all of her other sensational stories had been published anonymously or pseudonymously, the book was a revelation. The idea that the author of "moral pap" for children could also write something so lurid and thrilling boosted her reputation. The *Boston Evening Traveller* wrote that "it is quite probable that Miss Alcott's fame as an author will in the end rest more on this novel than on any other she has written."

Louisa's writing was slowed only by travel, continued health struggles, and motherhood (by adoption). She and May accompanied a friend of May's to Europe, staying in France, Switzerland, and Italy in 1870–71. The trip was supposed to improve Louisa's health, but it didn't. She suffered persistent leg pain. In December the girls learned of a death in the family: their brother-in-law, John Pratt, had passed away after ten years of marriage to Anna. To Louisa, he was her "dear, honest, tender, noble John."

He left two young boys behind, and Louisa determined to get back to work to secure their financial future. She returned to the world of the March family and finished *Little Men*. When she arrived in Boston after fourteen months abroad, her father and Thomas Niles met her in a carriage decorated with a "great red placard"—it was the publication day of *Little Men*. Niles reported advance sales of fifty thousand copies.

The decade continued to bring success to both father and daughter. Bronson was newly able to earn money from lecture tours in the Midwest, even in his seventies. In 1872, he followed *Tablets* with *Concord Days*, a book that brings together writings and observations of many years. It features deft sketches of Hawthorne, Emerson, Fuller, and Thoreau. It is a paean to Concord, to his house and family, to friends and conversation, to such thinkers as Plutarch, Plato, Coleridge, and Goethe, and to ideals: "Our instincts are idealists . . . they prompt us forth to the noblest aims and endeavors."

Concord Days overlaps in parts with *Tablets* and, like that book, includes extensive quotations and poems from Bronson's favorite writers. It mercifully includes even less of the speculations that troubled readers of *Tablets*. It came out in September, and by February 1873 Bronson was able to write that Thomas Niles "tells me my *Concord Days* has gone to a third edition and the last nearly sold. It has been received with almost universal favor, and is a success in the 'bookseller's sense,' a book running to a third edition being likely to run to five in a year or two."

During an 1874–75 lecture tour to Illinois (three cities), Iowa (twelve), and Wisconsin (nine), he made repeat visits and spoke scores of times in private and in public conversations, to enthusiastic crowds. It was his third western trip of the decade, each more successful than the last. In 1877, he published *Table-Talk*, a series of short entries on topics both "Practical" and "Speculative," based on his western conversations. It covered an enormous range in its 178 short pages, everything from "Books" and "Concord" to "Good and Evil" and "Immortality." Some of it is a rehash of *Tablets*, but this time, the speculative passages summarize his theology.

In the 1860s he had thought of founding a new church based on no doctrine or dogma, merely the assumption that truth would emerge from the free exchange of ideas among men and women in touch with the Spirit. After attending some church conferences at which doctrinal squabbles inevitably arose, he had given it up. Now he was preaching his own doctrine:

"It especially becomes Christians to free themselves from the exclusiveness of sects and creeds of every name and time." And: "Christians have no good reason for regarding with jealousy the Oriental religions. Christianity does not conflict with any, but complements them." He dismisses scripture of all types "since the Spirit alone divines the Spirit's teachings." Yet he does have a theology of sorts, which William T. Harris, the editor of the *Journal of Speculative Philosophy*, attempts to explain, in an essay that Bronson reproduced within the text:

"The first Principle, or God, is a Person." We all begin as pure souls—but we may "lapse." "Those that lapse create thereby bodies for themselves; and, lapsing still further, generate the lower animals; and, these continuing the lapse, beget the plant-world; and thence results the inorganic world." Perhaps, if a mosquito lost touch with its Spirit, it would reincarnate as a lower being, such as a fungus. Yet the reverse is also possible, as our individual spirits may ascend the ladder back to purity.

The good news: "The Person is immortal." Our pure souls will eventually enjoy "an eternity of fellowships." It is no wonder that Alcott rejected Darwin's theory—it just wasn't spiritual. Alcott was the last Transcendentalist alive.

Throughout these years Louisa faced new challenges to her health and reputation. Her right thumb became paralyzed, forcing her to write left-handed. She was writing *Work*, using impression paper to make three copies simultaneously, for her American and British book publishers and for the editor serializing it in the *Christian Union*. She had to press down hard with her pen. Reviewing her journal years later, she wrote, "This was the cause of the paralysis of my thumb, which disabled me for the rest of my life."

Her new fame also bedeviled her. "Reporters sit on the wall and take notes, artists sketch me as I pick pears in the garden, and strange women interview Johnny [her nephew] as he plays in the orchard. It looks like impertinent curiosity to me, but it is called 'fame,' and considered a blessing to be grateful for, I find. Let 'em try it."

Some years later she depicted this problem humorously in *Jo's Boys*, the third book in the March trilogy. Visitors barge into the house while Jo pretends to be a maid, dusting the furniture. At the time she also joked about it in a piece by "Tribulation Periwinkle" about Concord:

> It is said that a new hotel is about to be established, called "The Sphinx's Head," where pilgrims to this modern Mecca can be entertained in the most hospitable and appropriate style. Walden water, aesthetic tea, and "wine that never grew in the belly of the grape" will constantly be on tap for the refreshment of thirsty guests. Wild apples by the bushel, Orphic acorns by the peck, and Hawthorne's pumpkins, in the shape of pies, will be furnished at philosophic prices. The house will be filled with Alcott's rustic furniture, the beds made of Thoreau's pine boughs, and the sacred fires fed from the Emersonian wood pile. . . . Telescopes will be provided for the gifted eyes which desire to watch the soarings of the oversoul, when visible, and lassoes—with which the expert may catch untamed hermits, or poets on the wing.

She added a lament about all the reporters who were descending on the town. "No spot is safe, no hour is sacred, and fame is beginning to be considered an expensive luxury by the Concordians."

In 1877, after many years of decline, Abba Alcott died. Louisa's journal entries from the year are terse yet frenetic. In the spring she helped Anna purchased the Thoreau family home from the estate of Henry's late sister, Sophia, contributing $2,000 toward the $4,500 price. When the deal was done, she wrote that Anna "has *her* wish, and is happy. When shall I have mine?"

She was feeling better in the weeks afterward and began to hope she had "outlived the neuralgic worries and nervous woes born of the hospital fever and the hard years following." Yet by July she was laid up again for weeks. In September, "Marmee had a very ill turn, and the doctor told me it was the beginning of the end." Even as she nursed her mother, she finished volume four of *Aunt Jo's Scrap-Bag* and *Under the Lilacs*.

Possibly as a result of this burst of work, by October "I overdid [it] and was very ill,—in danger of my life for a week,—and feared to go before Marmee. But pulled through, and got up slowly to help her die." On November 25, Marmee died. Her last words to

Bronson were tender: "'You are laying a very soft pillow for me to go to sleep on.'"

Two years later the family grew by another grandchild. May Alcott had married Ernest Nieriker, a younger Swiss businessman, in 1878 while she was studying painting in England. They moved to a suburb of Paris, and Ernest began work at a trading firm. By early 1879 May was pregnant. On November 8 she gave birth to a daughter, naming her Louisa May Nieriker.

Louisa Alcott had hoped to be in France for the birth and to help her sister in the initial weeks of her niece's life, but her health wouldn't permit it. She recorded her regret: "Give up my hope & long cherished plan with grief. May sadly disappointed. I know I shall wish I had gone. It is my luck!"

45

Louisa May Nieriker in 1889, age ten. When she died in 1975, Lulu was likely the last living person who knew her famous aunt.

Much worse luck was to come. May suffered complications from the birth, and on December 29, she died. Two days later, a telegram from her husband brought the news to Emerson. Louisa wrote that she was at home, "alone when Mr E[merson] came. E[rnest Nieriker] sent to him knowing I was feeble & hoping Mr E. would soften the blow. I found him looking at May's portrait, pale & tearful with the paper in his hand. 'My child, I *wish* I could prepare you, but alas, alas!' there his voice failed & he gave me the telegram."

May's dying wish was that little Louisa be entrusted to her sister's care. At just shy of forty-eight, Louisa was to be a mother for the first time. She would need to fight through her illnesses. "I see now why I lived. To care for May's child & not leave Annie [Anna] all alone."

Lulu, as she called her niece, would live to be ninety-five, dying in 1975 as quite possibly the last living person who knew her famous aunt.

Bronson remained productive until 1882, his eighty-third year. In 1879, with the help of Franklin Sanborn, he founded the Concord School of Philosophy. That summer's classes were held in Orchard House, prompting Louisa, decidedly non-transcendental yet highly political, to write that "the town swarms with budding philosophers, & they roost on our step like hens, waiting for corn. Father revels in it, so we keep the hotel going & try to look as if we like it . . . speculation seems a waste of time when there is so much real work crying to be done. Why discuss the Unknowable till our poor are fed & the wicked saved?"

By the following year, with Louisa's financial assistance, the school had its own building on his property, decorated with marble busts of Plato, Pestalozzi, Emerson, and Bronson himself. As one historian notes, "Dozens of intellectuals delivered lectures over the next decade or so; thousands of students attended . . . The annual reading from Thoreau's unpublished journals quickly became the most popular event of the academy."

Bronson also continued to write, publishing *New Connecticut* in 1881 and *Sonnets and Canzonets* the following year. The former was

Bronson Alcott in 1880, on the steps of the Concord School of Philosophy, adjacent to Orchard House. 46

a sixty-four-page poem about his early life, originally intended only for friends and family. It covers his boyhood and years as a Yankee peddler. In some ways it completes the transition of his previous two books—there is nothing in it of transcendental ideals, nothing about education reform, nothing about politics. It is about simple, rural, virtuous living. He begins as a farmer and ends as "a fine gentleman."

Sonnets and Canzonets was published in April 1882. Its forty-nine original poems are almost all fourteen-line sonnets, and many of them are love poems to Abba. There are also poems to his unnamed daughters:

Glad tidings thence these angels downward bring,
As at their birth the heavenly choirs do sing.

One poem praises Louisa's wartime nursing. Others lament Lizzie's early death and May's still-fresh passing (the only time he inserts a family name: "Ah! gentle May, / Couldst thou not stay?"). In the later portion of the book, he salutes many of his friends, some by name. There are poems about Thoreau, Channing, Fuller, Hawthorne, and Brown.

The opening poem about Emerson is the most poignant of all. By now, his closest friend had suffered many years of mental decline. The poem is a "Proem," a preamble in verse, set off in the front matter of the book. It recalls conversations between the two friends from long ago, when Waldo would gently cut through Bronson's airy thinking and wording:

If I from Poesy could not all abstain,
He my poor verses oft did quite undress,
New wrapt in words my thought's veiled nakedness,
Or kindly clipt my steed's luxuriant mane:
'Twas my delight his searching eye to meet,
In days of genial versing, memories sweet.

By the end of the 1870s, Emerson was ready to give up lecturing. Reviewers of his recent appearances had been kind, but they could not pretend that all was well. One noted that he "read his lecture at a small desk . . . his faithful daughter guiding and prompting him whenever he lost his place, with his audience, of some two hundred persons, so thoroughly touched by his infirmities that they did not mind what they lost, provided only, they could look into his serene face and watch his varying expression."

One lecture that he gave as late as 1879 was on memory. It begins: "Memory is a primary and fundamental faculty, without which none other can work: The cement, the bitumen, the matrix, in which the other faculties are embedded; or, it is the thread on which the beads of man are strung, making the personal identity: and it is necessary to moral action. Without it, all life and thought were an unrelated succession." He had lost his.

In the early morning of July 24, 1872, a fire started in Emerson's attic. His neighbors rushed over and carried manuscripts, books, and many furnishings out to safety. Newspapers reported that the house was almost totally destroyed, except for its first-floor walls. Louisa recounted to a friend that she "saved some valuable papers for my Ralph, & most of their furniture, books & pictures were safe. The upper story is all gone & the lawn strewed with wrecks of beds, books & clothes." She found Emerson "pathetically funny that morning wandering about in his night gown, pants, old coat & no hose. His dear bald head lightly covered with his best hat, & an old pair of rubbers wobbling on his Platonic feet."

The Emersons moved back into the Old Manse. Their home was valued at $5,000 but insured for only half that. Friends and supporters stepped up. Francis Cabot Lowell, a Harvard classmate of Waldo's and the heir of a substantial textile and financial empire, handed Waldo an envelope with a check for $5,000. Judge Rockwood Hoar told him that an additional $10,000 had been raised. Ellen recalled that "Father said he did not see how he could accept so much. 'I don't know what you can do about it,' said the Judge, 'it is in the Bank to your credit. The best use you can make of it is to go to Egypt with it.'" And so they did, Waldo and Ellen together.

They stopped in London and Paris and reached Cairo in December. They traveled up the Nile and back. On the return journey they stopped in Florence, Rome, Paris, London, and Edinburgh. They returned to Concord in late May to an astonishing greeting: Bells were ringing. A band was playing. A huge crowd had gathered. An arch had been erected by the gate of their rebuilt home, where children sang "Home Sweet Home."

It was his last major trip. From then on, Waldo would lecture only rarely. With help from Ellen and James Cabot he published *Selected Poems* in 1876, his last book.

By 1881 Emerson's mental fog was near total. An ambitious young journalist, Edward Bok—he would go on to edit the *Ladies' Home Journal* for thirty years—came to Concord in hopes of meeting Louisa May.

She agreed to see him. He also wanted to meet Emerson, so she walked him over to Coolidge Castle. Ellen intercepted them at the door, saying "Father sees no one now, and I fear it might not be a pleasure if you did see him." Yet Louisa managed to get Bok into Emerson's study.

As Bok recalled, "No light of welcome came from those sad yet tender eyes." Emerson motioned for him to sit but then "walked away to the window and stood there softly whistling and looking out as if there were no one in the room." When Louisa tried to kindle a conversation, Emerson replied, "Did you speak to me, madam?"

Finally, Bok asked Emerson if he would sign his autograph book. Emerson didn't seem to know his own name. "Please write out the name you want, and I will copy it for you if I can."

Lidian and Ellen continued to care for him. Whitman came for a visit that year, and Bronson and Louisa joined him for a conversation at which Emerson sat silent. At dinner, according to Whitman, Emerson had "a healthy color in the cheeks, and good light in the eyes, cheery expression, and just the amount of talking that best suited, namely, a word or short phrase only where needed, and almost always with a smile."

His memory was so far gone that he would ask Lidian, ""What was the name of my best friend? 'Henry Thoreau,' she would answer. 'Oh yes, Henry Thoreau.'"

On April 27, 1882, Waldo died. He was buried in Sleepy Hollow, one of America's earliest examples of a natural-garden cemetery, with walkways that invite the living to contemplate the dead. Emerson had served on the committee that oversaw its design. Thoreau had excavated the site, and his family plot had been relocated there. Hawthorne was buried there. At the September 1855 consecration ceremony William Ellery Channing had read a poem, Frank Sanborn sang an ode, and Emerson had given a speech. "In all the multitudes of woodlands and hillsides, which within a few years have been laid out with a similar design, I have not known one so fitly named. *Sleepy Hollow*. In this quiet valley, as in the palm of Nature's hand, we shall sleep well when we have finished our day."

He purchased a large family plot on its high ground. After the cemetery opened he worked to bring friends and family to Concord, in death as in life. He convinced his aunt Mary that she should be buried there. When he tried to bring his older brother William from New York to Concord in William's final years, William refused. But William agreed to be buried in Sleepy Hollow. Near the Emerson plot are modest gravestones for the Alcotts, Hawthornes, and Thoreaus.

For his own marker, after "long deliberation," Emerson's family selected a large granite boulder that towers over the more conventional gravestones of Lidian and Ellen, on either side, as well as the other many Emersons in the plot. On it are inscribed two lines from his poem "The Problem" (a rejection of clergy and doctrine): "The passive master lent his hand / To the vast soul that o'er him planned."

47

Emerson's gravestone, with plaque. Lidian Emerson's stone is to the left. Eventually, their daughter Ellen's stone would be to the right.

The grave boulder is at once immodest and modest—its massive bulk sets Emerson apart from everyone else on what is now called Author's Ridge, yet its uncarved simplicity makes it the most naturalistic of all the markers there. Of all his acolytes, only Walt Whitman, buried in Camden, New Jersey, designed a more imposing mausoleum for himself.

Any attempt to summarize Emerson's achievements during his decades-long career is bound to be reductive. In some ways it is easier to state what he did *not* accomplish: He did not launch a new school of philosophical thought. He disliked the term "transcendentalism." His concept of the "Over-Soul" hasn't inspired any religious or philosophical movements. Academics only use the term in relation to its author.

He himself was quick to deny that he had any grand theory to offer. In "Experience" he wrote, "I know better than to claim any completeness for my picture. I am a fragment, and this is a fragment of me. I can very confidently announce one or another law, which throws itself into relief and form, but I am too young yet by some ages to compile a code."

Perhaps, in Isaiah Berlin's modern metaphor, he was the ultimate fox rather than the ultimate hedgehog: He knew many, many things rather than any one big thing. His essays and lectures contain epigrammatic wisdom on almost any imaginable topic. He examined issues from multiple perspectives and explored the limits of each of them. He rarely employed polemics, except when it came to abolitionism, slavery, the Trail of Tears, and women's rights.

Yet he was a hedgehog in one crucial sense: He constantly urged his listeners and readers to pursue the truth wherever it might take them, and he believed there was an ultimate truth, a moral law, accessible to all. From *Nature* and "Self-Reliance" to his 1860s lecture on "Truth," he admonishes us to be brave and refuse to buckle to popular opinions and traditions. As he says in that lecture: "We do not like those who unmask our illusions. Inestimable is the truth-speaker." To legions of new thinkers, he was an inspiration. Even Thoreau, who insisted on his own radical independence, had to admit that Emerson's "personal influence upon young persons [was] greater than any man's."

As the Victorian literary critic Matthew Arnold put it, Emerson was not "a great poet, a great writer, [nor] a great philosophy-maker. His relation to us is not that of one of those personages; yet it is a relation of, I think, even superior importance. . . . He is the friend and aider of those who would live in the spirit."

When he called for seeking eternal wisdom through nature, he inspired Thoreau. When he called for an original American poetry, he inspired Whitman. When the many varieties of utopians sought the truth through radical economic, sexual, or dietary experiments, it was Emerson's home to which they made a pilgrimage. He wasn't the first to call for the abolition of slavery, or for women's suffrage, but when he did so his voice was influential.

He captured the hopeful age of the early republic, and his decline coincided with the decline of reformism. In the decades after the Civil War, corruption flourished at every level: in cities, where political machines came to dominate local politics; at statehouses, where the explosive growth of the railroad industry set off a scramble for monopoly contracts; and in Washington, where the spoils system covered a vast number of jobs in the growing federal government. Reformers waged battles over civil service reform and women's suffrage, but the anything-is-possible spirit of the 1840s became buried beneath layers of political sludge.

Bronson Alcott visited Emerson just days before his friend died. Louisa wrote that Emerson "held his hand looking up at the tall, rosy old man, & saying with that smile of love that has been father's sunshine for so many years, '*you* are very well, Keep so, keep so.'"

Six months later, Bronson suffered a massive paralytic stroke. For several weeks he could not speak. The right side of his body was paralyzed. Louisa wrote that "his mind [is] in a very dim & feeble state." Yet he worked to recover, learning to write with his left hand just as Louisa had, and beginning to speak haltingly. Louisa wrote to a friend that he "seems to have difficulty in expressing even the disconnected thoughts that come & go in his bewildered yet active brain." By February 1883 she was able to report that he was better, and even mentally "bright," but he was bedridden. He would remain in this state, with good days and bad, for five years. His journaling and book-writing had come to an end.

Over time, Alcott's legacy would fade from the world's memory. Yet he had touched and inspired many people in his long life, even as he exasperated many of them. Thoreau may have put it best in his journals: "He is broad & genial but indefinite; some would say feeble; forever feeling about vainly in his speech & touching nothing . . . [yet] there are never any obstacles in the way of our meeting—he has no creed—He is not pledged to any institution—the sanest man I ever knew."

Louisa struggled to care for him while also raising Lulu. She tried hiring governesses for her daughter, but none satisfied her. She sold Orchard House to buy a cottage in Nonquitt, Massachusetts, on the South Shore, in hopes that it would be restorative for Bronson. During the winters she rented a town house in Boston.

She tried to finish *Jo's Boys*, but a burst of hard work made her ill for a week and she had to put it aside. In early 1885 she tried a series of some thirty "mind cure" sessions. As with Margaret Fuller's visits to a mesmerist in New York in the 1840s, she at first believed they worked. But she grew disillusioned, publishing a short article about it in *The Woman's Journal*. "When thirty treatments left the arm no better and the head much worse, I dared lose no more time, and returned to the homeopathy and massage from which I had been lured by the hope of finding a short and easy way to undo in a month the overwork of twenty years."

She finished *Jo's Boys* in July 1886. That fall she felt as ill as ever. In January she moved into a convalescent home while Anna remained at the town house with their father. Louisa steadily lost weight. She remained convinced that her health problems were caused by her Civil War illness and mercury treatments, though modern medical historians believe they were more likely to have been the result of some kind of autoimmune disease. In January 1888, at age fifty-six, she wrote to a friend, "I look about 70—grey & wrinkled & bent & lame."

On March 1 she drove to the town house to visit her father. She knelt next to him and spoke quietly. "Father, here is your Louy. What are you thinking of as you lie here so happily?" He took her hand, pointed upward, and said, "I am going up. Come with me." "Oh, I wish I could," she replied.

Bronson died on the fourth. Before the news could even reach her, Louisa slipped into a coma, presumably from a cerebral hemorrhage. On the sixth, she followed him.

Acknowledgments

Anyone who ventures to write about Emerson and his circle stands on the shoulders of an army of scholars, especially biographers: Robert D. Richardson Jr., Laura Dassow Walls, John Matteson, David S. Reynolds, Brenda Wineapple, and their many predecessors. I would like to thank one biographer in particular: Megan Marshall, whose careful reading of key portions of the manuscript yielded important insights and corrections. I am also deeply grateful to Robert A. Gross, who reviewed an entire draft and made many valuable suggestions. Any errors that remain in the text are solely my fault.

I would like to thank librarians and staff at the Houghton Library at Harvard, the New York Public Library, the Massachusetts Historical Society, and, especially, Jessie Hopper at the Concord Free Public Library. For assistance with illustrations, I am grateful to Sarah Hayes of the Archives & Research Center of the Trustees of Reservations of Massachusetts.

My literary agent, Tina Bennett, provided important advice and support throughout the conception and writing of this book. She also had the wisdom to place it in the hands of Ben Loehnen at Avid Reader Press, who believed in it from the start. Ben's astute comments improved every page, with editorial acumen matched only by his diplomatic communication skills. I am grateful to the entire team under Ben at Avid Reader: Carolyn Kelly, Alison Forner, Clay Smith, Sydney Newman, Allison Green, Hana Handzija, Douglas Johnson, Dominick Montalto, Ruth Lee-Mui, David Kass, Eva Kerins, Lily Soroka, Caroline McGregor, and Kayla Dee.

My wife, Sarah Cutler, to whom this book is dedicated, provided advice and counsel at every step, and tolerated more hours of conversation about antebellum America than she ever bargained for. I can never thank her enough.

A Note on Sources

Archival materials are identified in the notes by their call numbers preceded by initials indicating the archives:

CFPL	Concord Free Public Library
HL	Houghton Library at Harvard University
MHS	Massachusetts Historical Society

Frequently cited works by members of the Emerson circle are noted with these abbreviations:

BA *Journals The Journals of Bronson Alcott*, selected and edited by Odell Shepard (Boston: Little, Brown, 1938)

BA *Letters The Letters of A. Bronson Alcott*, edited by Richard L. Herrnstadt (Ames, IA: Iowa State University Press, 1969)

LMA *Journals The Journals of Louisa May Alcott*, edited by Joel Myerson and Daniel Shealy (Boston: Little, Brown, 1989)

LMA *Letters The Selected Letters of Louisa May Alcott*, edited by Joel Myerson and Daniel Shealy (Boston: Little, Brown, 1987)

RWE *Journals Journals of Ralph Waldo Emerson*, edited by Edward Waldo Emerson and Waldo Emerson Forbes (Boston: Houghton Mifflin, 1909–1914)

JMN *The Journals and Miscellaneous Notebooks of Ralph Waldo Emerson*, edited by William H. Gilman, Alfred R. Ferguson, George P. Clark, and Merrell R. Davis (Cambridge: Harvard University Press, 1960–1982)

RWE *Letters The Letters of Ralph Waldo Emerson*, six volumes, edited by Ralph L. Rusk (New York: Columbia University Press, 1939), plus three volumes edited by Eleanor M. Tilton (Columbia University Press, 1990)

RWE CW *The Complete Works of Ralph Waldo Emerson,* twelve volumes, edited by Edward Waldo Emerson (Boston: Houghton, Mifflin, 1903–1906)

LMF *The Letters of Margaret Fuller*, six volumes edited by Robert N. Hudspeth (Ithaca, NY: Cornell University Press, 1983–1994)

NH CE *Centenary Edition of the Works of Nathaniel Hawthorne*, twenty-three volumes, various editors (Columbus: The Ohio State University Press, 1963–1995)

HDT *Correspondence* Volumes 1 and 2, *The Writings of Henry D. Thoreau*, edited by Robert N. Hudspeth (Princeton: Princeton University Press, 2014, 2018)

HDT *Journal* Volumes 1–8, Henry Thoreau *Journal*, edited by John C. Broderick et al. (Princeton: Princeton University Press, 1981–)

HDT *Journals* Volumes VII–XX, *The Journal of Henry D. Thoreau*, edited by Bradford Torrey and Francis H. Allen (Boston: Houghton Mifflin, 1906)

HDT *Writings* Volumes I–XV, *The Writings of Henry D. Thoreau*, edited by J. Lyndon Shanley et al. (Princeton: Princeton University Press, 1971–2008)

WHM Volumes 1–15, *The Writings of Herman Melville*, edited by Thomas Tanelle et al. (Evanston, IL: Northwestern University Press, 1968–2017)

Articles from newspapers and academic journals are cited in full in the notes. All other citations refer to works listed in the bibliography.

Notes

Prologue

2 *"Christianity, the laws"*: Ralph Waldo Emerson, "Man the Reformer," *The Dial* 1, no. 4 (April 1841): 523–24.

3 *Transcendentalism has been described*: See the introduction to Perry Miller, ed., *The Transcendentalists: An Anthology* (Cambridge: Harvard University Press, 1950), 8.

3 *"the nation existed"*: "Life and Letters in New England," RWE CW 10:326.

Chapter 1: Waldo Emerson and Bronson Alcott

7 *"A great soul will be"*: "The American Scholar," RWE CW 1:99.

7 *Over his life he delivered*: William Charvat, *Emerson's American Lecture Engagements* (New York: The New York Public Library, 1961), 7.

9 *"the charm of his voice"*: James Russell Lowell, *My Study Windows* (Boston: Houghton, Mifflin/Riverside Press, 1883), 375.

9 *"see a perpendicular coffin"*: Ralph Waldo Emerson, *The Later Lectures of Ralph Waldo Emerson*, Ronald Bosco and Joel Myerson, eds. (Athens: University of Georgia Press, 2001), 103–4.

9 *"there arose"*: Emerson, *Later Lectures*, 82–83.

9 *"There is the saintly"*: Franklin B. Sanborn, "Mr. Emerson's Lectures," in Ronald Bosco and Joel Myerson, eds., *Emerson in His Own Time: A Biographical Chronicle of His Life, Drawn from Recollections, Interviews, and Memoirs by Family, Friends, and Associates* (Iowa City: University of Iowa Press, 2003), 43.

10 *"I was homesick"*: BA "Autobiography" in HL b MS Am 1130.9-1130.12, vol. 1.

10 *"They were born"*: Edward Waldo Emerson, *Emerson in Concord: A Memoir* (Boston: Houghton, Mifflin, 1888), 9.

11 *"gratitude, faith" . . . "beings holding a high rank"*: *Hints to Parents*, quoted in William Russell, *American Journal of Education for the Year 1829*, 4:56.

12 *"The business of school-keeping"*: Horace Mann, quoted in Robert B. Downs, *Horace Mann: Champion of Public Schools* (New York: Twayne Publishers, 1974), 31.

13 *four schools and five jobs*: HL "Autobiographical Index" MS Am 1130.9-1130.12, vol. 33.

13 *"anarchy and confusion"*: BA *Journals*, 4.

13 *"I have but limited faith"*: Ibid., 35.
13 *"There was nothing of artifice"*: Ibid., 12.
13 *"I walked with him"*: HL Memoir of Abigail (May) Alcott, MS Am 1130.10.
14 *"My husband is"*: Abigail May Alcott, letter of July 25, 1830, HL MS Am 1130.9-1130.12, Folder 1.
14 *"The vicissitudes"*: Abigail May Alcott, letter of September 1832, HL MS Am 1130.9-1130.12, Folder 1.
14 *"prose poem"*: Larry A. Carlson, "Bronson Alcott's 'Journal for 1837' (Part Two)," *Studies in the American Renaissance* (1982), 83, 99.
14 *"fortelleth and remembereth"*: HL MS Am 1130.10 (8), 2–3.
14 *"Winter reigneth"*: HL MS Am 1130.10 (8), 319.
14 *"Obedience has never"*: HL MS Am 1130.10 (vol. 6, pt. 1), 110.
15 *"I have now been four days"*: RWE *Journals*, 1:255.
15 *"Ellen Tucker Emerson died"*: Ibid., 356.
15 *"miserable apathy" . . . "I shall forget"*: Ibid., 357.
16 *"For what has imagination created"*: RWE *Journals*, 2:487.
16 *"The irresistible effect"*: Ibid., 490.
17 *"You have taken my Lord"*: Emerson, *Emerson in Concord*, 41.
17 *"Without a personal God"*: Mary Moody Emerson, *The Selected Letters of Mary Moody Emerson* (Athens: University of Georgia Press, 1993), 314.
18 *"Here we are impressed"*: RWE *Journals*, 2:163.
18 *some three thousand by 1845*: Lyceum statistics are from A. Augustus Wright, *Who's Who in the Lyceum* (Philadelphia: Pearson Brothers, 1906), 19.

Chapter 2: A Temple of Learning

19 *"[Alcott's] book is his school"*: RWE *Journals,* 3:559.
19 *At thirteen*: Statistic is from Megan Marshall, *The Peabody Sisters: Three Women Who Ignited American Romanticism* (Boston: Houghton Mifflin Harcourt, 2005), 91.
20 *"feels my infinite capacity"*: Elizabeth Palmer Peabody, quoted in Marshall, *The Peabody Sisters*, 327.
20 *"It is true that both of us" . . . "he had no bill"*: Franklin Sanborn, *The Genius and Character of Emerson* (Boston: James R. Osgood and Co., 1885), 150.
21 *"transcendentalism"*: Megan Marshall, *Margaret Fuller: A New American Life* (Boston: Houghton Mifflin Harcourt, 2013), 165.
21 *"elementary education needs"*: Elizabeth Palmer Peabody, in Russell, *American Journal of Education for the Year 1829*, 4:76.
22 *"creatures of instinct"*: Elizabeth Palmer Peabody, *Record of a School: Exhibiting the General Principles of Spiritual Culture*. Boston: Russell, Shattuck & Company, 1835, xvii.
23 *"The worst boys"*: Ibid., xix.

23 *"They declared"*: Ibid., 24.

24 *"Few men among us"*: BA *Journals*, 56.

24 *"almost equal to Mr. Emerson"*: Letter from Sarah Clarke to James Freeman Clarie, quoted in Ellen Tucker Emerson, *The Life of Lidian Jackson Emerson* (East Lansing: Michigan State University Press, 1992), 49.

24 *"It is in a mean place"*: RWE *Letters*, 1:447.

24 *"read with great delight"*: RWE *Journals*, 3:509–10.

25 *"Mr. E's fine"*: BA *Journals*, 69.

25 *"Every man"*: RWE *Journals*, 3:559–60.

25 *"Emerson is destined"*: Larry A. Carlson, "Bronson Alcott's 'Journal for 1837' (Part One)," *Studies in the American Renaissance* (1981), 47.

25 *"R. W. Emerson"*: LMF, 6:266.

Chapter 3: Margaret Fuller

26 *"I now know all the people"*: Margaret Fuller, *Memoirs of Margaret Fuller Ossoli*, Ralph Waldo Emerson, James Freeman Clarke, and William Henry Channing, eds. (Boston: Phillips, Sampson & Company, 1852) 1:234.

26 *"My father"*: "Autobiographical Romance," in Margaret Fuller, *The Essential Margaret Fuller*, Jeffrey Steele, ed. (New Brunswick, NJ: Rutgers University Press, 1992), 26.

27 *"For a long time"*: HL f MS Am 1086, Fuller Family Papers, 20:83.

27 *"should not be proud"*: HL MS Am 1086, Margaret Fuller Family Papers, vol. 5, letter of January 1818.

27 *"to acquire a taste"*: Ibid.

27 *"Give me the book"*: Ibid.

27 *"To excel in all things"*: HL MS Am 1086, Margaret Fuller Family Papers, vol. 5, letter of April 1820.

28 *"I read them in bed"*: HL f MS Am 1086, Fuller Family Papers, 20:23.

28 *In one letter*: LMF, 1:151.

29 *"I wish to study"*: LMF, 1:196

29 *"She was always conspicuous"*: Margaret Fuller, *Memoirs of Margaret Fuller Ossoli*, 1:94.

29 *"With what eagerness"*: Fuller, *Memoirs*, 1:62.

29 *"We both felt"*: Robert Habich, "Margaret Fuller's Journal for October 1842" in *Harvard Library Bulletin* 33, no. 3 (Summer 1985): 287.

29 *"It is so true that a woman"*: Habich, "Margaret Fuller's Journal for October 1842," 286–87.

30 *"Her extreme plainness"*: Fuller, *Memoirs*, 1:202–3.

30 *"quite an extraordinary person"*: RWE *Letters*, 2:32.

31 *"The spirit comes"*: Bronson Alcott, *Conversations with Children on the Gospels*, (Boston: James Munroe & Company, 1836), 68.

31 *"Dear Sir"*: LMF, 1:255–56.

32 *"of those who promise"*: Larry A. Carlson, "Bronson Alcott's 'Journal for 1837' (Part One)," *Studies in the American Renaissance* (1981), 48.

32 *"one third absurd"*: Andrews Norton, quoted in John Matteson, *Eden's Outcasts: The Story of Louisa May Alcott and Her Father* (New York: W. W. Norton, 2007), 80.

32 *"These conversations appear"*: Editor of the *Boston Daily Advertiser*, quoted in the introduction to "Bronson Alcott's 'Journal for 1837' (Part One)," *Studies in the American Renaissance* (1981), 30.

32 *"small men are ever in the way"*: Carlson, "Bronson Alcott's 'Journal for 1837' (Part One)," 103.

33 *"his book does him no justice"*: RWE *Letters*, 2:76

33 *"Our age is retrospective"*: Introduction to *Nature*, RWE CW, 1:3.

34 *"In the divine order"*: "The Method of Nature," RWE CW, 1:197.

34 *"Man is conscious"*: *Nature*, RWE CW, 1:27.

34 *"Standing on the bare ground"*: Ibid., 1:10.

34 *"a gem throughout"*: Bronson Alcott, quoted in Merton Sealts and Alfred R. Ferguson, *Emerson's Nature: Origin, Growth, Meaning* (Carbondale: Southern Illinois University Press, 1969), 74.

34 *"The work is a remarkable one"*: A reviewer in the *Western Messenger*, quoted ibid., 78.

35 *"To go into solitude"*: *Nature*, RWE CW, 1:9.

35 *"The greatest delight"*: Ibid., 1:13.

35 *"In no one essay"*: From Fuller's first article in the *New-York Daily Tribune*, December 7, 1844, collected in Judith Mattson Bean and Joel Myerson, eds., *Margaret Fuller, Critic: Writings from the New-York Tribune, 1844–1846* (New York: Columbia University Press, 2000), 5.

35 *"you may begin"*: Bronson Alcott, *Concord Days* (Boston: Roberts Brothers, 1872), 33.

36 *"The conversation was earnest"*: RWE *Journals*, 4:86–87.

36 *"an engine to undermine"*: "Farewell Address," *The Statesmanship of Andrew Jackson: As Told in his Writings and Speeches*, Francis Newton Thorpe, ed. (New York: The Tandy-Thomas Company, 1909), 509.

37 *"Mr. Fuller is as unlike"*: Margaret Fuller to Elizabeth Palmer Peabody, July 8, 1837, LMF, 1:291.

37 *"dreams and hopes"*: Margaret Fuller to William H. Channing, December 9, 1838, LMF, 1:354.

37 *"not forget the delight"*: Bronson Alcott, quoted in Kenneth Sacks, *Understanding Emerson: "The American Scholar" and His Struggle for Self-Reliance* (Princeton: University of Princeton Press, 2003), 17.

37 *"I do not know"*: Ibid., 19.

37 *"read God directly"*: "The American Scholar," RWE CW, 1:91.
37 *"A nation of men"*: Ibid., 115.

Chapter 4: Blasphemy

39 *"My life has been the poem"*: Henry David Thoreau, *A Week on the Concord and Merrimack Rivers*, HDT *Writings*, 5:343.
39 *"If life were long"*: RWE *Journals*, 3:460–61.
39 *"Emerson is too grand"*: HDT *Journal*, 4:309.
39 *"I think that I cannot preserve my health"*: "Walking," HDT *Writings*, 15:187.
40 *"I have much to learn"*: "The Allegash and East Branch," HDT *Writings*, 3:201.
40 *"I hate museums"*: HDT *Journal*, 2:77.
40 *"One man lies"*: HDT *Journal*, 5:145.
40 *"I think that the law"*: HDT *Journals*, 11:208.
40 *"In my experience"*: HDT *Journal*, 4:162.
40 *"Especially the transcendental"*: "Thomas Carlyle and His Works," HDT *Writings*, 4:103.
42 *"'What are you doing now?'"*: HDT *Journal*, 1:5.
42 *"Everything that boy"*: RWE *Journals*, 4:397.
43 *apart from the moral issues*: See Robert Gross, *The Transcendentalists and Their World* (New York: Farrar, Straus and Giroux, 2021), 468–69.
43 *Emerson had spoken*: For a full account, see Gross, *The Transcendentalists and Their World*, 525.
43 *"Almost the entire"*: The letter is reprinted in James Elliot Cabot, *A Memoir of Ralph Waldo Emerson* (Cambridge, MA: Riverside Press, 1887), 2: 697–702.
44 *"Mr. Emerson very unwillingly"*: Lidian Jackson Emerson, *The Selected Letters of Lidian Jackson Emerson* (Columbia: University of Missouri Press, 1987), 75.
44 *"If any person shall"*: Anonymous ("A Cosmopolite" identified as David Henshaw), *A Review of the Prosecution Against Abner Kneeland* (Boston, 1835), 3–4.
45 *"If thy mind"*: Abner Kneeland, *A Review of the Evidences of Christianity* (Boston: The Investigator, 1831), 1.
45 *"forging and lying"* . . . *"Is there a book in existence"*: Abner Kneeland, *A Review of the Evidences of Christianity* (Boston: Office of the Investigator, 1835), 1ff.
46 *"Universalists believe"*: *Commonwealth v. Abner Kneeland*, 37 Mass. 206 (Sup. Ct. Mass 1838).
47 *"Thus I have"*: Abner Kneeland, *A Review of the Trial, Conviction, and Final Imprisonment in the Common Jail of the County of Suffolk of Abner Kneeland for the Alleged Crime of Blasphemy* (Boston: George A. Chapman, 1838), 45.
47 *"indelible page of shame"*: The Boston *Advocate*, quoted in Commager, "The Blasphemy of Abner Kneeland," *The New England Quarterly* 8, no. 1 (March 1935): 39.
47 *"a 'Who's Who'"*: Leonard W. Levy, ed., *Blasphemy in Massachusetts: Freedom of*

Conscience and the Abner Kneeland Case: A Documentary Record (New York: Da Capo Press, 1973), xx.

47 *Indeed, during his time in prison*: August 7, 1838, letter by Theodore Parker, quoted in Franklin Sanborn and William T. Harris, *A. Bronson Alcott: His Life and Philosophy* (New York: Biblo and Tannen, 1965), 1:281.

47 *"I believe in the existence"*: Kneeland, *A Review of the Trial, Conviction, and Final Imprisonment*, 21.

48 *Emerson hoped the speech*: Some scholars argue that Emerson was deliberately provocative, but Robert E. Burkholder, in "Emerson, Kneeland, and the Divinity School Address" (*American Literature* 58, no. 1 [March 1986]: 1–14), makes a good case that the reverse is true.

48 *"The idioms of"*: "The Divinity School Address," RWE CW, 1:128–44

48 *"at war with" . . . "and is no longer a sectarian"*: *Boston Investigator*, October 12, 1838.

49 *"all belief in Christianity"*: Andrews Norton, quoted in Cabot, *A Memoir of Ralph Waldo Emerson*, 1:335.

49 *"we meet in a revolutionary" . . . "daring and crazy fanaticism"*: Andrews Norton, *A Discourse on the Latest Forms of Infidelity* (Cambridge, UK: John Owen, 1839), 4ff.

49 *"the miserable babble"*: JMN, 5:71.

50 *"Divine as the life"*: RWE *Journals*, September 29, 1839, 5:272.

Chapter 5: Coolidge Castle

51 *"All sorts of visitors"*: Ellen Tucker Emerson, *The Life of Lidian Jackson Emerson* (East Lansing: Michigan State University Press, 1992), 79–80.

51 *"I looked in to the parlour"*: Ibid., 80.

51 *"a whole company" . . . "looking hungrily"*: Ibid., 80.

51 *"a new course of study" . . . "A lady remembers"*: George P. Lathrop, "Literary and Social Boston," in *Harper's New Monthly Magazine* (February 1881): 383.

52 *"stiff, heady and rebellious"*: Ralph Waldo Emerson, quoted in Barbara Packer, "The Transcendentalists," in Sacvan Bercovitch, ed., *The Cambridge History of American Literature* (Cambridge: Cambridge University Press, 1995), 2:331.

53 *"I enjoyed the frank"*: JMN, 7:259.

53 *"prim and bloodless"*: James Eliot Cabot, *A Memoir of Ralph Waldo Emerson*, (Cambridge, MA: Riverside Press, 1887), 1:358.

53 *"She is superior"*: Emerson, quoted ibid., 1:379.

53 *"the most learned woman"*: Gamaliel Bradford, *Portraits of American Women* (Boston: Houghton Mifflin, 1919), 35.

53 *"How joyfully"*: JMN, 7:510.

54 *"Year by year"*: "Holidays," RWE CW, 9:136.

54 *"in the early 1840s"*: Robert Richardson Jr., *Emerson: The Mind on Fire* (Berkeley: University of California Press, 1995), 329.

54 *"Never hint"*: The full text of the "Transcendental Bible" is included in Ellen Tucker Emerson, *The Life of Lidian Jackson Emerson*, 81ff.

55 *"He seems not to be"*: BA *Journals*, 91.

55 *"a serious physical"*: Larry A. Carlson, "Bronson Alcott's 'Journal for 1837' (Part Two)," *Studies in the American Renaissance* (1982), 53.

56 *"I shall not always"*: BA *Journals*, 115.

56 *"My Patrons"*: HL "Autobiographical Index," MS Am 1130.9-1130.12, vol. 33.

56 *"God shall provide"*: Bronson Alcott, quoted in Cynthia H. Barton, *Transcendental Wife: The Life of Abigail May Alcott* (Lanham, MD: University Press of America, 1996), 66.

56 *"in the frankest manner"* . . . *"a more outward method"*: Quotes from Cheney's transcript from CFPL, A. Bronson Alcott Papers, 1843–1882, Vault A35, A.B. Alcott, Unit 1, Folder 1.

57 *"Miss Fuller's most important"*: A transcript of what were likely Elizabeth Palmer Peabody's notes from this 1839 conversation can be found in Nancy Craig Simmons's "Margaret Fuller's Boston Conversations: The 1839–1840 Series," *Studies in the American Renaissance*, 1994, 203.

57 *Her audiences may have included*: Elizabeth Cady Stanton, years later, wrote that she attended at least one Fuller conversation, but Megan Marshall questions the reliability of her remembered account (private correspondence with the author).

57 *"Margaret spoke well"*: Margaret Fuller, *Memoirs of Margaret Fuller Ossoli*, Ralph Waldo Emerson, James Freeman Clarke, and William Henry Channing eds. (Boston: Phillips, Sampson & Company, 1852), 348.

58 *"Thou art, my heart"*: Bronson Alcott, "Orphic Sayings," *The Dial* 1, no. 1 (July 1840): 85.

58 *"The poles of potatoes"*: New York *Knickerbocker*, "Gastric Sayings," quoted in Barbara Packer, "The Transcendentalists," in *The Cambridge History of American Literature*, 2:446.

58 *"you will not like"*: RWE *Letters*, 2:294.

58 *"should not be merely"*: Margaret Fuller, "A Short Essay on Critics," *The Dial* 1, no. 1 (July 1840): 7.

58 *"One of the most"*: *Boston Times*, July 17, 1840, quoted in Joel Myerson, *The New England Transcendentalists and The Dial*, 51.

59 *"the journal did not get"*: Fuller, *Memoirs*, 323.

59 *"woman possesses not"* . . . *"and an appendage"*: Sophia Ripley, "Woman," *The Dial* 1, no. 3 (January 1841): 362ff.

59 *"The essay is rich"*: Margaret Fuller, *"My Heart Is a Large Kingdom": Selected Letters of Margaret Fuller*, Robert N. Hudspeth, ed. (Ithaca, NY: Cornell University Press, 2001), 133.

59 *"Most things are"*: "The Service," HDT *Writings*, 3:5–6.
60 *"Now here are my wise"*: RWE *Journals*, 4:251.
61 *"Alcott seems to need"*: JMN, 7:298.
61 *"I cannot gee"*: Abigail May Alcott, quoted in Eve LaPlante, ed., *My Heart Is Boundless: Writings of Abigail May Alcott, Louisa's Mother* (New York: Free Press, 2012), 87.
62 *"little dewy nets"*: HDT *Journal*, 8:137–38.
62 *"affected me at first"*: RWE *Letters*, 7:404.
63 *"I will study to deserve"* . . . *"for a very long time"*: RWE *Letters*, 2:332ff.
63 *"friendship, like the immortality"*: "Friendship," RWE CW, 2:196, 199.
64 *"social reform and"*: George Ripley, *A Letter Addressed to the Congregational Church in Purchase Street, by Its Pastor*, 10.
64 *"talk was useless"*: Letter to Caroline Sturgis, October 18, 1840, LMF, 2:163.
64 *"My Dear Sir"* . . . *"to a future generation"*: The complete letter is in O. B. Frothingham, *George Ripley* (Boston: Houghton, Mifflin, 1882), 307–12.

Chapter 6: The Satirist in Paradise

66 *"The better life!"*: Nathaniel Hawthorne, *The Blithedale Romance*, NH CE, 3:10.
66 *"The ground of my decision"*: RWE *Letters*, 2:369.
66 *"Nature seems to exist"*: "Uses of Great Men," *Representative Men*, RWE CW, 4:3.
66 *"not pitched sufficiently"*: HL b MS Am 1130.10 (24), Folder 2.
67 *"I have not yet concluded"* . . . *"Satan may take them"*: NH CE, 15:138–39.
68 *"she was that wisest"*: "The Wedding Knell," NH CE, 9:29.
68 *"It is not merely"*: Margaret Fuller, "Hawthorne's 'Twice-Told Tales,'" *The Dial* 3, no. 1 (July 1842):130–31.
68 *"Oh Sophia"*: Elizabeth Palmer Peabody, quoted in Norman Holmes Pearson, "Elizabeth Peabody on Hawthorne," *Essex Institute Historical Collections* (July 1958): 264–65.
69 *"I have heard recently"*: NH CE, 15:270.
70 *"Often, while holding you"*: NH CE, 15:329.
70 *"now they are all ashes"*: NH CE, 8:552.
70 *"I was invited"*: NH CE, 15:382.
72 *"Amusement Group"*: Frothingham, *George Ripley*, 149, 155–56.
72 *"I strolled, after dinner"*: NH CE, 8:201–2.
73 *"The very liberality"*: Elizabeth Palmer Peabody, "Plan of the West Roxbury Community," *The Dial* 2, no. 3 (January 1842): 368–69.
73 *"Utopia it is impossible"*: Letter to William H. Channing, 1840, LMF, 2:109.
73 *"'And fools rush in'"*: RWE *Journals*, 6:491.
73 *"Here is thy poor husband"*: NH CE, 15:526.
73 *"We have eight"*: Ibid., 15:526–27.
74 *He complained about Ripley*: Ibid., 15:553.

74 *"Thou and I"*: Ibid., 15:563.

74 "CONCORD (Mass.), May, 1852" . . . "a most grievous wrong": NE CE 3:1–3.

74 *"not her real name"*: NH CE, 3:13.

74 *"noble courage" . . . "'Behold! here is a woman!'"*: NH CE, 3:12.

74 *"no friend who knew"*: RWE CW, 10:364.

74 *"A sketch to be given"*: NH CE, 8:10.

75 *"As soon as several of the inhabitants"*: Alexis de Tocqueville, *Democracy in America* (Chicago: University of Chicago Press, 2000), 410.

75 *"live with me & work"*: RWE *Letters*, 2:394.

75 *"I am glad"*: Letter to Ralph Waldo Emerson, April 1841, LMF, 2:208.

75 *"the civilized man"*: HDT *Writings*, 7:253.

75 *"an earnest thinker"*: Letter to Richard F. Fuller, May 25, 1841, LMF, 2:210.

75 *"a tinkling stream"*: HDT *Writings*, 6:272.

76 *"the whole institution of property"*: Emerson, "Man the Reformer," *The Dial* 2, no. 4 (April 1841): 526.

76 *"a ruthless criticism"*: See Letter to Arnold Ruge printed in the *Deutsch-Franzosische Jahrbucher* in 1844, *The Marx-Engels Reader*, second edition, Robert C. Tucker, ed. (New York: W. W. Norton, 1978), 13.

76 *"cannot content them"*: RWE *Letters*, 3:18.

76 *"Progress is not for society"*: Ralph Waldo Emerson, "The Individual," *The Early Lectures of Ralph Waldo Emerson* (Cambridge: Belknap/Harvard University Press, 1964), 2:176.

75 *"perhaps the most brilliant display"*: Gay Wilson Allen, *Waldo Emerson* (New York: Viking, 1981), 373.

77 *"Society everywhere" . . . "to that iron string"*: "Self-Reliance," RWE CW, 2:43ff.

77 *"The political parties"*: Ibid., 2:88–89.

78 *"We live in succession"*: "The Over-Soul," RWE CW, 2:269.

78 *"Polarity, or action and reaction"*: "Compensation," RWE CW, 2:96.

78 *"Mr. Emerson will give"*: *Boston Courier*, November 18, 1841.

78 *At least seven American journals*: See B. Bernard Cohen and Lucian A. Cohen, "A Penny Paper's Review of Emerson's Essays (1841)," *The New England Quarterly* 29, no. 4 (December 1956): 516.

78 *"the good river-god"*: RWE *Journals*, 5:558.

79 *"I am very familiar"*: JMN, 8:96.

79 *"Ellery . . . is a very imperfect"*: RWE *Journals*, 6:46.

79 *"I wish it to live"*: JMN, 8:203.

79 *"strange, cold-warm"*: Ibid., 8:87.

Chapter 7: Compensations

80 *"The South-wind brings"*: Ralph Waldo Emerson, "Threnody," RWE CE, 9:148.

80 *"My pleasure at getting home"*: RWE *Letters*, 3:4.

81 *"I was sent"*: Moncure Daniel Conway, *Emerson at Home and Abroad* (Boston: James Osgood, 1882), 141.
81 *"Death is beautiful when seen"*: HDT *Correspondence*, 1:105.
81 "Nature, who lost": Ralph Waldo Emerson, "Threnody," RWE CE, 9:149.
82 *"Here is a proposition"*: JMN, 8:172.
82 *"Happiness has no succession"*: NH CE, 8:315.
82 *"a singular character"*: Ibid., 353–54.
83 *"as reasonable"*: Ibid., 356.
83 *"Only imagine"*: Ibid., 317.
83 *"The mystic"*: Ibid., 336.
83 *"Margaret herself"* . . . *"high and low philosophy"*: Ibid., 341–43.
84 *"which would do away"*: Ibid., 367.
84 *"My expectations"*: "Margaret Fuller's 1842 Journal: At Concord with the Emersons," Joel Myerson, ed., *Harvard Library Bulletin* 21, no. 3 (July 1973): 324, 326.
84 *"The family were all present"* . . . *"I do not want you"*: "Margaret Fuller's 1842 Journal: At Concord with the Emersons," 331.
84 *"I dread and yet desire"*. . . *"no odor until crushed"*: HL MS Am 1130.14-1130.16, Abigail May Alcott diary for the years 1841–44.
85 *"a man of ideas"* . . . *"disgusts many"*: JMN, 8:210ff.
85 *"genial, innocent"*: Ralph Waldo Emerson, *The Correspondence of Emerson and Carlyle*, Joseph Slater, ed. (New York: Columbia University Press, 1964), 326.
85 *"the good Alcott"*: Ibid., 329.
85 *"all sounding brass"*: BA *Letters*, 74.
85 "*costly, elegant*": Ibid., 69.
85 *"the deepest, sharpest intellect"*: Ibid., 70.
85 *"the first man"* . . . *"that we might become"*: Ibid., 69.
86 *"abode of divine purposes"*: BA *Letters*, 68.
86 *"Britain, with all her resource"*: Ibid., 76.
86 *"will begin his labours"*: Ibid., 87.
87 *"a confused jumble of heads"*: HDT *Correspondence*, 1:160.
87 *"a whole continent"*: Ibid., 161.
87 *"a thousand times meaner"* Ibid., 181.
87 *"I must say I think"*: Ronald Bosco and Joel Myerson, eds., *Emerson in His Own Time: A Biographical Chronicle of His Life, Drawn from Recollections, Interviews, and Memoirs by Family, Friends, and Associates* (Iowa City: University of Iowa Press, 2003), 252.
88 *"I shall not hesitate"*: HDT *Correspondence*, 1:166.
88 *"to speak out"*: Ibid., 195.
88 *"did not impress me"*: Ibid., 180.
88 *"literature comes"*: Ibid., 233.

88 *"Whole families"*: HDT *Correspondence*, 1:239.

89 *Among other things*: See Augustine Sedgewick, "Thoreau's Pencils," *American Scholar* (Autumn 2024): 38–51.

89 *"I will give you"*: HDT *Correspondence*, 1:308.

89 *"with all his clothes"*: Whitelaw Reid, *Horace Greeley* (New York: Charles Scribner's Sons, 1879), 5.

89 *"entered into a conspiracy"*: Anonymous, *The New York Tribune: A Sketch of Its History* (New York: privately published, 1883), 6.

90 *"he lacked business thrift"*: Reid, *Horace Greeley*, 9.

Chapter 8: Utopia

91 *"We are all a little wild here"*: Emerson to Thomas Carlyle, October 30, 1840, *The Correspondence of Emerson and Carlyle*, Joseph Slater, ed., 283.

91 *"most of the noted"*: Nathaniel Hawthorne, "The Hall of Fantasy," NH CE, 9:180.

91 *"one theory"*: Ibid., 9:181.

92 *One scholar counted*: Otohiko Okigawa, cited in Christopher Clark, *The Communitarian Moment: The Radical Challenge of the Northampton Association* (Ithaca, NY: Cornell University Press, 1995), 2.

92 *"free lovers, nonlovers"*: Chris Jennings, *Paradise Now: The Story of American Utopianism* (New York: Random House, 2016), 190.

92 *one woman became convinced*: Sylvester Bliss, *Memoirs of William Miller* (Boston: Joshua V. Himes, 1853), 234–35.

92 *At one appearance*: Ibid., 249.

92 "*I* confess my error": Ibid., 256.

93 *"This Shop is closed"*: A Philadelphia tailor, quoted in Whitney Cross, *The Burned-Over District: The Social and Intellectual History of Enthusiastic Religion in Western New York, 1800–1850* (Ithaca, NY: Cornell University Press, 1950), 307.

94 *"became the manager"*: Whitney Cross, *The Burned-Over District*, 292–93.

95 *"When two Shakers walk"*: Jennings, *Paradise Now*, 74.

96 *"the flat broom"*: Ibid., 16.

98 *"I had studied"*: Redelia Brisbane, *Albert Brisbane: A Mental Biography with a Character Study* (Boston: Arena Publishing, 1893), 171–72.

98 *"a tall, slender man"*: Walt Whitman, quoted in Carl Guarneri, *The Utopian Alternative: Fourierism in Nineteenth-Century America* (Ithaca, NY: Cornell University Press, 1991), 25.

99 *"the presumptive cuckold"*: Charles Fourier, *The Hierarchies of Cuckoldry and Bankruptcy* (Cambridge, MA: Wakefield Press, 2011), 13.

100 *"a vast field of copulation"*: Charles Fourier, *Harmonian Man: Selected Writings of Charles Fourier*, Mark Poster, ed. (New York: Anchor Books, 1971), 8.

100 *"I am waiting to make"*: Ibid., 198.

100 *"as strong as the claws"*: Charles Fourier, quoted in Jonathan Beecher, *Charles Fourier: The Visionary and His World* (Berkeley: University of California Press, 1986), 340.

101 *"nine-tenths of all civilizees"*: Ibid., 221.

101 *"Civilizees may think"*: Ibid., 261–62.

101 *"a calculation how"*: "Historic Notes on Life and Letters in New England," RWE CW, 10:354.

102 *"When walking in the streets"*: Charles Pellerin, *The Life of Charles Fourier* (New York: William H. Graham, 1848), 97.

102 *"the love of lesbians"*: Beecher, *Charles Fourier*, 84.

102 *"His very mental constitution"*: Brisbane, *Albert Brisbane*, 7.

102 *"Fourier's fertile mind"*: Ibid., 194–95.

103 *"There is Horace Greeley"*: Ibid., 204.

103 *one source names*: Charles Madison, *Critics & Crusaders: A Century of American Protest* (New York: Henry Holt and Company, 1947), 124.

103 *"the members"*: Brisbane, *Albert Brisbane*, 44.

104 *"Mr. Brisbane pushes"*: Ralph Waldo Emerson, "Fourierism and the Socialists," *The Dial* 3, no. 1 (July 1842): 86ff.

104 *twenty-four attempts*: Sources vary, depending on the definition of Fourier communities. This number is from Guarneri, *The Utopian Alternative,* 60.

104 *one historian estimates*: Guarneri, *The Utopian Alternative*, 60.

105 *"the common view"*: Clark, *Communitarian Moment*, 11.

106 *"Happy days these!!!"*: HL MS Am 1130.14-1130.16, Abigail May Alcott diary for the years 1841–44.

106 *"this invasion"*: Ibid.

106 *"is far too great"*: Charles Lane, "A Day with the Shakers," *The Dial* 4, no. 2 (October 1843): 167.

106 *"A gay and pleasant sound"*: "Prudence," RWE CW, 2:228–29.

107 *"Good morning, damn you!"*: "Transcendental Wild Oats" in Louisa May Alcott, *Louisa May Alcott: An Intimate Anthology* (New York: Doubleday, 1997), 37.

107 *"infamous for free love"*: Nell Irvin Painter, *Sojourner Truth: A Life, a Symbol* (New York: W. W. Norton, 1996), 45.

108 *"second Sodom"*: Sojourner Truth, *Narrative of Sojourner Truth* (Boston: privately published, 1850), 100.

108 *"the air was full of isms"*: Frederick Douglass, "What I Found at the Northampton Association," in Charles Sheffield, ed., *The History of Florence, Massachusetts* (Florence, MA: 1895), 130.

108 *"Their whole doctrine"*: JMN, 8:310–11.

108 *"I will not prejudge"*: Ibid., 433.

108 *"I rose at five"*: LMA *Journals*, 45.

109 *"In the evening Mr. Lane"*: Ibid., 46–47.
110 *"Father and Mr. L."*: Ibid., 47.
110 *"lay down upon his bed"*: "Transcendental Wild Oats," Ibid., 43.
110 *"One a dark"* . . . *"In the early dawn"*: Ibid., 29ff.

Chapter 9: Transcendence Abroad

112 *"I have met with but"*: Henry David Thoreau, "Walking," HDT *Writings*, 15:185.
112 *"travels sell"*: George Palmer Putnam, quoted in Dona Brown, "Travel Books," in Robert Gross and Mary Kelley, eds., *A History of the Book in America, Vol. 2: An Extensive Republic: Print, Culture, and Society in the New Nation, 1790–1840* (Chapel Hill: University of North Carolina Press, 2010).
113 *"the aversion that the white man"*: Margaret Fuller, *Summer on the Lakes, in 1843* (Boston: Charles C. Little and James Brown, 1844), 115, 183.
113 *"The fashioning spirit"*: Ibid., 159.
113 *"Don't expect"*: LMF, 3:159–60.
113 *"it is much read"*: Ibid., 198.
114 *"Mr. Lane decided"* . . . *"ineffably comic"*: HDT *Correspondence*, 1:145–46.
115 *"Men do not fail"*: HDT *Writings*, 5:127.
115 *"The reform"*: Ibid.,127.
115 *"has done nothing"*: RWE *Letters*, 3:384.
115 *"let it lie"*: HDT *Correspondence*, 1:316.
116 *"The Concord and Merrimak"*: *The Athenaeum*, no. 1148 (October 27, 1849): 1086.
116 *"I have now"*: HDT *Journal*, 7:123.
116 *"clan & parish"*: RWE *Letters*, 4:151.
116 *"to see him's"*: James Russell Lowell, *A Fable for Critics* (New York: George P. Putnam, 1848), 30.
116 *"thrust themselves"*: James Russell Lowell, review of *A Week on the Concord and Merrimack Rivers, Massachusetts Quarterly Review* 3, no. 9 (December 1849): 47, 50.
116 *"I had a friend"*: HDT *Journal*, 3:26.
117 *He wrote in his journal*: JMN, 10:106–7.
117 *"And now another"*: HDT *Journals*, IX:249.
117 *"helpless prisoner"*: Ibid., 276.
117 *"Those whom we can love"*: Ibid., 279.
118 *"I do not ask"*: Ellery Sedgwick, *The Atlantic Monthly, 1857–1909: Yankee Humanism at High Tide and Ebb* (Amherst: University of Massachusetts Press, 1994), 60.
118 *"must withdraw"*: Henry David Thoreau, *A Week on the Concord and Merrimack Rivers*, HDT *Writings*, 5:272.
119 *"information more general"*: Ibid., 22.

119 *"I told him"*: Henry David Thoreau, *The Maine Woods*, HDT *Writings*, 2:168.
119 *a paradox that scholars*: See John J. Kucich, *Unsettling Thoreau: Native Americans, Settler Colonialism, and the Power of Place*, (Amherst: University of Massachusetts Press, 2024), 2.
119 *"I sit now"*: *A Week on the Concord and Merrimack Rivers*, HDT *Writings*, 5:153.
120 *"The Anglo-American"*: *The Maine Woods*, HDT *Writings*, 2:229.
120 *"In Wildness"*: Henry David Thoreau, "Walking," *The Atlantic Monthly*, June 1862.
120 *"Nature was here"*: *The Maine Woods*, HDT *Writings*, 2:70.
120 *"I knew that I was"*: *A Week on the Concord and Merrimack Rivers*, HDT *Writings*, 5:183.
121 *"I filled my dipper"*: Ibid., 5:180ff.
121 *"to put a board"*: Ibid., 5:186.
121 *"I once set fire"*: HDT *Journal*, 3:75–77.
121 *"As for Sandwich"*: *Cape Cod*, HDT *Writings*, 9:16–17.
122 *"A strict regard"* . . . *"But we respect"*: Ibid., 9:19.
122 *"I was fourteen"* . . . *"They said that"*: "The Wellfleet Oysterman" in *Cape Cod*, ibid., 9:62ff.
123 *"I have been into"*: *The Maine Woods*, HDT *Writings*, 2:122.
123 *"A journal is"*: HDT *Journal*, 8:134.
123 *"To the indifferent"*: HDT *Journal*, 2:78.
124 *"The fact is"*: HDT *Journal*, 5:469–70.
124 *"when Thoreau came"*: Edward Waldo Emerson, *Henry David Thoreau as Remembered by a Young Friend* (Boston: Houghton Mifflin, 1917), 107.
124 *" 'Tis healthy"*: HDT *Journal*, 3:178.
124 *"Wheels of the storm-chariots"*: HDT *Journals*, 8:88–89.
125 *"Why was there never"*: HDT *Journal*, 4:32.
125 *"How well-behaved"*: HDT *Journals*, X:166.
125 *"representations of things"*: Ralph Waldo Emerson, "The Transcendentalist," *The Dial*, no. 3 (January 1843): 297.
126 *"In reading Henry"*: RWE *Journals*, IX:522.

Chapter 10: How to Live at Home

127 *"Where do we find ourselves?"*: Ralph Waldo Emerson, "Experience," RWE CW, 3:45.
127 *"Illusion, Temperament"*: Ibid., 3:82–83.
127 *"we do not see directly"*: Ibid., 3:75.
127 *"The true romance"*: Ibid., 3:86.
128 *"Hawthorne intimates"*: Judith Mattson Bean and Joel Myerson, eds., *Margaret Fuller, Critic: Writings from the New-York Tribune, 1844–1846* (New York: Columbia University Press, 2000), 454.

128 *"moral shapes of men"* . . . *"wonderful magnetism"*: "The Old Manse," NH CE, 10:30.

129 *"the cheerless"*: "Fire-Worship," Ibid., 10:138.

129 *"the inventions of mankind"*: Ibid., 10:139.

129 *"an American author"*: "Earth's Holocaust," 388–89.

129 *"shall see good days"*: Ibid., 403.

129 *"they belong to"*: Edgar Allan Poe, *The Works of Edgar Allan Poe in One Volume* (New York: P. F. Collier & Son, 1927), 1290.

129 *"Indeed,* his *spirit"*: Edgar Allan Poe, "Tale-Writing: A Review," *Godey's Magazine and Lady's Book* 35 (November 1847): 254ff.

130 *"We christened"*: Frederick L. H. Willis, *Alcott Memoirs* (Boston: Richard G. Badger, 1915), 21–22.

130 *"full of spirit"*: Ibid., 35.

130 *"I am unwilling"* . . . *"vastly nobler aim"*: BA *Letters*, 111.

130 *"I cannot consent"*: Ibid., 115.

131 *"I wrote letters"*: Louisa May Alcott, "Recollections of My Childhood," in *Selected Fiction* (Boston: Little, Brown and Company, 1990), 474–75.

131 *"Two devils, as yet"*: BA *Journals*, 350.

132 *"I had three chairs"*: *Walden*, HDT *Writings*, 1:140.

132 *"I think he must be"*: Ibid., 1:268.

133 *"'Keep very still'"*: Willis, *Alcott Memoirs*, 91–92.

134 *"She really did wish to"*: HDT *Correspondence*, 1:316.

134 *"The society of young women"*: HDT *Journal*, 4:186.

134 *"there is a . . . crust"*: Henry David Thoreau, quoted in Walter Harding, "Thoreau's Sexuality," *Journal of Homosexuality* 21, no. 3 (1991): 24.

135 *"Did you ever"*: HDT *Correspondence*, 1:314.

135 *"if there is a misfortune"*: Margaret Fuller, "The Great Lawsuit: Man versus Men. Woman versus Women," *The Dial* 4, no. 1 (July 1843): 19.

136 *"husbands tell their"*: Margaret Fuller, *Woman in the Nineteenth Century*, in *The Essential Margaret Fuller*, Jeffrey Steele, ed. (New Brunswick, NJ: Rutgers University Press, 1992), 220.

136 *"the best instructed"*: Horace Greeley, *The Autobiography of Horace Greeley: or, Recollections of a Busy Life* (New York: E. B. Treat, 1872), 171.

136 *"woman is the weaker party"*: Margaret Fuller, *Woman in the Nineteenth Century*, 33.

136 *"Male and female represent"*: Ibid., 310.

137 *"Those who think"*: Ibid., 259.

137 *she had privately supported*: Noted in Charles Capper, *Margaret Fuller: An American Romantic Life, Vol. 2: The Public Years* (New York: Oxford University Press, 2007), 182.

137 *"But if you ask me"*: Fuller, *Woman in the Nineteenth Century*, 345.

137 *"felt a delightful"*: LMF, 3:241.

137 *"Never was punishment"*: Bean and Myerson, *Margaret Fuller, Critic*, 102.

138 *"their incorrigible habits"*: Margaret Fuller, "The Irish Character," in the *New-York Weekly Tribune*, June 28, 1845, p. 2.

138 *"It is an excellent"*: Bean and Myerson, *Margaret Fuller, Critic*, 131.

138 *"We must confess"*: Margaret Fuller, "Poems. By Henry Wadsworth Longfellow," *New-York Daily Tribune*, December 10, 1845, p 1.

138 *The scathing review*: See Capper, *Margaret Fuller: An American Romantic Life, Vol. 2*, 250–51.

138 *"radical reform is needed"*: Fuller, "The Rich Man—An Ideal Sketch," in Bean and Myerson *Margaret Fuller, Critic*, 359.

138 *"held his right hand"*: LMF, 4:61n.

138 *"a man of genuine excellence"*: Ibid., 4:46.

139 *"my mind has been enfolded"*: Ibid., 4:15.

139 *"I hear you with awe"*: Ibid., 4:19, 4:21.

139 *"yesterday was, perhaps"*: Ibid., 4:22–24.

139 *"You have touched"*: Ibid., 4:48.

139 *"the sweet little garden"*: Ibid., 4:44–47.

140 *"Was it an assault?"* Megan Marshall, *Margaret Fuller: A New American Life* (Boston: Houghton Mifflin Harcourt, 2013), 255.

Chapter 11: War, Part I

141 *"[When] a whole country"*: Henry David Thoreau, "On the Duty of Civil Disobedience," HDT *Writings*, 3:67.

143 *"People of the United States!"*: Horace Greeley, "Our Country, Right or Wrong!," *New-York Daily Tribune*, May 12, 1846, p. 2.

143 *"were fighting in defense"*: Margaret Fuller, review of Thomas L McKenney's *Memoirs Official and Personal* in *New-York Daily Tribune*, July 8, 1846, p. 1.

143 *"governments, creeds"*: Charles Lane, "English Reformers," *The Dial* 3, no. 2 (October 1842): 245.

143 *"Why should I need"*: BA *Journals*, 189.

143 *"I do not wish"*: Thoreau, quoted in Robert Gross, *The Transcendentalists and Their World* (New York: Farrar, Straus and Giroux, 2021), 502.

143 *"Henry knew that I"*: Samuel Arthur Jones, "Thoreau's Incarceration (As Told by His Jailer)," *The Inlander* IX (1898), 99.

144 *"he said, 'no* sir'": Thoreau, quoted in Laura Dassow Walls, *Henry David Thoreau: A Life* (Chicago: Chicago University Press, 2017), 209.

144 *"The state tax"*: RWE *Journals*, 7:223.

144 *"mean and skulking"*: BA *Journals*, 183–84.

144 *"when a sixth"*: Henry David Thoreau, "On the Duty of Civil Disobedience," HDT *Writings*, 10:137.

145 *"is of such a nature"*: Ibid., 10:146.

145 *"There will never be"*: Ibid., 10:169.

146 *"change of forms"*: RWE *Journals*, 4:430.

146 *"the streets full of bayonets"*: RWE *Letters*, 7:72–73.

147 *"I thought I should not"*: Margaret Fuller, "Things and Thoughts from Europe," no. 5, *New-York Daily Tribune*, November 13, 1846, p. 1.

147 *"you know of no other"*: HL MS Am 1086 Margaret Fuller Family Papers, vol. 10.

147 *"Miss F."*: HL MS Am 1086 Margaret Fuller Family Papers, vol. 10.

147 *"I care not"*: Margaret Fuller, *Love-Letters of Margaret Fuller, 1845–1846* (New York: D. Appleton and Company, 1903), 187.

148 *"What fixed my attention"*: Margaret Fuller, *Memoirs of Margaret Fuller Ossoli*, Ralph Waldo Emerson, James Freeman Clarke, and William Henry Channing, eds. (Boston: Phillips, Sampson & Company, 1852), 2:195.

148 *"You ask me if I love"*: LMF, 4:263.

148 *"the most beauteous person"*: Ibid., 4:240.

148 *"this hollow England"*: Margaret Fuller, "Things and Thoughts in Europe," no. 18, *New-York Daily Tribune*, January 1, 1848, p. 1.

149 *"were so tedious"* . . . *"achieve their purpose"*: Ibid.

150 *"with indescribable rapture"*: Margaret Fuller, "Things and Thoughts in Europe," no. 23, *New-York Daily Tribune*, May 4, 1848, p. 1.

150 *"the treacherous advice"*: Pope Pius IX, quoted in Mike Rapport, *1848: Year of Revolution* (New York: Basic Books, 2009), 163.

151 *"The work began"*: Margaret Fuller, "Things and Thoughts in Europe," no. 24, *New-York Daily Tribune*, June 15, 1848, p. 1.

151 *"He is not in any respect"*: LMF, 4:261.

151 *"I expect that to many"*: Ibid., 4:291.

151 *"say 'Povera'"*: LMF, 5:77.

151 *She wrote to*: See LMF, 5:103, 104, and 91. See also an unpublished letter to R. H. Manning, July 19, 1848, in the collection of Lucilla Fuller Marvel.

152 *"Dearest Husband"*: LMF, 5:111.

152 *"For the first time"*: Giuseppe Garibaldi, quoted in Rapport, *1848*, 253.

154 *"Between each"*: Margaret Fuller, "Things and Thoughts in Europe," no. 28, *New-York Daily Tribune*, April 4, 1849, p. 1.

154 *"When I think"*: LMF, 5:196.

155 *"I write you"*: Margaret Fuller, *New-York Daily Tribune*, June 5, 1849, p. 2.

155 *"War near at hand"*: Margaret Fuller, *New-York Daily Tribune*, June 23, 1849, p. 1.

Chapter 12: Death, Part I

156 *"I have in my pocket"*: HDT *Journals*, VIII:43.

156 *"nearly new" . . . "steamers is so great"*: LMF, 6:75.

156 *"I had intended"*: Ibid., 6:81.

157 *"I am absurdly fearful"*: Margaret Fuller, *Memoirs of Margaret Fuller Ossoli*, Ralph Waldo Emerson, James Freeman Clarke, and William Henry Channing eds. (Boston: Phillips, Sampson & Company, 1852), 2:337.

158 *"His eyes were closed"*: Ibid.

158 *"We must die" . . . "what, if I live"*: Ibid., 2:343ff.

159 *"and more than half"*: Letter of Bayard Taylor to the *New-York Daily Tribune*, July 23, 1850, reprinted in Margaret Fuller, *At Home and Abroad: or, Things and Thoughts in America and Europe*, Arthur Fuller, ed. (Boston: Crosby, Nichols, and Co., 1856), 447.

159 *"Once and again"*: Fuller, *Memoirs*, 2:346.

159 *"broken down by hardships" . . . "upon her shoulders"*: Fuller, *Memoirs*, 2:348–49.

160 *"to the last"*: RWE *Journals*, 7:115.

160 *"But she had only"*: Ibid., 7:116.

161 *Their daughter Ellen remembered*: Ellen Tucker Emerson, *The Life of Lidian Jackson Emerson* (East Lansing: Michigan State University Press, 1992), 124.

161 *"I have lost"*: JMN, 11:258.

161 *"America has produced"*: Horace Greeley, *New-York Daily Tribune*, July 23, 1850, p. 4.

161 *"Questions have lately been asked"*: Albert J. von Frank and Phyllis Cole, "Margaret Fuller: How She Haunts," *ESQ: A Journal of Nineteenth-Century American Literature and Culture* 64, no. 1 (2018): 68.

162 *"votes, offices and political equality"*: "Woman," RWE CW, 11:419.

162 *"a profound thinker" . . . "far more deeply"*: Margaret Fuller, "American Literature: Its Position in the Present Time, and Prospects for the Future," *New-York Daily Tribune*, September 23, 1846.

163 *"not of the finest"*: NH CE, 14:154.

163 *"He says that Ossoli's"*: Ibid., 14:155.

163 *"I do not understand"*: Ibid., 14:156.

164 *At least one scholar*: See Thomas R. Mitchell, *Hawthorne's Fuller Mystery* (Amherst: University of Massachusetts Press), 1998.

164 *"As one of those friends"*: Testimonials of James F. Clarke, etc., against the statements in "Nathaniel Hawthorne and his wife, by Julian Hawthorne," Boston, 1885, New York Public Library.

164 *"Margaret Fuller has at last"*: Ibid.

164 *No doubt the result*: Phyllis Cole, in "The Nineteenth-Century Women's Rights Movement and the Canonization of Margaret Fuller," reprinted in *Nineteenth-Century Literature Criticism* 310 (2015), suggests that feminist interest in Fuller declined in the 1890s as the movement turned toward pragmatic paths to achieve the vote.

Chapter 13: The Birth of American Literature

166 *"Great geniuses are parts"*: "Hawthorne and His Mosses," Herman Melville, *The Literary World*, August 17, 1850, p. 126.

166 *"to develop a genius"*: Margaret Fuller, "American Literature: Its Position in the Present Time, and Prospects for the Future," *New-York Daily Tribune*, September 23, 1846, p. 1.

167 *"the actual beginner"*: Walt Whitman, quoted by Harold Bloom in *The American Renaissance* (Broomall, PA: Chelsea House, 2004), 13.

167 *"Their tones were"*: F. O. Matthiessen, *American Renaissance: Art and Expression in the Age of Emerson and Whitman* (London: Oxford University Press, 1941), xv.

168 *"'The Scarlet Letter' is"*: LMA *Journals*, 63.

168 *"I am turned out of office!"*: Nathaniel Hawthorne, Letter to G. S. Hillard, June 8, 1849, NH CE, 16:273.

168 *"drew—what my troubles"*: Letter to G. S. Hilliard, January 20, 1850, NH CE, 16:309.

169 *"Hawthorne is one of them"*: James T. Fields, *Yesterdays with Authors* (London: Sampson Low, Marston, Low, and Searle, 1872), 49.

169 *"of anything you write" . . . "put into my hands"*: Ibid., 50.

169 *"somber"*: Letter to James T. Fields, January 20, 1850, NH CE, 16:307.

169 *"speaks of it"*: Letter to Horatio Bridge, February 4, 1850, NH CE, 16:311.

170 *"in no work has"*: *Massachusetts Quarterly Review 7*, quoted in Kenneth Clark, *Hawthorne Among His Contemporaries* (Hartford, CT: Transcendental Books, 1968), 8.

170 *"nauseous"*: Clark, *Hawthorne Among His Contemporaries*, 19.

170 *"the most decisive production"*: Ibid., 48.

170 *"entire, perfect creation"*: Evert Augustus Duyckinck, review of *The Scarlet Letter, The Literary World* 6, no. 165 (March 30, 1850): 323–24.

171 *"America is now wholly"*: Letter to William D. Ticknor, January 19, 1855, NH CE, 17:304.

171 *"was never able to complete"*: Julian Hawthorne, *Hawthorne and His Wife* (Boston: Houghton, Mifflin, 1884), 1:394.

171 *"Nathaniel Hawthorne's reputation"*: RWE *Journals*, 6:240.

172 *"has that freedom of view"*: Nathaniel Hawthorne, review of Herman Melville's *Typee*, March 25, 1846. NH CE, 23:235–36.

173 *"altered facts and dates"*: Introduction to Herman Melville, *Omoo: A Narrative of Adventures in the South Seas*, Harrison Hayford and Walter Blair, eds. (New York: Hendricks House, 1969), xx.

173 *"a born genius" . . . "thinly disguised"*: Horace Greeley, *New-York Weekly Tribune*, June 26, 1847, quoted in the introduction to the Hayford and Blair edition of *Omoo*.

173 *"Not long ago"*: WHM, 3:xvii.

173 *"story has no movement"*: George Ripley, quoted in Hershel Parker, *Herman Melville: A Biography*. 2 vols. (Baltimore: Johns Hopkins University Press, 2002), 1:632.

174 *"You see a human"*: WHM, 5:138.

174 *"evil is the chronic malady"*: WHM, 3:529.

174 *"We scrambled to the top"* . . . *"inevitable to all of us"*: Fields, *Yesterdays with Authors*, 52–53.

174 *"Ten per cent"*: Cornelius Mathews, "Several Days in Berkshire, Part II," *The Literary World* 7, no. 166 (August 31, 1850), 166.

175 *"I have read Melville's"*: Hawthorne to Evert Duyckinck, August 29, 1850, NH CE, 16:362.

175 *"humor so spiritually"* . . . *"manifestation of these things"*: Herman Melville, "Hawthorne and His Mosses," *The Literary World* 7, no. 185 (August 17, 1850): 125–27.

175 *"Now I do not say"*: Herman Melville, "Hawthorne and His Mosses," *The Literary World* 7, no. 186 (August 24, 1850): 125.

175 *"he has very keen perceptive power"*: Jay Leyda, *The Melville Log: A Documentary Life of Herman Melville, 1819–1891* (New York: Harcourt, Brace and Company, 1951), 1:393–94.

175 *"While thus engaged"*: Nathaniel Hawthorne, *American Notebooks*, NH CE, 8:447–48.

176 *"dollars damn me"*: Herman Melville, *The Writings of Herman Melville*, Harrison Hayford, Hershel Parker, and George Thomas Tanselle, eds. (Evanston, IL: Northwestern University Press, 1968), 14:191.

176 *"Shall I send"*: Ibid., 14:196.

176 *"Whence come you"*: Ibid., 14:212–13.

176 *"monstrous fable"*: WHM, 6:205.

176 *"at heart"*: Lewis Mumford, *The Golden Day: A Study in American Literature and Culture* (Boston: Beacon Press, 1957), 69.

177 *"more than a brilliant fellow"*: Melville to Evert Duyckinck, March 3, 1849, in Herman Melville, *The Letters of Herman Melville*, Merrell R. Davis and William H. Gilman, eds. (New Haven: Yale University Press, 1960), 78.

177 *"What a book"*: Hawthorne to Evert Duyckinck, December 1, 1851, NH CE, 16:508.

177 *"an ill-compounded mixture"*: *The Athenaeum*, quoted in Parker, *Herman Melville*, 2:18.

177 *"bulky and multifarious volume"* . . . *"idealized throughout"*: Evert Duyckinck, review of *Moby-Dick, or, The Whale*, in *The Literary World*, November 15 (9, no. 250) and 22 (9, no. 251), 1851.

177 *"We think it the best production"*: Horace Greeley, *New-York Tribune*, November 22, 1851, quoted in Parker, *Herman Melville*, 2:26.

179 *"Want of originality"*: "Literary Notices," *Harper's New Monthly Magazine* 4, no. 23 (April 1852): 711.

179 *"but he seems to think"*: Hawthorne to Evert Duyckinck, July 1, 1845, NH CE, 16:105–6.

181 *"a completer & truer account"*: Thoreau, quoted in James Lyndon Shanley, *The Making of Walden* (Chicago: University of Chicago Press, 1957), 7.

182 *"the earth expresses itself"*: *Walden*, HDT *Writings*, 1:306.

182 *Yet even this talk*: For a lengthy discussion of this passage and Thoreau's evolving thinking, see William Rossi, "Making Walden and Its Sandbank," *The Concord Saunterer* 30 (2022): 10–58.

182 *"There is never"*: *Walden*, HDT *Writings*, 1:218.

182 *"from exertion come wisdom"*: Ibid., 1:220.

182 *"If a man does not"*: Ibid., 1:326.

182 *"However mean"*: Ibid., 1:328.

182 *"Rather than love"*: Ibid., 1:330.

182 *"We regret"*: HDT *Correspondence*, 2:353.

183 *"All American kind"*: Emerson to George Partridge Bradford, August 28 and 30, 1854, RWE *Letters*, 4:459.

183 *"an original book"* . . . *"a gift to men"*: For reprints of initial reviews, see Bradley P. Dean and Gary Scharnhorst, "The Contemporary Reception of *Walden*," *Studies in the American Renaissance* (1990): 293–328.

183 *"We have yet had no genius"*: "The Poet," RWE CW, 3:37.

184 *"virtually all denominations"*: David Reynolds, *Walt Whitman's America: A Cultural Biography* (New York: Vintage Books, 1996), 35.

184 *"behavior to the children"*: See Reynolds, *Walt Whitman's America*, 70.

184 *Biographers disagree*: For the chief evidence of the sodomy claim, see Katherine Molinoff, *Walt Whitman at Southold* (privately published, 1966).

185 *"damned rot"*: Horace Traubel, *With Walt Whitman in Camden*, 1:93.

185 *"For vainly through"*: Walt Whitman, "The Love That Is Hereafter," *The Early Poems and the Fiction* (New York: New York University Press, 1963), 9.

185 *"one of the richest"* . . . *"matters than other men"*: Walt Whitman, *Walt Whitman of the New York Aurora*, Joseph Jay Rubin and Charles H. Brown, eds. (State College, PA: Bald Eagle Press, 1950), 105.

186 *"my ideas"*: Whitman quoted in William Sloane Kennedy, *Reminiscences of Walt Whitman* (London: Alexander Gardner, 1896), 83.

186 *"Witness of Anguish"*: Whitman, *The Early Poems and the Fiction*, 48.

187 *"of all the persons"* . . . *"it will abolish you"*: Walt Whitman, "The Eighteenth Presidency!," *Poetry and Prose* (New York: Library of America, 1982), 1309ff.

187 *"The United States themselves" . . . "the American poet"*: Walt Whitman, Preface, *Leaves of Grass* (Brooklyn, NY: privately published, 1855), 1ff.

188 *"Have you reckoned"*: Whitman, "Song of Myself," *Leaves of Grass*, 24.

188 *"As for its sensuality"*: Thoreau to Harrison Blake, December 7, 1856, HDT *Correspondence*, 2:488–89.

189 *"Walt Whitman, an American"*: Whitman, "Song of Myself," *Leaves of Grass*, 45.

189 *"my dinner, dress"*: Ibid., 26.

189 *"An American bard" . . . "a strange voice"*: For Whitman's self-reviews, see Milton Hindus, ed., *Walt Whitman: The Critical Heritage* (New York: Barnes & Noble, 1971), 34–48.

190 *"are certainly original" . . . "We can conceive"*: Ibid., 22ff.

190 *"Dear Sir"*: Ralph Waldo Emerson to Walt Whitman, July 21, 1855, reprinted in *Leaves of Grass,* second edition, 245–46.

191 *"A few years"*: Walt Whitman, *Leaves of Grass,* second edition, 346.

191 *"'There are parts'"*: Moncure Daniel Conway, *Autobiography: Memories and Experiences* (Boston: Houghton Mifflin, 1904), 1:216.

191 *"like two beasts"*: BA *Journals*, 290.

191 *"were much interested"*: Henry David Thoreau to Harrison Blake, November 19, 1856, HDT *Correspondence*, 2:484.

192 *"That Walt Whitman"*: Thoreau to Blake, December 7, 1856, Ibid., 2:488–89.

192 *"I will make a song"*: Walt Whitman, "Proto-Leaf," *Leaves of Grass* (Boston: Thayer and Eldridge, 1860), 10.

193 *"Limitless limpid jets"*: Ibid., 295.

193 *"During those two hours"*: Whitman, *Specimen Days,* quoted in Bosco and Myerson, *Emerson in His Own Time: A Biographical Chronicle of His Life, Drawn from Recollections, Interviews, and Memoirs by Family, Friends, and Associates* (Iowa City: University of Iowa Press, 2003), 82.

Chapter 14: The Great Cause

197 *"What should concern Massachusetts"*: Henry David Thoreau, "Slavery in Massachusetts," HDT *Writings,* 3:104.

198 *"There is sometimes"*: BA *Journals*, 25.

199 *"In the 1830s"*: Robert Gross, *The Transcendentalists and Their World* (New York: Farrar, Straus and Giroux, 2021), 514.

199 *"was an abolitionist"*: Louisa May Alcott, "Recollections of My Childhood," in Daniel Shealy, ed., *Alcott in Her Own Time: A Biographical Chronicle of Her Life, Drawn from Recollections, Interviews, & Memoirs by Family, Friends, & Associates* (Iowa City: University of Iowa Press, 2005), 33.

199 *"The Whole History"*: JMN, 7:58.

199 *"it is race"*: CFPL Journal HO, Box 2, Folder 35.

200 *"in this continent"*: RWE *Journals*, 7:116.

200 *"compassionately thought"*: CFPL Journal HO, Box 2, Folder 35.

200 *"When a zealot"*: Ralph Waldo Emerson, November 24, 1837, JMN, 5:437.

201 *"If the motto"*: James Elliot Cabot, *A Memoir of Ralph Waldo Emerson* (Cambridge, MA: Riverside Press, 1887), 2:425.

201 *"Our friend the fugitive"*: BA *Journals*, 190.

201 *"fugitive slaves were"*: LMA, "Recollections of My Childhood," 36.

202 *witnesses recalled him*: Fritz Oehlschlaeger and George Hendrick, eds., *Toward the Making of Thoreau's Modern Reputation: Selected Correspondence of S.A. Jones, A.W. Hosmer, H.S. Salt, H.G.O. Blake, and D. Ricketson* (Urbana: University of Illinois Press, 1979), 143. Robert Gross, conversely, is skeptical of these stories, given the location of Thoreau's cabin.

202 *"nearly every week"*: Edward Waldo Emerson 1892 interview with Ann Bigelow, from CFPL, Edward Waldo Emerson and Emerson Family Papers, 1845–1971, Vault A45, Box 1, Folder 2.

202 *Thanks to various accounts*: Sandra Harbert Petrulionis, *To Set This World Right: The Anti-Slavery Movement in Thoreau's Concord* (Ithaca, NY: Cornell University Press, 2006), 2.

202 *"Just put a fugitive slave"*: HDT *Journal*, 4:113.

203 *"For the negro"*: "Emancipation of the Negroes in the British West Indies," RWE CW, 11:102–3.

203 *"The blood is moral"*: Ibid., 104.

203 *Yet the speech left some radical*: See Kenneth Sacks, *Emerson's Civil Wars: Spirit and Society in the Age of Abolition* (New York: Cambridge University Press, 2025), 22.

204 *"It is possible"*: Thomas Wentworth Higginson, *Part of a Man's Life* (Boston: Houghton, Mifflin, 1905), 14.

205 *"the too great increase"*: HL MS Am 1280H Ralph Waldo Emerson journals and notebooks, Unspecified: BO.

205 *"If I were seriously"*: HDT *Journal*, 3:204.

205 *"On a given signal"*: James Horton and Lois Horton, *Black Bostonians: Family Life and Community Struggle in the Antebellum North* (New York: Holmes & Meier, 1979, reprinted 1999), 107.

206 *Within a month:* For details of the fugitive exodus, see R. J. M. Blackett, *The Captive's Quest for Freedom*, 46ff.

207 *"not because it was piracy" . . . "attitude of revolution"*: Thomas Wentworth Higginson, *Cheerful Yesterdays* (Cambridge: Riverside Press, 1898), 143–44.

207 *"I felt ready"*: LMA *Journals*, 65.

207 *"The question"*: BA *Journals*, 243–44.

207 *"the door would be"*: Charles Emery Stevens, *Anthony Burns: A History* (Boston: John P. Jewett and Company, 1856), 166.

209 *"mob of negroes"*: Higginson, *Cheerful Yesterdays*, 149–50.

209 *"I waited for"*: Ibid., 152–53.

209 *"There was room"*: Ibid., 153–54.

210 *"After a moment"*: Frederick L. H. Willis, *Alcott Memoirs* (Boston: Richard G. Badger, 1915), 73–74. See also Higginson, *Cheerful Yesterdays*, 158.

211 *"Here gape your great"*: Walt Whitman, *Leaves of Grass* (Brooklyn, NY: privately published, 1855), 127.

211 *"That law which God"*: Stevens, *Anthony Burns*, 282–83.

211 *Bronson joined in January*: MHS Boston Anti-Man-Hunting League Records, Box 1, Folder 5, Fol. 4, Applicants List, 1854–1856.

213 *One member believed*: Henry Bowditch's description of the Anti-Man-Hunting League can be found in Vincent Bowditch, *Life and Correspondence of Henry Ingersoll Bowditch* (Boston: Houghton Mifflin, 1902), 1:271ff.

213 *"The whole military force"*: Henry Thoreau, "Slavery in Massachusetts," HDT *Writings*, 3:91ff.

Chapter 15: The Trials of Louisa May

215 *"Being willful, I said"*: Louisa May Alcott, 1862 journal entry, LMA *Journals*, 109.

215 *prejudice against Bronson*: Frederick Dahlstrand, *Amos Bronson Alcott: An Intellectual Biography* (Rutherford, NJ: Farleigh Dickinson University Press, 1982), 215.

216 *"Further talk"*: BA *Journals*, 230–31.

216 *"hard to be cheerful"*: LMA *Journals*, 661–62.

216 *"poor as rats"* Ibid., 65.

216 *"I go to Dedham"*: Ibid., 65.

216 *"a very nervous"* . . . *"rubbish"*: Louisa May Alcott, *Alternative Alcott*, Elaine Showalter, ed. (New Brunswick, NJ: Rutgers University Press, 1988), 355ff.

217 *"My first story"*: LMA *Journals*, 67.

217 *"In February"* . . . *"I call that doing"*: Ibid., 71.

219 *"Now that women"*: Kenneth Walter Cameron, *Concord Literary Renaissance* (Hartford, CT: Transcendental Books, 1888), 119. See also Madeleine Stern, "Louisa May Alcott and the Boston *Saturday Evening Gazette*," *American Periodicals* 2 (Fall 1992): 64–78.

220 *"Wonder if I"*: LMA *Journals*, 85.

220 *"Lizzie much worse"*: Ibid., 88.

220 *"A curious thing happened"*: Ibid., 89.

221 *"friendly and wonderful"*: Ibid.

221 *"My courage"*: LMA *Letters*, 34.

221 *"The world looked very dark"*: Louisa May Alcott, *Work: A Story of Experience* (Boston: Roberts Brothers, 1873), 150, 157–58.

222 *"I did not like"*: LMA *Letters*, 177.

222 *new candidates have been proposed*: See Max L. Chapnick, "New Louisa May Alcott Pieces: Radical Sensation in a Culture of Ambiguous Attribution," *J19: The Journal of Nineteenth-Century Americanists* 11, no. 1 (2023): 171–85.

223 *"my fifty dollars"*: LMA *Journals*, 95.

223 *"Genius burned"*: Ibid., 99.

223 *"my head was dizzy"*: Ibid., 104.

223 *"Where did you get"*: Ibid.

223 *"very tired of this"*: Ibid., 108.

223 *"Stick to your teaching"*: Ibid., 109.

223 *"Mr. L. says"*: Ibid.

223 *"Mind grammar"*: LMA *Letters*, 231.

224 *"I like a camp"*: LMA *Journals*, 95.

224 *"I like the stir"*: Ibid., 109.

Chapter 16: War, Part II

225 *"A man of rare common-sense"*: Henry David Thoreau, "A Plea for Captain John Brown," HDT *Writings*, 5:115.

225 *"In May 1854"*: See Nicole Etcheson, *Bleeding Kansas*, 29.

226 *"than in a hundred Bibles"*: "Sharp's Rifles as a Moral Agent," *New-York Daily Tribune*, February 8, 1856, p. 6.

226 *Ellen Tucker Emerson reported*: Ellen Tucker Emerson, *The Letters of Ellen Tucker Emerson* (Kent, OH: The Kent State University Press, 1982), 118–19.

226 *"We hear the screams"*: "Speech on Affairs in Kansas," RWE CW, 11:255ff.

227 *"the first transcendentalist in arms"*: George Fredrickson, *The Inner Civil War: Northern Intellectuals and the Crisis of the Union* (New York: Harper & Row, 1965), 37.

227 *"precisely like waking up"*: Thomas Wentworth Higginson, *Letters and Journals of Thomas Wentworth Higginson* (Boston: Houghton Mifflin, 1921), 142–43.

228 *"with a rod"*: Stephen Oates, *To Purge This Land with Blood: A Biography of John Brown* (New York: Harper & Row, 1970), 17.

228 *a conspiracy that is still debated*: See Michael P. Johnson, "Denmark Vesey and His Co-Conspirators," *The William and Mary Quarterly* 58, no. 4 (October 2001): 915–76.

230 *"Pro-Slavery Falsehoods"*: "From Kansas: Pro-Slavery Falsehoods," *New-York Daily Tribune*, May 31, 1856, p. 7.

230 *"victims were most horribly mutilated"*: "From Kansas," *New-York Daily Tribune*, June 3, 1856, p. 5.

231 *"fame was"*: Franklin Sanborn, *The Life and Letters of John Brown: Liberator of Kansas, and Martyr of Virginia* (London: Sampson Low, Marston, Searle, & Rivington, 1885), 279.

231 *"John Brown of Osawatomie"*: Wendell Phillips, *Wendell Phillips on Civil Rights and Freedom*, Louis Filler, ed. (New York: Hill and Wang, 1965), 105.
232 *"Such a deed"*: Sanborn, *Life and Letters of John Brown*, 248.
232 *"gave a good account"*: RWE *Journals*, 16:81–82.
232 *"had a perfect right"*: HDT *Writings*, 4:414.
233 *"BY FAR"*: John Brown quoted in Oates, *To Purge This Land with Blood*, 225.
233 *"with surpassing simplicity"*: BA *Journals*, 315–16.
233 *"till I confess"*: Frederick Douglass, quoted in David Blight, *Frederick Douglass*, 297–98.
233 *"Virginia would blow"*: Ibid., 302.
234 *"I am worth"*: John Brown, quoted in Oates, *To Purge This Land with Blood*, 335.
234 *"What are your ideas"*: LMA *Letters*, 49.
234 *"martyrdom, if he shall"*: "Courage," RWE CW, 7:427.
234 *"glorious, like a cross"*: John J. McDonald, "Emerson and John Brown," *The New England Quarterly* 44, no. 3 (September 1971): 387.
234 *"a transcendentalist above all"* . . . *"No man in America"*: Henry David Thoreau, "A Plea for Captain John Brown," *Reform Papers*, HDT *Writings*, 3:115, 3:125.
234 *"Some eighteen hundred"*: Ibid., 3:137.
235 *"I bequeath"*: Sandra Harbert Petrulionis, *To Set This World Right: The Anti-Slavery Movement in Thoreau's Concord* (Ithaca, NY: Cornell University Press, 2006), 140.
235 *"My hands were powerless"* . . . *the way to Lexington*: Franklin Sanborn, *Recollections of Seventy Years*, 1:209ff.
236 *"from Bangor to"* . . . *"illegal behavior"*: Randall Fuller, *The Book That Changed America: How Darwin's Theory of Evolution Ignited a Nation* (New York: Viking, 2017), 171.
236 *"We are wafted"*: Emerson, quoted in James Eliot Cabot, *A Memoir of Ralph Waldo Emerson*, 2 vols. (Cambridge, MA: Riverside Press, 1887), 2:600–601.
236 *"it was God's doing"*: Ibid., 2:605.
237 *"War news bad"*: LMA *Journals*, 109.
237 *"optimism had fled"*: Moncure Daniel Conway, *Autobiography: Memories and Experiences* (Boston: Houghton Mifflin, 1904), 1:335.
238 *"We regret the innuendo"*: Nathaniel Hawthorne, "Chiefly About War Matters, By a Peaceable Man," *The Atlantic Monthly*, July 1862.
238 *"A solemn time"*: LMA *Journals*, 110.
239 *"I hardly think"*: George Washington Whitman, *Civil War Letters of George Washington* Whitman, Jerome M. Loving, ed. (Durham, NC: Duke University Press, 1975), 74.
239 *"Out doors"*: Walt Whitman, *Memoranda During the War*, 8.

240 *"Up at six"*: LMA *Journals*, 113–14.

241 *"so riddled"*: Louisa May Alcott, "Hospital Sketches," *The Sketches of Louisa May Alcott* (Queens, NY: Isis, 2001), 31.

241 *"all persons held as slaves"*: For the full text of the proclamation, see the website of the US National Archives and Records Administration, https://www.archives.gov/exhibits/american_originals_iv/sections/transcript_preliminary_emancipation.html.

242 *"these are acts"*: Ralph Waldo Emerson, "The President's Proclamation," *The Atlantic Monthly*, November 1862.

242 *"complete conversion"*: George Fredrickson, *The Inner Civil War*, 120.

242 *"the transformation of genius"*: Emerson "Experience," RWE CW, 3:86.

242 *"with more eagerness"*: Alcott, *The Sketches of Louisa May Alcott*, 87.

243 *"active, interested"*: BA *Journals*, 352.

243 *"I had married"*: LMA *Journals*, 116.

243 *"the doctor says"*: Walt Whitman, *The Correspondence* (New York: New York University Press, 1961–1969), 2:86.

Chapter 17: Death, Part II

244 *"It is time to be old"*: Ralph Waldo Emerson, "Terminus" RWE CW, 9:251.

245 *he may have been aiming*: See Robert D. Richardson, *Henry David Thoreau: A Life of the Mind* (Berkeley: University of California Press, 1986), 343. Laura Dassow Walls, in *Seeing New Worlds*, makes the point that there was no clear separation between science and holistic understanding in Thoreau's day.

246 *"A nation of 20 millions"*: Henry Thoreau, letter of March 31, 1861, quoted in Sandra Harbert Petrulionis, *To Set This World Right: The Anti-Slavery Movement in Thoreau's Concord* (Ithaca, NY: Cornell University Press, 2006), 155.

246 *"Read not the Times" . . . "moral tyrant"*: "Life Without Principle," HDT *Writings*, 3:173, 174.

247 *"I love Henry"*: Elizabeth Hoar, quoted in JMN, 8:375.

247 *"A party of great people"*: LMA *Letters*, 77.

248 *"He was a born protestant" . . . "I so much regret"*: Ralph Waldo Emerson, "Thoreau," *The Atlantic Monthly*, August 1862.

248 *"Better for me"*: HDT *Journals*, IX:37.

248 *"He knew the country"*: Emerson, "Thoreau," *The Atlantic Monthly*.

249 *"The bluebird"*: HDT *Journal*, 4:423.

249 *"The tanager"*: based on HDT *Journal*, 6:139.

249 *"Poetry is not"*: LMA *Letters*, 84.

249 *"During all the time"*: Bronson Alcott, *Concord Days* (Boston: Roberts Brothers, 1872), 193–95.

251 *"There dwelt a sage"*: Caroline Ticknor, *May Alcott: A Memoir* (Boston: Little, Brown and Company, 1928), 53.

251 *"would have been the greatest"*: James T. Fields, *Yesterdays with Authors* (London: Sampson Low, Marston, Low, and Searle, 1872), 96.

252 *"so haggard"*: Ibid., 118–19.

252 *"a beautiful soul"*: LMA *Letters*, 321.

252 *"the painful solitude"*: RWE *Journals*, 10:40.

Chapter 18: A Child Shall Lead

253 *"My dear—dearest Miss Alcott!"*: Thomas Niles, publisher of *Little Women*, to Louisa May Alcott, from Julian Hawthorne, "The Woman Who Wrote *Little Women*," in Daniel Shealy, ed., *Alcott in Her Own Time: A Biographical Chronicle of Her Life, Drawn from Recollections, Interviews, & Memoirs by Family, Friends, & Associates* (Iowa City: University of Iowa Press, 2005), 201.

254 *"challenge to the tournament"*: Louisa May Alcott, "Pauline's Passion and Punishment," *Louisa May Alcott Unmasked*, Madeleine Stern, ed. (Boston: Northeastern University Press, 1995), 16.

254 *"a story of"*: Frank Leslie, "Our Prize Stories," *Frank Leslie's Illustrated Newspaper*, December 27, 1862, p. 210.

254 *"was small at home"*: Review of George Ticknor's *History of Spanish Literature, The Atlantic Monthly*, November 1863, p. 662.

255 *"I see nothing"*: BA *Journals*, 357.

255 *"surprise & delight"*: LMA *Journals*, 119.

255 *"A way to shorten"*: Ibid., 132.

256 *"Unhappy marriages"*: Louisa May Alcott, *Moods* (Boston: Loring, 1864), 201.

256 *"for a week"*: LMA *Journals*, 133.

256 *"mostly favorable"*: Ibid., 138.

256 *"artless"* . . . *"there is no reason"*: For reviews of *Moods*, see Beverly Lyon Clark, ed., *Louisa May Alcott: The Contemporary Reviews* (Cambridge, UK: Cambridge University Press, 2004), 27ff.

257 *"paling spirits"*: BA *Journals*, 373.

257 *"best to suit & serve"*: LMA *Journals*, 142.

257 *"tall, white, spectral"*: Ibid., 143.

257 *"motley collection of lodgers"*: Louisa May Alcott, "Life in a Pension," in *The Sketches of Louisa May Alcott* (Queens, NY: Ironweed Press, 2001), 196.

258 *"two hiccups and a sneeze"* . . . *"the memory of certain"*: Louisa May Alcott, *Aunt Jo's Scrap-Bag: My Boys, etc.* (Boston: Roberts Brothers, 1872), 20.

258 *"a little romance"* . . . *"Couldn't be"*: LMA *Journals*, 145, 148.

258 *"Bon voyage"*: Alcott, *Aunt Jo's Scrap-Bag*, 23.

258 *"feeling as happy"*: LMA *Journals*, 151.

258 *"tired, bewildered" . . . "good as home"*: Alcott, *Aunt Jo's Scrap-Bag*, 23–24.
259 *"it is hardly necessary"*: Ibid., 34.
259 *"placid as ever"*: LMA *Journals*, 152.
260 *"Sick from too hard work"*: Ibid., 157.
260 *"Niles, partner of"*: Ibid., 158.
260 *"began at once"*: Ibid.
260 *"eight long tales"*: Ibid., 165.
261 *"One does not half"*: Louise Chandler Moulton, in Elizabeth Stuart Phelps, *Our Famous Women* (Hartford, CT: A. D. Worthington & Co., 1884), 41.
261 *"superior women who"*: Louisa May Alcott, *Alternative Alcott* (New Brunswick, NJ: Rutgers University Press, 1988), 203.
261 *"poor, plain" . . . "a strongly individual type"*: Alcott, *Alternative Alcott*, 204, 205.
261 *"If love comes"*: Ibid., 206.
261 *"curious jumble"*: LMA *Journals*, 165.
261 *"I spoke of"*: BA *Letters*, 427.
262 *"So I plod away"*: LMA *Journals*, 165–66.
262 *"He thought it* dull": Ibid., 166.
263 *"it reads better"*: Ibid.
263 *"caused much perplexity"*: Franklin Sanborn, *A. Bronson Alcott: His Life and Philosophy* (New York: Biblo and Tannen, 1965), 2:642.
263 *"I may be scholarly"*: Bronson Alcott, *Tablets* (Boston: Roberts Brothers, 1868), 14–15.
263 *"Life, when hospitably taken"*: Ibid., 41.
264 *"constancy, fidelity" . . . "Good books"*: Ibid., 89, 127.
264 "Tablets *are like windows"*: *Boston Daily Advertiser*, quoted in Frederick Dahlstrand, *Amos Bronson Alcott: An Intellectual Biography* (Rutherford, NJ: Farleigh Dickinson University Press, 1982), 290.
264 *"whole life and utterances"*: *The Republican*, HL b MS Am 1130.9-1130.12, volume 43 (7), p. 36.
264 *"all civil rights"*: Madeleine B. Stern, ed., *L. M. Alcott: Signature of Reform* (Boston: Northeastern University Press, 2002), 209.
264 *"this was the initiation"*: BA "Autobiographical Collections," b MS Am 1130.9-1130.12, volume 43 (7), 115.
265 *"must help make the Laws"*: Abba May Alcott, quoted in Eve LaPlante, *Marmee & Louisa: The Untold Story of Louisa May Alcott and Her Mother* (New York: Free Press), 253.
265 *"We elected"*: LMA *Journals*, 225.
265 *"I can do a chapter"*: Ibid., 167.
265 *"I am so full"*: Ibid.

265 *"amusing exaggeration" . . . "My dear—dearest Miss Alcott"*: Daniel Shealy, ed., *Alcott in Her Own Time*, 200–201.

267 *"'Jo' should have remained"*: LMA *Letters*, 125.

267 *"Dear Miss Alcott"*: A reader, quoted in Phelps, *Our Famous Women*, 43.

268 *"the 19th* 000*"*: Bronson Alcott, quoted in Madeleine Stern, ed., *Critical Essays on Louisa May Alcott* (Boston: G. K. Hall, 1984), 262.

268 *"fresh, sparkling"*: *Boston Evening Transcript*, reprinted in Clark, *Louisa May Alcott: The Contemporary Reviews*, 61.

268 *"'Little Women' is"*: *Eclectic Magazine*, quoted in Clark, *Louisa May* Alcott, 76.

Chapter 19: We Are in Life

269 *"In the midst of death"*: HDT *Journals* XIV:109.

269 *"I trim myself"*: Ralph Waldo Emerson, "Terminus," RWE CW 9:252.

269 *"it almost startled me"*: Edward Emerson in RWE CW, 9:489.

270 *"wrote nothing but"*: LMA *Journals*, 172.

270 *"She is a satirist"*: Henry James, quoted in Beverly Lyon Clark, *Louisa May Alcott: The Contemporary Reviews* (Cambridge, UK: Cambridge University Press, 2004), 246–47.

271 *"E[merson] gave me"*: Ednah Cheney, *Louisa May Alcott: Her Life, Letters, and Journals* (Boston: Roberts Brothers, 1889), 398.

271 *"had been simmering"*: LMA *Journals*, 204.

271 *"it does not seem"*: Thomas Niles, quoted in Louisa May Alcott, *A Modern Mephistopheles and Taming a Tartar*, Madeleine Stern, ed. (New York: Praeger Publishers, 1987), xix.

272 *"probably by Mrs. Prescott" . . . "it is quite probable"*: For reviews of *A Modern Mephistopheles*, see Clark, *Louisa May Alcott: The Contemporary Reviews*, 285ff.

272 *"dear, honest, tender"*: LMA *Letters*, 153.

272 *"great red placard"*: LMA *Journals*, 178.

273 *"Our instincts are"*: Bronson Alcott, *Concord Days* (Boston: Roberts Brothers, 1872), 270.

273 *"tells me my* Concord Days*"*: BA *Journals*, 430.

273 *"It especially becomes"*: Bronson Alcott, *Table-Talk* (Boston: Roberts Brothers, 1877), 98.

273 *"Christians have no good reason"*: Ibid., 99.

274 *"since the Spirit"*: Ibid., 103.

274 *"The first Principle"*: William T. Harris, ibid., 116–17.

274 *"The Person is immortal"*: Alcott, *Table-Talk*, 173.

274 *"This was the cause"*: LMA *Journals*, 184.

274 *"Reporters sit on the wall"*: Ibid., 183.

275 *"It is said that"* . . . *"No spot is safe"*: Letter to the *Springfield Republican*, May 4, 1869, from LMA *Letters*, 127–28.

275 *"has* her *wish"*: LMA *Journals*, 204.

275 *"Marmee had a very ill turn"* . . . *"'You are laying'"*: Ibid., 206.

276 *"Give up my hope"*: Ibid., 217.

277 *"alone when"*: Ibid., 218.

277 *"I see now"*: Ibid., 219.

277 *"the town swarms"*: Ibid., 216.

277 *"Dozens of intellectuals"*: Randall Fuller, *The Book That Changed America: How Darwin's Theory of Evolution Ignited a Nation* (New York: Viking, 2017), 236.

278 *"a fine gentleman"*: Bronson Alcott, *New Connecticut: An Autobiographical Poem* (Boston: privately published, 1881), 71.

278 *"Glad tidings"*: Bronson Alcott, *Sonnets and Canzonets* (Boston: Roberts Brothers, 1882), 69.

279 *"Ah! gentle May"*: Ibid., 77.

279 *"If I from Poesy"*: Ibid., 39.

279 *"read his lecture"*: An audience member, quoted in Ralph Waldo Emerson, *The Later Lectures of Ralph Waldo Emerson* (Athens: University of Georgia Press, 2001), 2:100.

279 *"Memory is a primary"*: Emerson, "Memory," *Later Lectures*, 2:101.

280 *"saved some valuable"* . . . *"pathetically funny"*: LMA *Letters*, 166–67.

280 *"Father said he"*: Ellen Tucker Emerson, *The Life of Lidian Jackson Emerson* (East Lansing: Michigan State University Press, 1992), 160.

281 *"Father sees no one"* . . . *"Please write out"*: Edward Bok, *The Americanization of Edward Bok: The Autobiography of a Dutch Boy Fifty Years After* (New York: Charles Scribner's Sons, 1921), 54–57.

281 *"a healthy color"*: Quoted in Ronald A. Bosco and Joel Myerson, eds, *Emerson in His Own Time: A Biographical Chronicle of His Life, Drawn from Recollections, Interviews, and Memoirs by Family, Friends, and Associates* (Iowa City: University of Iowa Press, 2003), 81.

281 *"'What was the name'"*: Clara Barrus, *Whitman and Burroughs: Comrades* (Boston: Houghton Mifflin Company, 1931), 181–82.

281 *"In all the multitudes"*: Ralph Waldo Emerson, Speech at the Consecration of Sleepy Hollow Cemetery, September 29, 1855, RWE CW, 11:434.

282 *"long deliberation"*: John McAleer, *Ralph Waldo Emerson: Days of Encounter* (Boston: Little, Brown, 1984), 665.

283 *"The passive master"*: Emerson, "The Problem," RWE CW, 9:8.

283 *"I know better"*: "Experience," RWE CW, 3:83.

283 *"We do not like those"*: Emerson, *Later Lectures*, 2:256.

284 *"personal influence"*: HDT *Journal*, 2:224.

284 *"a great poet"*: Matthew Arnold, *Discourses in America* (London: Macmillan and Co., 1885), 196.

284 *"held his hand"*: LMA *Journals*, 233–34.

284 *"his mind"*: LMA *Letters*, 261.

285 *"seems to have difficulty"*: Ibid., 263.

285 *"bright"*: Ibid., 268.

285 *"He is broad"*: HDT *Journal*, 6:101.

285 *"When thirty treatments"*: Louisa May Alcott, "Miss Alcott on Mind-Cure," *The Woman's Journal* 16, no. 16 (April 18, 1885): 1.

285 *modern medical historians*: Norbert Hirschhorn and Ian A. Greaves, "Louisa May Alcott: Her Mysterious Illness," *Perspectives in Biology and Medicine* 50, no. 2 (Spring 2007): 243–59.

286 *"I look about 70"*: LMA *Letters*, 330.

286 *"Father, here is your Louy"*: Louisa May Alcott, quoted in Madeleine Stern, *Louisa May Alcott* (Norman: Oklahoma University Press, 1950), 330–31.

Bibliography

Alcott, Bronson. *Concord Days*. Boston: Roberts Brothers, 1872.

———. *Conversations with Children on the Gospels*. Boston: James Munroe & Company, 1836.

———. *New Connecticut: An Autobiographical Poem*. Boston: privately published, 1881.

———. *Sonnets and Canzonets*. Boston: Roberts Brothers, 1882.

———. *Table-Talk*. Boston: Roberts Brothers, 1877.

———. *Tablets*. Boston: Roberts Brothers, 1868.

Alcott, Louisa May. *Alternative Alcott*. Edited by Elaine Showalter. New Brunswick, NJ: Rutgers University Press, 1988.

———. *Aunt Jo's Scrap-Bag: My Boys, etc*. Boston: Roberts Brothers, 1872.

———. *Flower Fables*. Boston: George W. Briggs & Co., 1855.

———. *Little Women: An Annotated Edition*. Edited by Daniel Shealy. Cambridge, MA: Belknap Press/Harvard University Press, 2013.

———. *Louisa May Alcott: An Intimate Anthology*. New York: Doubleday, 1997.

———. *Louisa May Alcott Unmasked: Collected Thrillers*. Edited by Madeleine Stern. Boston: Northeastern University Press, 1995.

———. *A Modern Mephistopheles and Taming a Tartar*. Edited by Madeleine Stern. New York: Praeger Publishers, 1987.

———. *Moods*. Boston: Loring, 1864.

———. *Moods*. Boston: Roberts Brothers, 1882.

———. *Selected Fiction*. Edited by Daniel Shealy, Madeleine B. Stern, and Joel Myerson. Boston: Little, Brown and Company, 1990.

———. *The Sketches of Louisa May Alcott*. Oxford, UK: Isis, 2001.

———. *Work: A Story of Experience*. Boston: Roberts Brothers, 1873.

Allen, Gay Wilson. *The Solitary Singer: A Critical Biography of Walt Whitman*. New York: Macmillan, 1955.

———. *Waldo Emerson*. New York: Viking, 1981.

Anonymous. *The Boston Slave Riot, and Trial of Anthony Burns*. Boston: Fetridge, 1854.

Anonymous. *The New York Tribune: A Sketch of Its History*. New York: privately published, 1883.

Anonymous ("A Cosmopolite" identified as David Henshaw). *A Review of the Prosecution Against Abner Kneeland*. Boston, 1835.

Anthony, Katharine. *Louisa May Alcott*. New York: Alfred A. Knopf, 1938.

Arnold, Matthew. *Discourses in America*. London: Macmillan and Co., 1885.

Arvin, Newton. *Hawthorne*. Boston: Little, Brown and Company, 1929.

Baker, Carlos. *Emerson Among the Eccentrics: A Group Portrait*. New York: Viking, 1996.

Barrus, Clara. *Whitman and Burroughs: Comrades*. Boston: Houghton Mifflin Company, 1931.

Barton, Cynthia H. *Transcendental Wife: The Life of Abigail May Alcott*. Lanham, MD: University Press of America, 1996.

Bedell, Madelon. *The Alcotts: Biography of a Family*. New York: Clarkson Potter, 1980.

Beecher, Jonathan. *Charles Fourier: The Visionary and His World*. Berkeley: University of California Press, 1986.

Bercovitch, Sacvan, ed. *The Cambridge History of American Literature*, Vol. 2. Cambridge, UK: Cambridge University Press, 1995.

Blackett, R. J. M. *The Captive's Quest for Freedom: Fugitive Slaves, the 1850 Fugitive Slave Law, and the Politics of Slavery*. New York: Cambridge University Press, 2018.

Blight, David W. *Frederick Douglass: Prophet of Freedom*. New York: Simon & Schuster, 2018.

Bliss, Sylvester. *Memoirs of William Miller*. Boston: Joshua V. Himes, 1853.

Bloom, Harold, ed. *The American Renaissance*. Broomall, PA: Chelsea House, 2004.

Bode, Carl. *The American Lyceum: Town Meeting of the Mind*. New York: Oxford University Press, 1956.

Bok, Edward. *The Americanization of Edward Bok: The Autobiography of a Dutch Boy Fifty Years After*. New York: Charles Scribner's Sons, 1921.

Bonstelle, Jessie, and Marian de Forest, eds. *Little Women Letters from the House of Alcott*. Boston: Little, Brown, and Company, 1914.

Bordewich, Fergus M. *Bound for Canaan: The Underground Railroad and the War for the Soul of America*. New York: Amistad Books, 2005.

Bosco, Ronald A., and Joel Myerson, eds. *Emerson in His Own Time: A Biographical Chronicle of His Life, Drawn from Recollections, Interviews, and Memoirs by Family, Friends, and Associates*. Iowa City: University of Iowa Press, 2003.

Bowditch, Vincent Y. *Life and Correspondence of Henry Ingersoll Bowditch*. 2 vols. Boston: Houghton Mifflin, 1902.

Bradford, Gamaliel. *Portraits of American Women*. Boston: Houghton Mifflin, 1919.

Brisbane, Albert. *Association: or, a Concise Exposition of the Practical Part of Fourier's Social Science*. New York: Greeley & McElrath, 1843.

———. *Social Destiny of Man, or, Association and Reorganization of Industry*. Philadelphia: C. F. Stollmeyer, 1840.

Brisbane, Redelia. *Albert Brisbane: A Mental Biography with a Character Study*. Boston: Arena Publishing, 1893.

Brooks, Van Wyck. *The Flowering of New England, 1815–1865*. New York: E. P. Dutton & Co., 1937.

Brown, Dona. *Inventing New England: Regional Tourism in the Nineteenth Century*. Washington, D.C.: Smithsonian Institution Press, 1995.

Buehrens, John A. *Conflagration: How the Transcendentalists Sparked the American Struggle for Racial, Gender, and Social Justice*. Boston: Beacon Press, 2020.

Buell, Lawrence. *Emerson*. Cambridge, MA: Belknap Press/Harvard University Press, 2003.

———. *Henry David Thoreau: Thinking Disobediently*. New York: Oxford University Press, 2023.

———. *Literary Transcendentalism: Style and Vision in the American Renaissance*. Ithaca, NY: Cornell University Press, 1973.

Cabot, James Elliot. *A Memoir of Ralph Waldo Emerson*. 2 vols. Cambridge, MA: Riverside Press, 1887.

Cameron, Christopher. *To Plead Our Own Cause: African Americans in Massachusetts and the Making of the Antislavery Movement*. Kent, OH: The Kent State University Press, 2014.

Cameron, Kenneth Walter. *Concord Literary Renaissance*. Hartford, CT: Transcendental Books, 1888.

———. *Hawthorne Among His Contemporaries*. Hartford, CT: Transcendental Books, 1968.

Capper, Charles. *Margaret Fuller: An American Romantic Life, Vol. 1: The Private Years*. New York: Oxford University Press, 1992.

Capper, Charles, and Conrad Edick Wright, eds. *Transient and Permanent: The Transcendentalist Movement and Its Contexts*. Boston: Massachusetts Historical Society, 1999.

———. *Margaret Fuller: An American Romantic Life, Vol. 2: The Public Years*. New York: Oxford University Press, 2007.

Charvat, William. *Emerson's American Lecture Engagements*. New York: The New York Public Library, 1961.

Cheever, Susan. *American Bloomsbury: Louisa May Alcott, Ralph Waldo Emerson, Margaret Fuller, Nathaniel Hawthorne, and Henry David Thoreau: Their Lives, Their Loves, Their Work*. New York: Simon & Schuster, 2006.

———. *Louisa May Alcott: A Personal Biography*. New York: Simon & Schuster, 2010.

Cheney, Ednah D., ed. *Louisa May Alcott: Her Life, Letters, and Journals*. Boston: Roberts Brothers, 1889.

Clark, Beverly Lyon, ed. *Louisa May Alcott: The Contemporary Reviews*. Cambridge, UK: Cambridge University Press, 2004.

Clark, Christopher. *The Communitarian Moment: The Radical Challenge of the Northampton Association*. Ithaca, NY: Cornell University Press, 1995.

Clark, Kenneth, *Hawthorne Among His Contemporaries*. Hartford, CT: Transcendental Books, 1968.

Conway, Moncure Daniel. *Autobiography: Memories and Experiences*. 2 vols. Boston: Houghton Mifflin, 1904.

———. *Emerson at Home and Abroad*. Boston: James Osgood, 1882.

Cramer, Jeffrey S. *Solid Seasons: The Friendship of Henry David Thoreau and Ralph Waldo Emerson*. Berkeley: Counterpoint, 2019.

Cross, Whitney R. *The Burned-Over District: The Social and Intellectual History of Enthusiastic Religion in Western New York, 1800–1850*. Ithaca, NY: Cornell University Press, 1950.

Dahlstrand, Frederick C. *Amos Bronson Alcott: An Intellectual Biography*. Rutherford, NJ: Farleigh Dickinson University Press, 1982.

De Tocqueville, Alexis. *Democracy in America*. Translated, edited, and with an introduction by Harvey C. Mansfield and Delba Winthrop. Chicago: University of Chicago Press, 2000.

Deiss, Joseph Jay. *The Roman Years of Margaret Fuller: A Biography*. New York: Thomas Y. Crowell Company, 1969.

Delano, Sterling F. *Brook Farm: The Dark Side of Utopia*. Cambridge, MA: Belknap Press/Harvard University Press, 2004.

Dowling, David. *Emerson's Protégés: Mentoring and Marketing Transcendentalism's Future*. New Haven: Yale University Press, 2014.

Downs, Robert B. *Horace Mann: Champion of Public Schools*. New York: Twayne Publishers, 1974.

Earle, Jonathan, and Diane Mutti Burke, eds. *Bleeding Kansas, Bleeding Missouri: The Long Civil War on the Border*. Lawrence: University Press of Kansas, 2013.

Edelstein, Tilden G. *Strange Enthusiasm: A Life of Thomas Wentworth Higginson*. New Haven: Yale University Press, 1968.

Emerson, Edward Waldo. *Emerson in Concord: A Memoir*. Boston: Houghton, Mifflin, 1888.

———. *Henry David Thoreau as Remembered by a Young Friend*. Boston: Houghton Mifflin, 1917.

Emerson, Ellen Tucker. *The Letters of Ellen Tucker Emerson*. Edited by Edith E. W. Gregg. Kent, OH: The Kent State University Press, 1982.

———. *The Life of Lidian Jackson Emerson*. Edited by Delores Bird Carpenter. East Lansing: Michigan State University Press, 1992.

Emerson, Lidian Jackson. *The Selected Letters of Lidian Jackson Emerson*. Edited and with an introduction by Delores Bird Carpenter. Columbia: University of Missouri Press, 1987.

Emerson, Mary Moody. *The Selected Letters of Mary Moody Emerson*. Edited by Nancy Craig Simmons. Athens: University of Georgia Press, 1993.

Emerson, Ralph Waldo. *The Annotated Emerson*. Edited by David Mikics. Cambridge, MA: Belknap Press/Harvard University Press, 2012.

———. *The Complete Sermons of Ralph Waldo Emerson*. Edited by Albert J. von Frank. Columbia: University of Missouri Press, 1989–1992.

———. *The Correspondence of Emerson and Carlyle*. Edited by Joseph Slater. New York: Columbia University Press, 1964.

———. *The Early Lectures of Ralph Waldo Emerson*. Edited by Stephen Whicher, Robert Spiller, and Wallace Williams. 3 vols. Cambridge: Belknap/Harvard University Press, 1964.

———. *Essays and Lectures*. Edited by Joel Porte. New York: Library of America, 1983.

———. *The Later Lectures of Ralph Waldo Emerson*. Edited by Ronald A. Bosco and Joel Myerson. 2 vols. Athens: University of Georgia Press, 2001.

Etcheson, Nicole. *Bleeding Kansas: Contested Liberty in the Civil War Era*. Lawrence: University Press of Kansas, 2004.

Fields, Annie. *Authors and Friends*. Boston: Houghton, Mifflin, 1897.

———. *James T. Fields: Biographical Notes and Personal Sketches*. Boston: Houghton, Mifflin, 1881.

Fields, James T. *Yesterdays with Authors*. London: Sampson Low, Marston, Low, and Searle, 1872.

Foner, Eric. *Gateway to Freedom: The Hidden History of the Underground Railroad*. New York: W. W. Norton, 2015.

Fourier, Charles, *Harmonian Man: Selected Writings of Charles Fourier*. Translated by Susan Hanson. Edited by Mark Poster. New York: Doubleday, 1971.

———. *Hierarchies of Cuckoldry and Bankruptcy*. Translated by Geoffrey Longnecker. Cambridge, MA: Wakefield Press, 2011.

———. *Oeuvres Complètes de Charles Fourier*. Paris: Éditions Anthropos, 1968.

———. *The Theory of the Four Movements*. Edited by Gareth Stedman Jones and Ian Patterson. Cambridge, UK: Cambridge University Press, 1996.

———. *The Utopian Vision of Charles Fourier: Selected Texts on Work, Love, and Passionate Attraction*. Translated, edited, and with an introduction by Jonathan Beecher and Richard Bienvenu. Boston: Beacon Press, 1971.

Francis, Richard. *Fruitlands: The Alcott Family and Their Search for Utopia*. New Haven: Yale University Press, 2010.

Fredrickson, George M. *The Inner Civil War: Northern Intellectuals and the Crisis of the Union*. New York: Harper & Row, 1965.

Frothingham, O. B. *George Ripley*. Boston: Houghton, Mifflin, 1882.

Fuller, Margaret. *At Home and Abroad: or, Things and Thoughts in America and Europe*. Edited by Arthur Fuller. Boston: Crosby, Nichols, and Co., 1856.

———. *The Essential Margaret Fuller*. Edited by Jeffrey Steele. New Brunswick, NJ: Rutgers University Press, 1992.

———. *Love-Letters of Margaret Fuller, 1845–1846*. With an introduction by Julia Ward Howe. New York: D. Appleton and Company, 1903.

———. *Margaret Fuller, Critic: Writings from the New-York Tribune, 1844–1846*. Edited by Judith Mattson Bean and Joel Myerson. New York: Columbia University Press, 2000.

———. *Margaret Fuller's New York Journalism: A Biographical Essay and Key Writings*. Edited by Catherine C. Mitchell. Knoxville: University of Tennessee Press, 1995.

———. *Memoirs of Margaret Fuller Ossoli*. Edited by Ralph Waldo Emerson, James Freeman Clarke, and William Henry Channing 2 vols. Boston: Phillips, Sampson & Company, 1852.

———. *"My Heart Is a Large Kingdom": Selected Letters of Margaret Fuller*. Edited by Robert N. Hudspeth. Ithaca, NY: Cornell University Press, 2001.

———. *Summer on the Lakes, in 1843*. Boston: Charles C. Little and James Brown, 1844.

———. *These Sad but Glorious Days: Dispatches from Europe, 1846–1850*. Edited by Larry J. Reynolds and Susan Belasco Smith. New Haven: Yale University Press, 1991.

Fuller, Randall. *The Book That Changed America: How Darwin's Theory of Evolution Ignited a Nation*. New York: Viking, 2017.

———. *Bright Circle: Five Remarkable Women in the Age of Transcendentalism*. New York: Oxford University Press, 2025.

———. *Emerson's Ghosts: Literature, Politics, and the Making of Americanists*. New York: Oxford University Press, 2007.

Greeley, Horace. *The Autobiography of Horace Greeley: or, Recollections of a Busy Life*. New York: E. B. Treat, 1872.

Gross, Robert A. *The Transcendentalists and Their World*. New York: Farrar, Straus and Giroux, 2021.

Gross, Robert A., and Mary Kelley, eds. *A History of the Book in America, Vol. 2: An Extensive Republic: Print, Culture, and Society in the New Nation, 1790–1840*. Chapel Hill: University of North Carolina Press, 2010.

Guarneri, Carl J. *The Utopian Alternative: Fourierism in Nineteenth-Century America*. Ithaca, NY: Cornell University Press, 1991.

Gura, Philip F. *American Transcendentalism: A History*. New York: Hill and Wang, 2007.

Hale, Edward Everett. *Memories of a Hundred Years*. 2 vols. New York: Macmillan, 1902.

Hale, William Harlan. *Horace Greeley: Voice of the People*. New York: Harper & Brothers, 1950.

Harding, Walter Roy. *The Days of Henry Thoreau*. New York: Alfred A. Knopf, 1965, revised and reprinted 1992.

———, ed. *Thoreau as Seen by His Contemporaries*. New York: Dover, 1989.

Harding, Walter Roy, and Michael Meyer, eds. *The New Thoreau Handbook*. New York: New York University Press, 1980.

Hawthorne, Julian. *Hawthorne and His Circle*. New York: Harper & Brothers, 1903.

———. *Nathaniel Hawthorne and His Wife*. 2 vols. Boston: Houghton, Mifflin, 1884.

Hawthorne, Nathaniel. *Selected Letters of Nathaniel Hawthorne*. Edited by Joel Myerson. Columbus: The Ohio State University Press, 2002.

———. *Our Old Home*. Boston: Houghton, Mifflin, 1901.

Higginson, Thomas Wentworth. *A Ride Through Kanzas* (New York: American Anti-Slavery Society, 1856).

———. *Cheerful Yesterdays*. Cambridge: Riverside Press, 1898.

———. *Letters and Journals of Thomas Wentworth Higginson*. Edited by Mary Thacher Higginson. Boston: Houghton Mifflin, 1921.

———. *Part of a Man's Life*. Boston: Houghton, Mifflin, 1905.

Hindus, Milton, ed. *Walt Whitman: The Critical Heritage*. New York: Barnes & Noble, 1971.

Horton, James, and Lois Horton. *Black Bostonians: Family Life and Community Struggle in the Antebellum North*. New York: Holmes & Meier, 1979, reprinted 1999.

Howe, Irving. *The American Newness: Culture and Politics in the Age of Emerson*. Cambridge: Harvard University Press, 1986.

Jennings, Chris. *Paradise Now: The Story of American Utopianism*. New York: Random House, 2016.

Kaplan, Justin. *Walt Whitman: A Life*. New York: Simon & Schuster, 1980.

Kennedy, William Sloane. *Reminiscences of Walt Whitman*. London: Alexander Gardner, 1896.

Kneeland, Abner. *A Review of the Evidences of Christianity*. Boston: Office of the Investigator, 1835.

———. *A Review of the Trial, Conviction, and Final Imprisonment in the Common Jail of the County of Suffolk of Abner Kneeland for the Alleged Crime of Blasphemy*. Boston: George A. Chapman, 1838.

Kucich, John J. *Unsettling Thoreau: Native Americans, Settler Colonialism, and the Power of Place*. Amherst: University of Massachusetts Press, 2024.

LaPlante, Eve. *Marmee & Louisa: The Untold Story of Louisa May Alcott and Her Mother*. New York: Free Press, 2012.

———, ed. *My Heart Is Boundless: Writings of Abigail May Alcott, Louisa's Mother*. New York: Free Press, 2012.

Levine, Lawrence W. *Highbrow/Lowbrow: The Emergence of Cultural Hierarchy in America*. Cambridge: Harvard University Press, 1988.

Levy, Leonard W., ed. *Blasphemy in Massachusetts: Freedom of Conscience and the Abner Kneeland Case: A Documentary Record*. New York: Da Capo Press, 1973.

Leyda, Jay. *The Melville Log: A Documentary Life of Herman Melville, 1819–1891*. New York: Harcourt, Brace and Company, 1951.

Loving, Jerome. *Walt Whitman: The Song of Himself*. Berkeley: University of California Press, 1999.

Lowell, James Russell. *A Fable for Critics*. New York: George P. Putnam, 1848.

———. *My Study Windows*. Boston: Houghton, Mifflin/Riverside Press, 1883.

Macy, John. *The Spirit of American Literature*. Garden City: Doubleday, Page & Company, 1913.

Madison, Charles A. *Critics & Crusaders: A Century of American Protest*. New York: Henry Holt and Company, 1947.

Malin, James C. *John Brown and the Legend of Fifty-Six*. New York: Haskell House, 1971.

Marcus, James. *Glad to the Brink of Fear: A Portrait of Ralph Waldo Emerson*. Princeton: Princeton University Press, 2024.

Marshall, Megan. *Margaret Fuller: A New American Life*. Boston: Houghton Mifflin Harcourt, 2013.

———. *The Peabody Sisters: Three Women Who Ignited American Romanticism*. Boston: Houghton Mifflin Harcourt, 2005.

Matteson, John. *Eden's Outcasts: The Story of Louisa May Alcott and Her Father*. New York: W. W. Norton, 2007.

———. *The Lives of Margaret Fuller: A Biography*. New York: W. W. Norton, 2012.

Matthiessen, F. O. *American Renaissance: Art and Expression in the Age of Emerson and Whitman*. London: Oxford University Press, 1941.

McAleer, John. *Ralph Waldo Emerson: Days of Encounter*. Boston: Little, Brown, 1984.

Mead, Edwin D. *The Influence of Emerson*. Boston: American Unitarian Association, 1903.

Mellow, James R. *Hawthorne in His Times*. Boston: Houghton Mifflin Harcourt, 1980.

Melville, Herman. *The Letters of Herman Melville*. Edited by Merrell R. Davis and William H. Gilman. New Haven: Yale University Press, 1960.

———. *Mardi: And a Voyage Thither*. New York: Harper & Brothers, 1849.

———. *Moby-Dick: or, the Whale*. New York: Harper & Brothers, 1851.

———. *Narrative of a Four Months' Residence Among the Natives of a Valley of the Marquesas Islands; or, A Peep at Polynesian Life*. London: John Murray, 1846.

———. *Omoo: A Narrative of Adventures in the South Seas*. Edited by Harrison Hayford and Walter Blair. New York: Hendricks House, 1969.

———. *White-Jacket: or, the World in a Man-of-War*. New York: Harper & Brothers, 1855.

Miller, Edwin Haviland. *Salem Is My Dwelling Place: A Life of Nathaniel Hawthorne*. Iowa City: University of Iowa Press, 1991.

Miller, F. DeWolfe. *Christopher Pearse Cranch: and His Caricatures of New England Transcendentalism*. Cambridge: Harvard University Press, 1951.

Miller, Perry. *The Raven and the Whale: The War of Words and Wits in the Era of Poe and Melville*. New York: Harcourt, Brace and Company, 1956.

———, ed. *The Transcendentalists: An Anthology*. Cambridge: Harvard University Press, 1950.

Mitchell, Thomas R. *Hawthorne's Fuller Mystery*. Amherst: University of Massachusetts Press, 1998.

Molinoff, Katherine. *Walt Whitman at Southold*. Smithtown: not published, 1966.

Mumford, Lewis. *The Golden Day: A Study in American Literature and Culture*. Boston: Beacon Press, 1957.

Myerson, Joel, ed. *A Historical Guide to Ralph Waldo Emerson*. New York: Oxford University Press, 2000.

———, ed. *The Brook Farm Book: A Collection of First-Hand Accounts of the Community*. New York: Garland Publishing, 1987.

———, ed. *The Transcendentalists: A Review of Research and Criticism*. New York: Modern Language Association of America, 1984.

———, ed. *Emerson Centenary Essays*. Carbondale: Southern Illinois University Press, 1982.

———. *The New England Transcendentalists and the Dial*. Rutherford, NJ: Fairleigh Dickinson University Press, 1980.

Nelson, Liz. *Concord: Stories to be Told*. Beverly, MA: Commonwealth Editions, 2002.

Norton, Andrews. *A Discourse on the Latest Forms of Infidelity*. Cambridge, UK: John Owen, 1839.

Oates, Stephen B. *To Purge This Land with Blood: A Biography of John Brown*. New York: Harper & Row, 1970.

Oehlschlaeger, Fritz, and George Hendrick, eds. *Toward the Making of Thoreau's Modern Reputation: Selected Correspondence of S.A. Jones, A.W. Hosmer, H.S. Salt, H.G.O. Blake, and D. Ricketson*. Urbana: University of Illinois Press, 1979.

Painter, Nell Irvin. *Sojourner Truth: A Life, a Symbol*. New York: W. W. Norton, 1996.

Parker, Hershel. *Herman Melville: A Biography*. 2 vols. Baltimore: Johns Hopkins University Press, 2002.

Payne, Alma. *Louisa May Alcott: A Reference Guide*. Boston: G. K. Hall & Co., 1980.

Peabody, Elizabeth Palmer. *Record of a School: Exhibiting the General Principles of Spiritual Culture*. Boston: Russell, Shattuck & Company, 1835.

———. *The Letters of Elizabeth Palmer Peabody, American Renaissance Woman*. Edited by Bruce Ronda. Middletown, CT: Wesleyan University Press, 1984.

Pellarin, Charles. *The Life of Charles Fourier*. New York: William H. Graham, 1848.

Petrulionis, Sandra Harbert. *To Set This World Right: The Anti-Slavery Movement in Thoreau's Concord*. Ithaca, NY: Cornell University Press, 2006.

———, ed. *Thoreau in His Own Time: A Biographical Chronicle of His Life, Drawn from Recollections, Interviews, and Memoirs by Family, Friends, and Associates*. Iowa City: University of Iowa Press, 2012.

Phelps, Elizabeth Stuart. *Our Famous Women*. Hartford, CT: A. D. Worthington & Co., 1884.

Phillips, Wendell. *Wendell Phillips on Civil Rights and Freedom*. Edited by Louis Filler. New York: Hill and Wang, 1965.

Poe, Edgar Allan. *Essays and Reviews*. Edited by G. R. Thompson. New York: Library of America, 1984.

———. *The Works of Edgar Allan Poe in One Volume*. New York: P. F. Collier & Son, 1927.

Rapport, Mike. *1848: Year of Revolution*. New York: Basic Books, 2009.

Reid, Whitelaw. *Horace Greeley*. New York: Charles Scribner's Sons, 1879.

Reisen, Harriet. *Louisa May Alcott: The Woman Behind Little Women*. New York: Henry Holt and Company, 2009.

Reynolds, David S. *Beneath the American Renaissance: The Subversive Imagination in the Age of Emerson and Melville*. New York: Alfred A. Knopf, 1988.

———. *John Brown, Abolitionist*. New York: Alfred A. Knopf, 2005.

———. *Walt Whitman's America: A Cultural Biography*. New York: Vintage Books, 1996.

Richardson, Robert D., Jr. *Emerson: The Mind on Fire*. Berkeley: University of California Press, 1995.

———. *Henry David Thoreau: A Life of the Mind*. Berkeley: University of California Press, 1986.

Ripley, George. *A Letter Addressed to the Congregational Church in Purchase Street, by Its Pastor*. Boston: privately published, 1840.

Ronda, Bruce A. *Elizabeth Palmer Peabody: A Reformer on Her Own Terms*. Cambridge: Harvard University Press, 1999.

Rusk, Ralph L. *The Life of Ralph Waldo Emerson*. New York: Charles Scribner's Sons, 1949.

Sacks, Kenneth S. *Emerson's Civil Wars: Spirit and Society in the Age of Abolition*. New York: Cambridge University Press, 2025.

———. *Understanding Emerson: "The American Scholar" and His Struggle for Self-Reliance*. Princeton: University of Princeton Press, 2003.

Sanborn, Franklin B., and William T. Harris. *A. Bronson Alcott: His Life and Philosophy*. 2 vols. New York: Biblo and Tannen, 1965.

Sanborn, Franklin B. *The Genius and Character of Emerson*. Boston: James R. Osgood and Co., 1885.

———. *The Life of Henry David Thoreau*. Boston: Houghton Mifflin, 1917.

———. *The Life and Letters of John Brown, Liberator of Kansas, and Martyr of Virginia*. London: Sampson Low, Marston, Searle, & Rivington, 1885.

———. *Recollections of Seventy Years*. 2 vols. Boston: Richard Badger, 1909.

Sealts, Merton, and Alfred R. Ferguson. *Emerson's Nature: Origin, Growth, Meaning*. Carbondale: Southern Illinois University Press, 1969.

Sears, Clara Endicott, ed. *Bronson Alcott's Fruitlands*. Boston: Houghton Mifflin, 1915.

Sedgwick, Ellery. *The Atlantic Monthly, 1857–1909: Yankee Humanism at High Tide and Ebb*. Amherst: University of Massachusetts Press, 1994.

Seitz, Don Carlos. *Horace Greeley: Founder of The New York Tribune*. New York: AMS Press, 1970.

Shanley, James Lyndon. *The Making of Walden*. Chicago: University of Chicago Press, 1957.

Shealy, Daniel, ed. *Alcott in Her Own Time: A Biographical Chronicle of Her Life, Drawn from Recollections, Interviews, & Memoirs by Family, Friends, & Associates*. Iowa City: University of Iowa Press, 2005.

Sheffield, Charles A., ed. *The History of Florence, Massachusetts*. Florence, MA: privately published, 1895.

Sinha, Manisha. *The Slave's Cause: A History of Abolition*. New Haven: Yale University Press, 2016.

Smith, Harmon. *My Friend, My Friend: The Story of Thoreau's Relationship with Emerson*. Amherst: University of Massachusetts Press, 1999.

Stern, Madeleine B. *Louisa May Alcott*. Norman: Oklahoma University Press, 1950.

———, ed. *L. M. Alcott: Signature of Reform*. Boston: Northeastern University Press, 2002.

———, ed. *Critical Essays on Louisa May Alcott*. Boston: G. K. Hall, 1984.

Stevens, Charles Emery. *Anthony Burns: A History*. Boston: John P. Jewett and Company, 1856.

Still, William. *The Underground Railroad*. New York: Arno Press and *The New York Times*, 1968.

Stowell, Robert F. *A Thoreau Gazetteer*. Princeton: Princeton University Press, 1970.

Thayer, William R. *The Influence of Emerson*. Boston: Cupples, Upham, and Company, 1886.

Thoreau, Henry David. *The Correspondence of Henry David Thoreau*. Edited by Walter Harding and Carl Bode. New York: New York University Press, 1958.

Ticknor, Caroline. *May Alcott: A Memoir*. Boston: Little, Brown and Company, 1928.

Traubel, Horace. *With Walt Whitman in Camden*. Vols. 1–3: New York: Rowman and Littlefield, 1961; Vols. 4–7: Carbondale: Southern Illinois University Press, 1953–1992.

Truth, Sojourner. *Narrative of Sojourner Truth*. Edited by Olive Gilbert. Boston: privately published, 1878.

Tryon, Warren S. *Parnassus Corner: A Life of James T. Fields, Publisher to the Victorians*. Boston: Houghton Mifflin, 1963.

Von Frank, Albert J. *The Trials of Anthony Burns: Freedom and Slavery in Emerson's Boston*. Cambridge: Harvard University Press, 1998.

Von Mehren, Joan. *Minerva and the Muse: A Life of Margaret Fuller*. Amherst: University of Massachusetts Press, 1994.

Walls, Laura Dassow. *Henry David Thoreau: A Life*. Chicago: Chicago University Press, 2017.

———. *Seeing New Worlds: Henry David Thoreau and Nineteenth-Century Natural Science*. Madison: University of Wisconsin Press, 1995.

Whitman, George Washington. *Civil War Letters of George Washington Whitman*. Edited by Jerome M. Loving. Durham, NC: Duke University Press, 1975.

Whitman, Walt. *Leaves of Grass* (first edition). Brooklyn, NY: privately published, 1855.

———. *Leaves of Grass* (second edition). Brooklyn, NY: privately published, 1856.

———. *Memoranda During the War*. New York: Oxford University Press, 2004.

———. *Poetry and Prose*. Edited by Justin Kaplan. New York: Library of America, 1982.

———. *The Correspondence*. Edited by Edwin Haviland Miller. 5 vols. New York: New York University Press, 1961–1969.

———. *The Early Poems and the Fiction*. Edited by Thomas L. Brasher. New York: New York University Press, 1963.

———. *Walt Whitman of the New York Aurora*. Edited by Joseph Jay Rubin and Charles H. Brown. State College, PA: Bald Eagle Press, 1950.

Willis, Frederick L. H. *Alcott Memoirs*. Boston: Richard G. Badger, 1915.

Wineapple, Brenda. *Hawthorne: A Life*. New York: Alfred A. Knopf, 2003.

Wirzbicki, Peter. *Fighting for the Higher Law: Black and White Transcendentalists Against Slavery*. Philadelphia: University of Pennsylvania Press, 2021.

Wright, A. Augustus, ed. *Who's Who in the Lyceum*. Philadelphia: Pearson Brothers, 1906.

Young, Philip. *Hawthorne's Secret: An Untold Tale*. Boston: David Godine, 1984.

Illustration Credits

1. Courtesy Concord Free Public Library
2. Folger Shakespeare Library
3. No credit
4. Library of Congress
5. Fruitlands Museum Collections, The Trustees of Reservations
6. New York Public Library, Miriam and Ira D. Wallach Division of Art, Prints and Photographs, Photograph Collection
7. No credit
8. Metropolitan Museum of Art
9. Courtesy Concord Free Public Library
10. Courtesy Concord Free Public Library
11. New-York Historical Society
12. Courtesy Concord Free Public Library
13. Courtesy Concord Free Public Library
14. Courtesy Concord Free Public Library
15. Peabody Essex Museum
16. Collection of the Massachusetts Historical Society
17. Flute, Meacham and Pond, Albany, NY, 1828–1832. Concord Museum Collection, Gift of Mr. Walton Ricketson and Miss Anna Ricketson; Th40.
18. Fruitlands Museum Collections, The Trustees of Reservations
19. Library of Congress
20. National Portrait Gallery, Smithsonian Institution
21. Bibliothèque Nationale de France
22. Frick Collection
23. No credit
24. Fruitlands Museum Collections, The Trustees of Reservations
25. Massachusetts Historical Society
26. Courtesy Concord Free Public Library
27. Creative Commons
28. Courtesy Concord Free Public Library
29. British National Portrait Gallery
30. Pictorial Press Ltd./Alamy Stock Photo

31. National Portrait Gallery, Smithsonian Institution
32. Courtesy Concord Free Public Library
33. Library of Congress
34. Courtesy Concord Free Public Library
35. No credit
36. Courtesy of the Camden County Historical Society
37. Collection of the Massachusetts Historical Society
38. Used by permission of Louisa May Alcott's Orchard House
39. Fruitlands Museum Collections, The Trustees of Reservations
40. Boston Athenaeum
41. National Library of Medicine, Prints and Photographs
42. No credit
43. Used by permission of Louisa May Alcott's Orchard House
44. Used by permission of Louisa May Alcott's Orchard House
45. Used by permission of Louisa May Alcott's Orchard House
46. Used by permission of Louisa May Alcott's Orchard House
47. Courtesy Concord Free Public Library

Index

About the Author

BRUCE NICHOLS grew up in a Unitarian household twenty minutes from Concord, Massachusetts. During an almost forty-year career in publishing, he served as publisher of both Houghton Mifflin Harcourt (HMH) and Little, Brown and Company, the original publishers of Thoreau, Hawthorne, and Louisa May Alcott. At HMH, he regularly reissued Thoreau's works.